Criminal Justice
Recent Scholarship

Edited by
Marilyn McShane and Frank P. Williams III

A Series from LFB Scholarly

Criminal Justice and the Placement of Abused Children

Diane R. Martell

LFB Scholarly Publishing LLC
New York 2005

Library of Congress Cataloging-in-Publication Data

Martell, Diane R., 1957-
  Criminal justice and the placement of abused children / Diane R.
Martell.
    p. cm. -- (Criminal justice)
  Includes bibliographical references and index.
  ISBN 1-59332-059-0 (alk. paper)
  1. Child abuse--United States--Prevention. 2. Abused children--
Services for--United States. 3. Criminal justice, Administration of--
United States. 4. Child abuse--Investigation--United States. I. Title.
II. Series: Criminal justice (LFB Scholarly Publishing LLC)
  HV741.M37 2005
  364.15'554'0973--dc22

2005021537

ISBN 1-59332-059-0

Printed on acid-free 250-year-life paper.

Manufactured in the United States of America.

Table of Contents

List of Tables

Acknowledgements

This book developed out of my dissertation, which was written as part of my studies at the Florence Heller Graduate School for Advanced Studies in Social Welfare at Brandeis University. I am indebted to many people at Brandeis, especially Ted Cross and Jim Callahan. Without their guidance and friendship, I would not have engaged in the research that became the basis for this book. I would also like to express my appreciation to the National Center on Child Abuse and Neglect, for their financial support of the project, and to Jane Willan and Lori Herz for their research and formatting assistance. Finally, I would like to thank the social workers, area directors, victim/witness advocates, assistance district attorneys and support staff within the Massachusetts Department of Social Services and the Child Abuse Unit of the Suffolk County District Attorney's Office, particularly, Janis Lynch, Janet Fine, Susan Goldfarb and David Deakin. Without the cooperation of these individuals, it would not have been possible to study the impact of system interventions on child abuse cases. Their commitment to providing assistance and support to maltreated children and their families is commendable and I am grateful for their guidance and support throughout the project.

CHAPTER 1

Introduction

Child abuse is one of the most serious problems facing our society today. In 2001, nearly 1 million children across the nation were found to be victims of maltreatment by child protection agencies (United States Department of Health and Human Services, U.S.D.H.H.S., 2003b). Fifty-seven percent of these substantiated cases involved child neglect, 19% involved physical abuse, 10% involved sexual abuse, and 27% involved other types of maltreatment[1]. During the same year, approximately one-fifth or 19% of these maltreated children were removed from their homes (U.S.D.H.H.S., 2003b).

The two primary systems involved in child abuse cases are criminal justice and child protection. When an incident of abuse is reported, both of these systems are often required to respond. Protective services must investigate incidents of intra-familial or caretaker abuse, assessing the validity of the complaint, the safety of the living environment, the physical and mental health of the child, and the level of familial support. The criminal justice system must investigate all cases in which criminal behavior is alleged and decide which cases to accept for prosecution.

The two systems have distinct, but overlapping, mandates and procedures. Protective services seeks to protect abused children by providing services or removing them from the home whereas the criminal justice system seeks to protect society through the arrest and criminal prosecution of offenders (Besharov, 1990). In many of the cases in which both systems become involved, the processes of each are initiated simultaneously or within a short time period of each other.

1These percentages include reports of multiple forms of maltreatment.

When reported cases of child abuse enter both the child protection and criminal justice systems, it is likely that the steps taken by these two separate systems can influence the interventions and/or outcomes of the other. For example, the criminal justice decision to prosecute or decline a case may have a direct impact on the safety of an abused child (i.e. through the issuance of a restraining order or the incarceration of the perpetrator) and therefore, influence the need for child placement outside the home. Alternatively, the disruption, isolation and trauma that can result from a child's removal from the home may make it more difficult for the child to act as a witness, thereby weakening the ability of the criminal justice system to prosecute the case. At least one study of child sexual abuse (Cross, Martell & McDonald, 1995) has found a strong relationship between child placement outside the home and cases not being prosecuted by criminal justice agencies.

To date, research on interventions in child abuse cases have focused almost exclusively on the processes and outcomes of only one system. Studies have examined child abuse from the perspective of protective service agencies, law enforcement organizations, health and mental health providers and juvenile and criminal courts. Until recently, little research has been conducted on the responses of more than one system to the same reports of abuse. This has resulted in a paucity of information regarding the true costs and benefits of system interventions and a lack of accurate data regarding the interaction and influence of multiple systems on a particular case (National Research Council, 1993).

This book begins to address these gaps in knowledge by examining the relationship between the interventions of the criminal justice system and the child protection system as they respond to the same cases of child abuse. The first two chapters provide an overview of child maltreatment and policy and practice in both the criminal justice and child protection systems. A theoretical framework for assessment the ability systems to engage in collaborative processes is described in Chapter 3 and Chapter 4 summarizes those factors that influence the case prosecution and child placement decisions. In Chapter 5, I describe a 1997-1998 study that examined incidents of child abuse that were investigated by both criminal justice and child protection in Massachusetts. This dual-system sample allowed for an analysis of the decision-making of two intervening agencies regarding the same cases of child maltreatment; an investigation that has not been undertaken by previous studies. Specifically, the study examines whether there is an association between the criminal justice prosecution decision and the protective service placement decision for cases of child abuse under investigation by both systems. The results of the study are reviewed in Chapter 6. Finally, in Chapter 7, implications for policy and practice are outlined.

An examination of the potential relationship between the placement and prosecution decision is important to efforts to improve the quality of life of abused children. If arrest or prosecution of an offender can negate the need for child removal or, the preservation of the family can help prosecution, then cooperative practices may be developed to increase the likelihood of positive outcomes within both the child protection and criminal justice systems. Likewise, if there is an identifiable group of cases most at risk for non-prosecution and child removal, dual agency collaboration may help to address their specific needs. Essentially, it is hoped that this research will provide useful information that can be helpful in the formation of more effective policies and practices for both systems.

Understanding the impact of multi-systemic responses to child abuse will enhance our ability, as a society, to respond appropriately and effectively to violence against children. Over the past ten years, our country has witnessed a dramatic growth in children's advocacy centers, which represent a new, collaborative, child-centered model for responding to reports of child abuse. Children's advocacy centers coordinate teams of child protection, law enforcement, criminal justice, and mental and medical health professionals to work collaboratively on child abuse cases (Walsh, Jones, & Cross, 2003). Children's advocacy centers provide us with the opportunity to examine how multidisciplinary teams can work together to best meet the needs of abused children (Cramer, 1985). Research currently being conducted on the effectiveness of these organizations is likely to result in very useful information regarding relationships between the interventions of different systems and how interdisciplinary coordination can best provide positive outcomes for child victims (Walsh et al., 2003).

CHAPTER 2

Child Maltreatment: An Overview

A History of Child Abuse

Child abuse and neglect was not recognized as a major social problem in the United States until the latter part of the nineteenth century. Before that time, the needs of abandoned or neglected children were addressed by religious groups, charitable organizations or local governments. Indigent, homeless or neglected children were apprenticed or placed in homes or institutions, such as almshouses or orphanages (McCauley, Schwartz-Kenney, Epstein, & Tucker, 2001). For the most part, the individuals who directed these early initiatives were not primarily concerned with child well-being. Their goal was to create useful and hard working adult citizens within their community by removing children from immoral and impoverished environments. Although reported criminal cases involving child abuse were recorded as early as 1655, public and private interventions with abused children did not regularly occur until the early 1800's (Watkins, 1990b). At that time, states began to afford to social welfare agencies the right to remove children suffering from abuse from their homes (Pecora, Whittaker, Maluccio & Barth, 2000).

In the late 1800's, cases of serious child maltreatment began to receive public attention. In 1874, public outrage over the court case involving Mary Ellen Wilson, a child who was seriously abused by her caretaker for over seven years, resulted in the establishment of the New York Society for the Prevention of Cruelty to Children (Watkins, 1990b). Soon thereafter, responsibility for the care of dependent children began to shift from private organizations to state and federal government. A number of states created their own institutions to serve as both home and school for children in need and the federal government began to study the problem and search for remedies.

In 1909, President Roosevelt held the first White House Conference on the Care of Dependent Children which ended with the resolution that a secure and loving home should be acquired for every child. The event signaled the beginning of the formation of a complex child welfare system that would incorporate both public and private organizations. The first federal Children's Bureau was established in 1912 and in 1920, the Child Welfare League of America began advocating for familial services and support and the temporary placement of children in cases of child maltreatment. The allocation of federal funding to states for child welfare services and authorization of voluntary reporting of suspected child abuse and neglect occurred for the first time in 1935, as part of the Social Security Act (Pecora et al., 2000). Shortly thereafter, a formal foster care system, involving emergency shelters, foster family homes and group homes, began to evolve. However, significant public attention did not turn again to child abuse until the 1960s with the publication of the article, "The Battered Child Syndrome" by the American Medical Association (Kempe, Silverman, Steele, Proegmueller & Silver, 1962).

By 1967, all fifty states had passed either mandatory or voluntary child abuse reporting laws and the number of official reports of child maltreatment significantly increased. By 1974, widespread public concern about the problem of physical child abuse and neglect resulted in the first piece of major legislation that addressed the issue, the passage of the Child Abuse Prevention and Treatment Act (C.A.P.T.A.). C.A.P.T.A. established a federal definition for child maltreatment and outlined standards for state mandatory reporting laws (Pecora et al., 2000). The codification of the mandatory reporting laws in the 1970's resulted in a significant increase in the number of children reported for potential maltreatment

The passage of C.A.P.T.A. also brought about public acknowledgement that child sexual abuse was a serious problem. Despite longstanding laws prohibiting molestation and rape in the United States, cases of child sexual abuse were often met with public and professional hostility and skepticism (Myers, Diedrich, Lee, Fincher & Stern, 1999). The passage of C.A.P.T.A., in concert with the rise of the feminist and victim's rights movements, growth of the child protection field and publication of research on the prevalence of sexual violence, catapulted child sexual abuse to the forefront of American consciousness (Myers et al., 1999).

As public opinion about both physical and sexual child abuse began to shift, laws and policies relating to all types of family violence came under question (Finkelhor & Ormrod, 2001). After the passage of C.A.P.T.A., numerous reforms have been implemented within the child welfare, law enforcement and criminal justice systems in efforts to improve systemic responses and outcomes and more effectively address the needs of children and families impacted by maltreatment and other forms of family violence.

Definitions for child abuse and neglect also changed over this time period. The 1974 C.A.P.T.A. originally defined child abuse as the "physical or mental injury, sexual abuse, negligent treatment, or maltreatment of a child under the age of 18 by a person who is responsible for the child's welfare under the circumstances which indicate the child's health or welfare is harmed or threatened" (Child Abuse Prevention and Treatment Act, 1974).

This definition was so broad that it was difficult for protective service agencies to enforce the legislation. In 1996, the federal government amended the statute to allow states to limit maltreatment to serious harm caused to a child by a caretaker. Currently, the law states that "any recent act or failure to act on the part of a parent or caretaker, which results in death, serious physical or emotional harm, sexual abuse or exploitation, or an act or failure to act which presents an imminent risk of serious harm" (Child Abuse Prevention and Treatment Act, 1996, p. 44). The C.A.P.T.A. definition is important because in order for states to qualify for federal child welfare funds, they must utilize definitions of child maltreatment that meet the federal standard.

Incidence and Prevalence

Over the past 25 years, researchers have attempted to estimate the rate of child maltreatment in the United States. However, determining the extent of child abuse is a difficult task because definitions for child maltreatment vary between the fields of medicine, psychology, criminal law and child welfare and the ambiguity of the statutory definitions leaves a great deal of room for interpretation (Portwood, 1999). In addition, there is wide disparity in terms of community and cultural beliefs about what behaviors are indicative of abuse versus poor parenting (Portwood, 1999). For example, corporal punishment (ie. spanking) is viewed as an acceptable disciplinary practice by many communities but it meets the criteria for abuse in others. Therefore, attempts to estimate abuse are most successful when specific behavioral definitions are used in the counting of incidents.

Studies that examine cases of abuse reported to state agencies must rely on definitions found in state statutes. There are two types of statutes in which definitions of abuse can be found, civil and criminal statutes. Civil statutes are general and guide child protection interventions. Criminal statutes are much more specific, often delineating the level of the crime by the age of the child, the level of force used, and the type of abusive act. Criminal statutes guide law enforcement and criminal justice decision-making. There is great variation between states in their civil and criminal definitions for abuse and this, in turn, limits research that attempts to aggregate state-by-state data (U.S.D.H.H.S., 2003a).

Various techniques have been used to estimate child abuse in US. Studies prior to the enactment of nationwide mandatory reporting, such as David Gil's 1967 nationwide inventory of physical child abuse, resulted in low estimates and wide variation. In 1973, DeFrancis estimated that between 30,000 to 40, 000 incidents of serious abuse 1975, Nagi found 167,000 reported and 91,000 unreported cases of abuse (Gelles, 1998).

Since 1976, national data on child abuse has been collected to determine both the incidence and prevalence of child maltreatment in the United States (Widom, 2001). Incidence refers to the number of children reported as having experienced child abuse in a specific year. The prevalence of maltreatment is the number of children who have ever experienced a form of child abuse.

The primary sources of current information on child neglect and physical, sexual and emotional abuse have been the National Child Abuse and Neglect Data System (N.C.A.N.D.S.) and the National Incidence Study (N.I.S.). N.C.A.N.D.S. is a national data collection system that counts and categorizes the official reports of maltreatment to child welfare agencies in the fifty states and District of Columbia.

In 2002, N.C.A.N.D.S. found that the states received approximately 2.6 million referrals for 4.5 million children regarding child maltreatment. It is estimated that state child protection agencies screened in approximately 1,800,000 or 67.1 percent of these cases. Approximately 30 percent of these cases were found to be substantiated, indicating the occurrence of child maltreatment. It is estimated that one-fifth (265,000) of these child victims were removed from their home following the child protection investigation (U.S.D.H.H.S., 2004).

In 2002, 65% of the substantiated reports were for child neglect, 18.6 involved physical abuse, 9.9 were cases of sexual abuse, 6.5% involved emotional abuse and 18.9 involved other types of maltreatment such as abandonment. Twenty percent of the cases involved multiple forms of maltreatment (U.S.D.H.H.S., 2004).

N.C.A.N.D.S. also found that child victims under the age of 3 had the highest victimization rate (16%) in 2002. Forty-eight percent of the child victims were male. Most of the children involved in the reports were white (54.2%), a quarter (26%) were African-American, and one-tenth (11%) were Hispanic. However, an examination of incidence by ethnic groups revealed that Native American and African-American children had the highest rates of victimization, 21.7% and 20.2% respectively. Mothers of child victims comprised 40% of the perpetrators. In 20% of the cases, the father was the offender and 18% of the cases involved both mother and father. Thirteen percent of the cases involved a sole perpetrator who was not a parent (U.S.D.H.H.S., 2004).

Approximately 1,400 children died of maltreatment in 2002. The majority of the fatalities involved children under the age of four (75%). Over one-third of the fatalities were attributed to neglect, approximately 30% were caused by physical abuse and 28.9 % were related to multiple forms of maltreatment (U.S.D.H.H.S., 2004).

The rate of victimization has fluctuated over the past 15 years. Data from N.C.A.N.D.S. indicates that the national annual rate of child victimization increased significantly from 1990 to 1993, peaking at 15.3 children per 1,000, and decreased to 11.8 per 1,000 in 1999. In 2000, there was a slight increase to 12.2 child victims per 1,000 children but it is unclear whether this growth in reports represents a new trend (U.S.D.H.H.S., 2004).

In contrast, N.C.A.N.D.S. also found that the number of sexual abuse cases substantiated by protective services dropped significantly between 1992 and 2000, from 150,000 to 89,500. The reasons for this change are unknown, however, there is some evidence that the decrease may relate to changes in protective service procedures and/or a real decline in the incidence of sexual abuse (Finkelhor & Jones, 2004).

The N.C.A.N.D.S. data provides an excellent overview of those cases that come under the purview of state child welfare agencies. However, it is limited as a national data source in that there is variation in the statutory definitions and reporting and substantiation procedures utilized by the different states (Finkelhor & Hashima, 2001). In addition, NCCANDS data cannot provide information about cases of child maltreatment that do not come to the attention of child protection or are not screened in by the protective service agency. In contrast, the National Incidence Study of Child Abuse and Neglect (N.I.S.) is able to provide information about child maltreatment that comes to the attention of human service professionals, whether or not there is protective service involvement.

The National Incidence Study of Child Abuse and Neglect (N.I.S.) is a congressionally-mandated survey that periodically collects data on child abuse from human service agencies and professionals (Finkelhor & Hashima, 2001). N.I.S. uses a nationally representative statistical sample to collect information from professionals on incidents of abuse and neglect in which they have been involved during a specific time period.

Three consecutive surveys designed to measure the national incidence of reported child maltreatment were administered in 1979, 1986 and 1993/94. The most recent, N.I.S.-3, findings were based on a nationally representative sample of over 5,600 professional in 842 agencies serving 42 states. The study collected data using both a harm standard (children who had experienced abuse or neglect) and an endangerment standard (children who were at risk of harm). Using both of these standards, N.I.S.-3 found that in 1993, there had been a considerable increase (67%) from the 1986 data in the number of children who had experienced maltreatment. N.I.S.-3 estimated that 1,553,800 children were abused or neglected in 1993. Significant increases were found for both abused and neglected children (Continuing Medical Education, 2001).

It was estimated by N.I.S.-3 that 381,700 children were physically abused in 1993, versus 269,700 in 1986. Similarly, the approximate number of children reported to have experienced sexual abuse in 1986 (9,200) increased 83% (217,700) in 1993 and the number of neglected children rose from 167,800 (N.I.S.-2) to 338,900 (N.I.S.-3) (Continuing Medical Education, 2001).

In 1993, N.I.S.-3 found that protective services investigated only 28% of the children who met the harm standard, versus 44% of this same group in 1986 (Continuing Medical Education, 2001). These findings indicate that as many as 72 percent of children identified by professionals as being maltreated in 1993 were not investigated by child protection agencies (Orr, 1999). The N.I.S. data is very useful in that it allows for the tracking of cases outside the child protection system and for comparisons over time. However, it also has limitations such as variation in involvement by the participating agencies.

Researchers have attempted to supplement attempts to gather national data with empirical studies that estimate the occurrence of different types of maltreatment (Finkelhor, Moore, Hamby, & Strauss, 1997: Moore, Gallup & Schussel, 1995: Strauss & Gelles, 1990). Empirical studies can provide useful information about maltreatment, however, the stigma associated with child abuse can impact the ability of researchers to obtain a sample that truly represents the overall population (Kinard, 2001).

National self report surveys conducted by Gelles and Straus (Gelles, 1998) asked parents to report acts of physical violence towards their children. They found that 1.5 % of parents reported kicking, biting or punching their child every year. Data indicated that more than 20 in 1000 parents (2.3%) exhibited abusive violence during 1984. The findings indicated that the actual rate of physical abuse may be much higher than most estimates based on official reports.

Likewise, Finkelhor, Hotaling, Lewis and Smith (1990) conducted the first national telephone survey to estimate the prevalence of child sexual abuse. Of the 2,626 Americans questioned regarding prior sexual abuse, victimization was reported by 27 percent of the women and 16 percent of the men. Of those participants who confirmed childhood sexual abuse, 42 percent of the women and 33 percent of the men reported that they had never disclosed the abuse to anyone (Finkelhor et al.)

Definitions

Child abuse is generally defined as any act or failure to act on the part of a child's caretaker which results in "physical or emotional harm, sexual abuse or exploitation" (National Clearinghouse on Child Abuse and Neglect Information, 2000). Child maltreatment is typically divided into four categories, physical abuse, sexual abuse, emotional abuse and child neglect. Within all types of maltreatment, there is a wide range of behaviors and great variation in terms of severity of the abuse and its impact on the child victim.

Physical abuse may be defined as the nonaccidental acts that inflict physical injury on a child. It includes behaviors such as punching, beating, kicking, shaking, throwing, stabbing, choking or otherwise physically harming a child. Child sexual abuse refers to nonconsensual sexual contact, usually between a child and an adult (Kendall-Tackett & Marshall, 1998). It includes both noncontact sexual abuse such as sexual comments and voyeurism and contact abuse such as fondling, digital or object penetration, oral sex, and penile penetration (Faller, 1990).

Emotional or psychological abuse is more difficult to define. Psychological maltreatment usually refers to parental behavior patterns that as the "repeated pattern of caregiver behavior or extreme incidents that communicate to children that they are defective, unwanted, and/or of little value. Psychological abuse may include parent actions such as rejecting, isolating, terrorizing, ignoring, corrupting, verbally assaulting, and exploiting (Hamarman, Pope & Czaja, 2002). Definitions for emotional abuse across states vary considerably which makes it difficult for this form of maltreatment to be identified in a consistent manner (Hamarman et al.).

Although physical, sexual and emotional abuse receive the most public attention, more children experience and suffer from neglect than any other form of child maltreatment (Cantwell, 1997). Child neglect is a form of child maltreatment that is usually categorized separately from other forms of child abuse. Despite the high occurrence of neglect, it has been the focus of less research than other forms of maltreatment. This may be in part because it is difficult to define and often co-occurs with other forms of maltreatment (Garbarino & Collins, 1999).

Neglect refers to unmet basic develpmental needs of child, regardless of cause (Dubowitz, Black, Starr & Zuravin, 1993). Unlike abuse, neglect is typically defined as an act of omission versus an act of commission (Dubowitz et al.). There are three general forms of neglect; physical, educational and emotional. Physical neglect refers to the failure of a caretaker to meet the basic needs for food, shelter, clothing, safety and medical and mental health care (Downs, Moore, McFadden, & Costin, 2000). Included under physical neglect is the nonorganic failure to thrive. Educational neglect involves the failure to enroll a child in school, permitting a child to miss school, and/or failing to address the special educational needs of a child. Emotional neglect refers to acts of omission regarding psychological needs, for example, the need for love and nurturing (Gelles, 1999). Neglect tends to be long term and chronic, therefore statistics on neglect usually refer to its prevalence (Gaudin, 1993).

Causes of Maltreatment

The origins of child abuse are complex. Numerous theories, such as individual pathology, social learning, and ecological and structural conditions, have been utilized to better understand the root causes of child maltreatment (Winton & Mara, 2001). Given that there are multiple causes of child abuse, a combined psycho-social approach to maltreatment can most effectively summarize those factors that are associated with abusive behavior (Winton & Mara, 2001).

Individual pathology is often the focus of inquiries into why adults maltreat children, however, most people who abuse children are not diagnosed with a psychiatric disorder (Gelles, 1998). Individual characteristics found to be associated with child abuse include depression, anxiety, low frustration tolerance, low self-esteem, deficits in empathy, anger control and problem-solving skills, and antisocial behavior (National Research Council, 1993). Difficulties relating to attachment and empathy have been associated with perpetrators of sexual abuse (Faller, 1990). Ward (2003) postulates that sexually abusive behavior may occur when both psychological and cognitive disorders and specific environmental conditions are present.

Families in which there is substance abuse, a lack of social supports and/or poverty have been found to be associated with all forms of child abuse. There is also a high rate of co-occurrence between child maltreatment and domestic violence (Daro, Edlson, & Pinderhughes, 2004). Neglectful parents are often found to suffer from both depression and substance abuse, however, these individuals are also likely to be socially isolated and lack social skills (Miller-Perrin & Perrin, 1999).

Family and parenting difficulties are also associated with child abuse. Spousal conflicts or abuse, unrealistic expectations of children, disregard for children's needs and difficulties with child management are often found in home in which child maltreatment is occurring (Barnett, Miller & Perrin, 2004). Physical abuse, in particular, has been found to be related to a lack of interpersonal and social skills (DiLauro, 2004).

In contrast to theories focusing on pathology, the social learning approach focuses on the ways in which individuals learn abusive behavior. The results of many studies support the supposition that abusive behavior is handed down from one generation to the next (Doumas et al., 1994; Ethier, Courture & Lacharite, 2004; Hotaling & Sugarman, 1986; Simons et al., 1991, as cited in Markowitz, 2001). In many cases, adults who abuse children may themselves, as children, have experienced or witnessed, violence, deprivation, and/or trauma. However, in a recent study of ex-offenders and the general population, Markowitz (2001) found that attitudes toward violence can significantly impact abusive behavior in adulthood, in individuals who had experienced violence while growing up. Why some people who experience early violence and/or dysfunctional environments engage in abusive behaviors as adults, and others do not, is a complex question that deserves further attention.

Research on the roots of sexual abuse have also utilized the social learning approach. Two of the four preconditions identified by Finkelhor (1984) for the occurrence of sexual abuse are the presence of a sexual attraction to young children and the willingness to act on that attraction. Childhood experiences with sexual trauma can lead to identification with the assailant in order to lessen feelings of vulnerability (Faller, 1990). According to behavioral theorists, a learned condition of sexual arousal from sexual abuse can be difficult to change. However, in recent years, it has become clear that the motivating factors of many sexual abusers are often very similar to those of parents who physically maltreat children. Many adults abuse children in an attempt to assert their power and gain a feeling of control over life stressors and circumstances (Ryan, 1997).

Ecological approaches to understanding child maltreatment focus on the interactions between individuals and their environment, the family, social groups, work, school, the neighborhood, and larger social, political and economic institutions. People who lack access to necessary resources may become disengaged from the mainstream society, creating frustration and hopelessness. For example, in a review of research on child neglect, Connell-Carrick (2003) found that poverty, a large number of people in the home, single-parenthood and deficits in family functioning have all been highly correlated to neglect.

Environmental stressors can result in poor family functioning which impacts parenting ability. It has been hypothesized that stress can lead to child abuse in a number of ways (Salzinger et al., 2002). Parents may not have the cognitive or psychological capacity to cope with stress. Alternatively, parents may have the personal capacity to cope but may not perceive that there are adequate resources to support family functioning resulting in caretaker distress. Salzinger (et al., 2002) suggests that familial stress increases the risk for partner violence, which raises the risk of child maltreatment.

The characteristics of neighborhoods have also been found to be related to all forms of child maltreatment. Urban, densely populated neighborhoods lacking economic and social resources have been found to be highly associated with higher reports of child neglect and physical abuse (Ernst, 2000). Although abuse is found in families at every socioeconomic level, poverty is one of the most highly correlated factors (Drake & Pandey, 1996).

Poverty has been found to be directly related to neglect (DiLauro, 2004). Neglect is highest among the poor. Our society does not provide adequate social and economic supports and resources to poor families (Garbarino, 1992). These parents have an overall pattern of depression, disengagement, and retreating from the stressful demands of children, family and the outside environment. They have poor coping skills and perceive that there are few resources or support systems available to them (Gaines, Sandgrund, Green, & Power, 1978).

However, poverty does not equal neglect. Although children in poor families are much more likely to be neglected than children with adequate family incomes, only a small portion, three percent, of families in poverty are reported to neglect their children (Sedlack & Broadhurst, 1996).

Consequences of Maltreatment

Over the past 30 years, the detrimental effects that maltreatment can have on children have been documented by numerous medical and mental health practitioners and researchers (Helfer, Kempe, & Krugman, 1997). Child victimization can be very traumatic. It is difficult to predict how childhood incidents of abuse will impact a child, in both the immediate future and later in adulthood (Johnson, 1998).

The consequences of childhood trauma can be mediated by the presence of protective factors. Child factors, such as high intelligence and academic achievement, as well as the type of intervention that occurs, such as child placement in a supportive setting, can help a child gain effective coping skills and build resilience. Research indicates that one of the most effective protective factors is the presence of a knowledgeable, caring and consistent adult in life of child. A positive support network can help to lessen the negative impact of maltreatment (Garmezy, 1981; Kendall-Tackett & Marshall, 1998).

Different forms of child abuse often co-occur with other forms of maltreatment as well as familial and social environment stressors (Higgins & McCabe, 2003). Therefore, it is difficult to clearly identify the consequences of specific types of maltreatment (Johnson, 1998).

Child abuse is highly correlated with many physical, psychological and behavioral problems. Data from N.I.S.-3 indicates that over the course of one year, 565,000 abused children experienced long term or life-threatening injuries and 822,000 child victims suffered from moderate injuries (Sedlak & Broadhurst, 1996). Clearly, physical violence toward a child can cause minor and major injuries to the victim of abuse (Widom, 2001). Physical abuse and physical neglect can also result in growth impairments, disability, and death (Gaudin, 1999).

In the past five years, researchers have also discovered serious neurobiological impairments in child victims of abuse and/or neglect. In children, especially young children, the brain is still in the process of forming and developing. Exposure to traumatic experiences can cause impairments in brain functioning. Child victims of abuse often develop an automatic, maladaptive fear response. This results in severe hyper-vigilance, anxiety, aggression and behavioral impulsivity. Impaired neurodevelopment, including the suppression of cell growth, decreased development of the left hemisphere, and limbic irritability, can severely impact emotional stability, problem-solving, language-based learning, general information processing and cognitive ability (Hagberg & Greer, 2004). Cognitive difficulties in maltreated children often present as learning disorders, attention disorders and behavioral disorders (Widom, 2001; Ford et al., 2000).

The psychological harm associated with child abuse and neglect can also have a long lasting effect on a child. Child symptoms can vary according to the gender (Banyard, Williams & Siegel, 2004) and developmental level of the child (Kendall-Tackett & Marshall, 1998; Herrenkohl & Russo, 2001). Psychological consequences of maltreatment can range from mild symptoms, such as a lowered sense of self-esteem, to serious conditions, for example, a psychiatric disorder. Acute reactions to child physical and sexual abuse include emotional shock, confusion, sleep disturbances, loss of appetite, guilt anxiety, memory problems, and hyperactivity (Johnson, 1998; Kendall-Tackett & Marshall, 1998). Children who experience abuse may immediately present maladaptive behaviors such as suicide attempts, running away, academic difficulties, delinquent behavior and drug and alcohol abuse (Johnson, 1998; Kendall-Tackett & Marshall, 1998; Malmgren & Meisel, 2004; Widom, 2001).

There are also a number of long term psychological reactions to abuse. Anxiety, post-traumatic stress disorder, depression, attachment disorders, regression, low self-esteem and interpersonal difficulties have all been found to be highly associated with maltreatment. (Haugaard, 2004; Johnson, 1998; Kendall-Tackett & Marshall, 1998; Runyon & Kenny, 2002). Children who experience both sexual and physical child abuse have been found to be at high risk for the most severe psychological symptoms (Naar-King, Silvern, Ryan & Sebring, 2002).

Child victims can present a variety of symptoms depending on their age, gender, developmental level, and the type of abuse they experienced, as well as a number of characteristics relating to family environment (Higgins & McCabe, 2003). For example, children who are sexually abused are vulnerable to revictimization (Grauerholz, 2000) and may exhibit inappropriate sexual behavior (Kendall-Tackett & Marshall, 1998). They also appear to be particularly vulnerable to psychiatric disorders. These include phobias, affective disorder, post-traumatic stress disorder and depression (Saunder, Villeponteaux, Lipovsky, Kilpatrick, & Veronen, 1992). In contrast, physically abused children are prone to depression, aggression and bullying behavior toward other children (Johnson et al., 2002; Winton and Mara, 2001).

Experiencing maltreatment as a child can significantly impact later functioning in adulthood. Adults who were victimized as children can suffer from numerous psychological and social problems including difficulties in parenting and in other interpersonal relationships. For example, researchers have found a potential association between the development and functioning of non-offending parents and intergenerational sexual abuse. In a study of 570 children of battered women, Avery, Hutchinson and Whitaker (2002) found that the mother's of child sexual abuse victims were much more likely to have been sexually abused as children. This suggests that psychological, developmental and/or social challenges that can result from sexual abuse may have long-term ramifications for future generations.

Psychological maltreatment and neglect have also been associated with significant adjustment problems and impairments in adult development (Higgins & McCabe, 2003). The quality of the family environment, in terms of parental attitudes and familial relationships, has been found to be related to adjustment difficulties in adulthood (Higgins & McCabe).

Child neglect alone can result in serious physical, psychological and developmental impairments. A lack of adequate food, housing or health care can cause a child to suffer from any number of health related problems. In addition, children who are raised in an unsafe environment without appropriate supervision are at risk for exposure to abuse, violence, alcohol and/or drugs at an early age (Cantwell, 1997).

The quality of parent-child interactions can also greatly impact young children. Children can be severely harmed by the behavior of psychologically distant and emotionally unavailable parents (English, 1995). Children who do not receive stimulation or engage in regular, positive interactions with their primary caretakers often have difficulties in cognitive and social-emotional functioning (Polansky, Gaudin, Ammons & Davis, 1985). They may suffer from low self-esteem, depression and attachment disorders, and present numerous behavioral problems, including limited social skills, a lack of cooperation and disinterest in engaging with other children or adults (Erikson, Egeland & Pianta, 1996). The experience of neglect as a child, has also been found to be related to functioning difficulties in adulthood. As adults, these individuals report chronic symptoms relating to trauma such as anxiety, depression, substance abuse, dissociation and sleep disturbances (Bevan & Higgins, 2002; Crittendon, 1999). In addition, childhood neglect has been found to be associated with physically abusive behaviors by men towards their spouses in adulthood (Bevan & Higgins, 2002).

Widom (2000) has pointed out that child maltreatment has consequences not only for the children and families directly involved but also society itself. The problems of maltreated children, including health or mental health problems, developmental delays, incomplete or inadequate education, and/or substance abuse, result in considerable costs to society. Detrimental behaviors such as delinquency and criminal activity result in significant societal outlays.

A study by Miller (as cited in Finkelhor & Hashima, 2001) has estimated that each case of reported child sexual abuse costs on average $5,800 for mental health care and $1,100 for social services. For each child abuse victim, the monetary estimate for loss in quality of life is calculated at $52,000. Interventions by public agencies that respond to reports of abuse is also costly. For example, in 1995, the combined federal and state expenditure for each child placed in foster care was approximately $29,092 annually (Courtney, 1998). Services provided by law enforcement, child welfare, crisis intervention centers and mental health providers, as well as juvenile and criminal court procedures result in incalculable costs to the public.

Societal Interventions

Numerous agencies, including child protection, law enforcement, crisis intervention, health and mental health care agencies, as well as the juvenile and criminal courts, respond to reports of child maltreatment. Protective service is usually the initial system to respond to reports of child maltreatment by a parent or caretaker. In contrast, the criminal justice system is required to respond to any form of child maltreatment reported to their agency that involves criminal activity. Although the two systems have distinct and separate roles, their caseloads frequently overlap.

Child welfare agencies are public agencies mandated to protect and provide care for the needs of abused and neglected children in a state or county. Within these child welfare agencies, protective services is the department that assesses, investigates and substantiates reports of child maltreatment inflicted by a family member or caretaker.

The goal of child protection is to ensure child well-being by protecting children from abuse and providing families with support

(Pecora et al., 2000). Despite this broad mission, until recently the primary focus of child protection has been the detection, investigation and placement outside the home. Although placement in a foster home was officially considered a temporary service, in reality many dependent children who entered the system were never reunited by their parents or adopted. These children spent most of their childhoods moving from foster home to foster home. This 'foster care drift' gave rise to a debate within child welfare over the contrasting needs of child victims, the need to be protected from maltreatment versus the importance of permanency and families of origin in children's lives.

The purpose of placement is to provide adequate care for the child and eliminate the risk of further abuse. Out-of-home placement, however, also carries risks to the child that must be balanced against the safety of the child's home environment. Although placement outside the home is designed to protect the child from further abuse, it can also disrupt the child's attachment to their family of origin and increase their chance of additional psychological trauma (Fanshel & Shinn, 1978).

Changes in child welfare legislation reflect attempts to balance these competing needs. In 1980, the Adoption Assistance and Child Welfare Act (PL-96-272) with its 1983 amendments made funding for foster care dependent on the utilization of reasonable efforts by states to keep maltreated children in the home or reunify them with their families, and instituted case review and court oversight procedures (U.S.D.H.H.S., 2000). The Multi-Ethnic Placement Act (PL 103-382) of 1994, amended in 1996, attempted to reduce the length of time children spend in out-of-home care and ensure that race, culture or ethnicity is not used to deny placement to a child (U.S.D.H.H.S., 2000). More recently, the Adoption and Safe Families Act of 1997 (PL 105-89), was enacted to swiftly move children in foster care into permanent placements by clarifying the circumstances under which reasonable efforts to reunify were not required and establishing firm timelines for showing a reduced likelihood of maltreatment, and for making decisions regarding permanent placements (U.S.D.H.H.S., 2000).

These changes in child welfare practice have attempted to provide necessary safeguards to meet the needs of children, however, they have also diminished the amount of time available to provide support services to families. Child welfare staff often find themselves lacking the necessary time or resources required by families impacted by multiple problems (Dawson & Berry, 2002).

Many of these reforms have been difficult to operationalize. For example, given increasing caseloads, many states find it difficult to adhere to mandated time frames regarding response time and investigation (Kopels, Chariton, & Wells, 2003). A recent New York Times ("U.S. Finds Fault", 2004) article reported that over the past three years, no state child welfare agency has been found in full compliance with the federal standards regarding child safety and permanency planning.

The procedures of the child protection system are fairly uniform across counties and states. Reports of maltreatment come to protective services from mandated reporters as well as law enforcement, parents, third parties, and child victims themselves. Mandatory reporters are groups of individuals who are required to report suspected incidents of child abuse when there is reason to believe that a child has been harmed or is at risk for harm. State laws vary in terms of who is designated to report, however, in most states mandatory reporters include medical professionals, mental health professionals, social workers, school and child care personnel, and law enforcement officers. Today, just slightly more than half of all reports of maltreatment are filed by mandatory reporters. In 1997, the median state reporting rate for abuse was 42 per 1,000 children (Pecora et al., 2000).

Incoming reports of maltreatment are first screened by agency personnel to determine if the requirements of protective service involvement are met. The abuse must have involved a caretaker or family member and be of a serious nature. Caretaker is defined broadly and includes anyone who is entrusted to be responsible for the child such as parents, household members, foster parents, babysitters, camp counselors, teachers and others. Those cases that fall within the protective service mandate are then referred for an investigation. The investigation, which may include both interviews with family members and other witnesses as well as a home visit, is the process by which the nature, extent and cause of the child's injuries are evaluated (Pecora et al., 2000). At this step, a determination is made as to whether or not the report of maltreatment can be substantiated or indicated. Following substantiation, cases are referred to a protective service case manager who develops service plans for the child and/or family and monitors the well being of the child and the progress of the family in the provision of adequate care.   Given the potential for serious and immediate harm in some cases of child maltreatment, protective service departments must have the ability to receive and respond to reports 24 hours a day (Pecora et al., 2000).

All substantiated cases of abuse are forwarded to a caseworker within the child welfare agency for a needs assessment and the development of a child and family service plan. The purpose of the service plan is to outline the types of resources protective services will provide to the child and family (i.e. case management, counseling) and clarify the expectations that the department has of both the child and family (Pecora et al., 2000).

Protective service caseworkers examine a number of factors in the development of a service plan for a child and family. The severity and duration of the abuse, the age and developmental functioning of the child, and any history of abuse or neglect in the family must be considered.   In addition, the caseworker must identify barriers that interfere with healthy family functioning (for example, domestic violence) and provide referrals to resources that help to ameliorate these problems. The agency is mandated to review the service plan at least every six months to determine if changes are required (Pecora et al., 2000).

Although case managers are required by federal law to make reasonable efforts to keep abused and neglected children with their families (Mori, 1994), they are also mandated, under AFSA, to develop permanency plans and, in many states, engage in family-centered practice.   Family-centered practice refers to a family-oriented, culturally competent, strengths-based approach that emphasizes parental accountability, agency transparency and a partnership approach to permanency planning (Pecora et al., 2000).

In some cases, the provision of support services or resources can address the maltreatment and other family problems adequately. However, when parents are not able to meet minimal standards of care, necessary services are not forthcoming, or it is determined that the risk of further maltreatment is likely, a recommendation of child removal from the home is often the most common course of action.

Children may be removed from their homes 'voluntarily', either by parents who request placement services or by primary caretakers who, following   an   investigation,   choose   to   cooperate   with   the recommendations of protective services to avoid a removal order by the juvenile court. However, most children are involuntarily removed from their home. Protective services can immediately remove a child on a temporary basis if the child is determined to be in imminent danger. For example, in cases of serious maltreatment such as child abandonment or life-threatening physical injury, protective service workers can take immediate custody of children without a court order. Following these emergency removals, the caseworker must write a report stating the reasons for the emergency removal and file a juvenile court petition within a short time period (Myers, 1998).

Court hearings to consider the need for child placement are usually conducted by a juvenile or family court judge. Oftentimes, a child welfare investigator files the child protection petition to initiate the hearing. The findings of the protective service investigation are of great importance in the juvenile court hearing (Davidson, 1997).

The goal of the juvenile court judge in dependency cases is to assess how to best provide protection and care to children. Children have the right to certain entitlements such as food, housing, medical care, education and protection. The best interest standard means that in many cases of maltreatment, the needs and rights of the child victim should be given priority. Determining the needs of the child can be difficult and complex concept. In any given case, there will be varying and opposing viewpoints. The judge hearing the case must sort through the evidence and determine whether the petition is true, whether the child should be removed and/or declared a dependent of the court. Later in the process, the judge must approve of both a dispositional plan for the child, and a permanency plan for the child. Each court hearing must be held according to strict timelines to ensure that the cases of dependent children do not languish in the system (Sagatun & Edwards, 1995; Woodhouse, 2001).

When child protective proceedings are initiated by protective services due to the emergency removal of a child, court action must occur within 24-72 hours if the child remains in placement. This preliminary hearing focuses on the whether or not the child needs a continuation of the placement (Davidson, 1997). If there is a finding that the child is in need of continued placement and no informal resolution is negotiated, a formal adjudicatory hearing will be scheduled. If the court finds that abuse or neglect has occurred, a disposition hearing is arranged in which child and family permanency and treatment plans are mandated (Davidson, 1997).

The criminal courts become involved in cases of child maltreatment when abusive behavior constitutes criminal activity. The criminal dispensation of child abuse cases is based upon the concept of 'parens patriae,' which established the state's ability to override parental authority and defend the rights of children and other people who are incapable of defending themselves (Haugaard, 1988; Myers, 1998). The adjudication of child abuse cases operates on the basic supposition that children have the right to be protected from abuse and that perpetrators of child abuse should be punished. The process of the criminal court is adversarial in nature and the authority of the court is confined to the alleged offender (Watkins, 1990a; Myers, 1998).

Under criminal law, acts of child maltreatment include both the physical battering of a child and sexual activity between adults and children. State statutes define child physical and sexual abuse under a variety of criminal codes. Severe acts of abuse are usually categorized as felonies whereas less serious incidents are considered misdemeanors. Acts of child abuse are technically considered crimes against the state, not against the child. The injury suffered by the victim of child abuse is prosecuted because of the harm it inflicts on a member of our society. Therefore, the complaint is brought forth by the office of the state's attorney and the child victims and witnesses testify on behalf of the state (Wilber, 1987).

The initial criminal investigation of a report of maltreatment is usually handled by law enforcement. Reports of abuse come to the police from child protection agencies, parents, child victims and third parties. As with child protection agencies, police departments must investigate all complaints of child abuse received by their organization. The investigator is responsible for contacting medical and crisis intervention services in emergency cases, securing the scene of the crime, collecting evidence, conducting background investigations, and interviewing the victim, witnesses and suspects (Shephard, 1997). Law enforcement officers can also use their legal authority to arrest the suspected perpetrator of the crime (Shephard, 1997). If they are the first responder, a police officer may also be charged with the removal of a child from the home in cases of serious risk (Shephard, 1997).

Although the role of law enforcement to the criminal justice system is clear, its relationship to the child welfare system is more variable depending upon state law and interagency protocols. In following up on reports of maltreatment, police officers may conduct sole investigations, joint investigations, or simply provide support to the child protection investigator who is taking the lead on the case. In many states, law enforcement works hand in hand with child protection in regards to reports of abuse. In other jurisdictions, a separate, and at times, adversarial, relationship exists (Finkelhor & Ormrod, 2001).

The criminal justice process in child abuse crimes involves several stages including the reporting or detection of the crime, the victim interview and investigation, the filing of formal charges, arrest, prosecution, adjudication and sentencing (Louthan, 1985). Reports of criminal abuse are forwarded to the district offices of the state's attorney and, if appropriate, to child protection. The right of the state's attorney to file criminal charges is known as prosecutorial discretion (Myers, 1998). For misdemeanors or minor felonies, a prosecutor may file charges but in serious felony cases, evidence is often presented to a grand jury to initiate indictment.

Criminal investigations of child abuse often take more time than other types of cases and require specialized training (American Prosecutors Research Institute-APRI, 2004; Froum & Kendall-Tackett, 1998; Portwood, Grady & Dutton, 2000). At a number of points in this process, decisions are made that impact how the case proceeds. For example, decisions by law enforcement, the state's attorney and criminal court personnel can determine whether a case will be dropped or move forward, be diverted, be settled by plea bargain or move forward to trial. The findings of the investigation will greatly influence whether or not an alleged offender will be arrested, charged, and prosecuted (Besharov, 1990). Information from the investigation will also inform the prosecutor's decision as to whether or not to negotiate a plea bargain or recommend that the case be diverted.

Child abuse cases involving immediate arrests are more likely to be prosecuted, for two reasons. First, they often involve physical and/or medical evidence and eyewitness testimony which can support successful case prosecution. Second, an arrest puts a case in motion in the judicial process. Following an arrest, the assigned prosecutor must take steps to halt prosecution of a case, otherwise, it simply goes forward. In cases in which an immediate arrest does not occur, prosecutors often confer with the police on the strength of the evidence and the credibility of witnesses prior to making a decision regarding prosecution.

There are two methods of indictment (or charging a person of a criminal act), through 'an information' or via a grand jury indictment. An information, or the initiation of criminal charges either by an immediate arrest or through the filing of a complaint in a district court, sets in motion the criminal justice process. The filing of charges allows police to keep the alleged perpetrator in jail until the arraignment, which is the formal presentation of charges in open court, and the setting of bail. In contrast, a grand jury indictment is an indictment that occurs when the evidence is presented to a panel of citizens by the prosecutor. The grand jury must decide if there is probable cause to believe that the crime was committed, and that it was committed by the accused individual. The prosecutor presents evidence and the grand jury members must decide if it is sufficient to indict the accused (Myers, 1998).

An immediate arrest and district court indictment can sometimes help with successful prosecution, especially in cases of physical abuse. If a physical abuse perpetrator is immediately arrested, the child may be freed from the pressure of an abusive parent and the prosecutor can work with the child on testifying and assist in getting services provided to the nonoffending parent. When physically abusive parents are not arrested but are called into court for an arraignment at a later date, it is possible that the child will refuse to testify due to pressure from the alleged perpetrator and out of fear for his or her physical safety. However, an arrest followed by a swift indictment can also interfere with successful prosecution because it may give the Assistant District Attorney little time to gather evidence and interview witnesses (D. Deakin, personal communication, August 1, 1998).

In a grand jury indictment, the prosecutor typically has more control over the charging process. A grand jury indictment allows the prosecutor the ability to determine the charges against the individual and interview the child victim prior to the accused having any awareness of the impending complaint. It also gives him or her additional time to collect evidence, interview witnesses, assess the level of cooperation likely to be received from the child and family and determine if interventions other than prosecution (e.g. treatment) are most appropriate (Davidson, 1997). Technically, the decision to go forward with a prosecution can be made without the consent or cooperation of the child or family, however, the cooperation of the child and family is often needed for a case to be successfully prosecuted (Suffolk County District Attorney's Office, 1996b).

Child abuse can be difficult to prosecute (Costin, Karger, Stoesz, 1996; A.P.R.I., 2004). This can be especially true when the perpetrator of the abuse is a family member (Finkelhor & Hashima, 2001). Prosecutors indicate that a number of factors influence their decision to prosecute a case including the emotional well-being of child, cooperation of the parent, credibility of the child as a witness, availability of corroborating evidence, nature and severity of the maltreatment and degree of publicity focused on the case (A.P.R.I., 2004).

The decision to accept or reject a case of child abuse for prosecution is often based on the likelihood that the prosecution will be successful. Prosecutors must assess the strength of the evidence and the ability of the child to serve as a witness (Myers, 1998). Unlike other types of crimes, corroborating physical and medical evidence is often lacking and the case often rests on the victims ability to describe maltreatment and stand up under questioning (Faller,1990; McCauley et al., 2001; National Research Council, 1993). The statements of the child regarding the abuse to family or other adults, the statements made in formal interviews, child behavioral symptoms following the abuse, and a therapist's evaluation may all be considered. The prosecutor must also consider whether evidence relating to the defendant, such as an opportunity to commit the crime, a history of prior maltreatment of children, polygraph results, or a partial admission is helpful (A.P.R.I., 2004).

The effectiveness of the child victim as a witness is impacted by her or his ability to recall and answer questions about the abusive incident(s). The environment of the courtroom and the developmental level and cognitive skills of the child can greatly influence the child's performance in the courtroom (Ceci & Bruck, 1995).

In some jurisdictions, the competency of children to testify must be determined in a pretrial hearing (Bulkley, Feller, Stern & Roe, 1996; A.P.R.I., 2004). These child witnesses must demonstrate their ability to tell the difference between a lie and the truth (McCauley et al., 2001). Another barrier to successful prosecution can be the child's retraction of the accusation of abuse, often due to pressure exerted by the family on the child (Bulkley, 1988).

The criminal courts do not easily accommodate the complaints of child victims of abuse. Our legal structures and procedures were designed with adult witnesses in mind (Goodman et al., 1992). Since the criminal adjudication of child abuse cases can result in a loss of liberty for the accused, the alleged offender is provided many legal protections. A defendant in a criminal case has certain constitutional rights including the right to confront and cross-examine witnesses, the right to reasonable bail, the right to a jury trial and the right to appeal (Sagatun & Edwards, 1995).

It can be difficult for victims and their family members to understand why a prosecutor may decide to not file charges against an alleged offender. Although a prosecutor may believe that a crime has been committed, he or she may still decline the case because they do not foresee that they will be able to produce sufficient evidence to meet a standard of proof beyond a reasonable doubt (A.P.R.I., 2004; Myers, 1998).

Court reforms and innovative procedures that support the child ability to give testimony have been implemented in numerous states. These include: information sharing and joint investigations by multidisciplinary teams; coordination between the juvenile and criminal courts; child and family courtroom visits prior to the trial; educational programs that teach children and their families about the criminal court procedures; training attorneys and judges about child witnesses; reducing the number of continuances granted; the exclusion of spectators from the courtroom; the use of victim-advocates and court-appointed special advocates to provide support to the child prior to and during the trial; sequestration of witnesses during the child's testimony; the use of videotaped testimony; and the use of closed circuit television or one-way mirrors to shelter the child from testifying in open court (A.P.R.I., 2004; Bulkley et al., 1996; Myers, 1996; Saywitz & Snyder, 1993; Watkins, 1990a). Professionals in the field of child welfare report that these innovative reforms are helpful in increasing the chances of successful prosecution, however, little empirical research is available currently to better inform us of their effectiveness.

Some child advocates have raised concerns regarding the impact of prosecution and a trial on the well-being of a child victim. Researchers have found that involvement in court processes can have both positive and negative effects on the mental health of maltreated children

(Goodman et al., 1992; Runyan, Everson, Edelsohn, Hunter & Coulter, 1988). Children can become stressed by numerous interviews, having to tell their story to a judge and jury, and facing an intimating defense attorney. However, prosecution of a case can also validate to the child and their family that the behavior of the offender was not acceptable (Harshbarger, 1987). In addition, testifying has been found to help some children to recover from the trauma of abuse, whether or not there is a conviction (Henry, 1997). Runyan (et al., 1988) found children who testified in juvenile court better able to initiate closure regarding the abuse than children who had not testified. However, the same study found that child abuse cases that moved slowly through the criminal justice system were more likely to result in poor mental health outcomes for children.

Mental health professionals have also argued that the treatment of child abuse offenders can be undermined by criminal court involvement (Steele, 1975, Westcott & Page, 2002). However, many professionals within child protection and criminal justice see benefits to children, families and offenders arising from judicial interventions. Protective service workers frustration regarding their inability to intervene with some abusive families in any way other than child removal. They see criminal justice involvement in child abuse cases as essential in terms of providing some type of influence and control over the alleged perpetrator (Wilbur, 1987). Whether or not prosecution is successful, arrest and indictment can be helpful in separating the offender from the child. The perpetrator's fear of prosecution and incarceration can help child protection to get offenders to comply with service plans. Criminal justice involvement can also strengthen external constraints on an offender by supporting the child's understanding of the abuse act as a crime, helping the child to resist future abuse and encouraging the nonoffending parent to perceive the abuse as serious and damaging to the child (Wilbur, 1987).

Health, mental health and crisis intervention agencies also play important roles in our societal response to reports of maltreatment. Professionals within these organizations are often critical in the identification of child abuse and neglect. As mandated reporters, these professionals are required to report both confirmed and suspected abuse to child protection. In addition, crisis intervention centers provide 24-hour information, referral and victim advocacy to children and their families. Mental health service providers may serve not only as therapist for the child victim and family, but also be called upon to testify in juvenile or criminal court and participate in multidisciplinary case reviews (Faller, 1990). Physicians and nurses also act as service providers to abused children and their families. Medical personnel diagnose abuse; conduct forensic exams to collect evidence; provide health care for injuries; conduct forensic exams for the collection of evidence; consult with protective services and law enforcement; testify in court; and participate on multidisciplinary teams to manage and investigate child abuse (Starling and Boos, 2003). Unfortunately, many health professionals are not adequately trained to diagnose maltreatment or/and conduct forensic exams, especially in regards to child sexual abuse (Lentsch & Johnson, 2000).

Over the past fifteen years, multidisciplinary, community-based interventions have been developed to address the numerous needs of child victims (Weber, 1997). The concurrent involvement of child protection, criminal justice, medical and mental health agencies in child abuse cases necessitates the need for systemic coordination to ensure the best possible child and case outcomes. Many agencies have established formal protocols that outlined the role of each and guidelines to support collaboration between organizations.

Agency protocols that allow or mandate early case referral to outside agencies and case review meetings can be particularly beneficial. Early case referral can enable law enforcement and protective service to conduct joint investigations of reports of maltreatment. Multi-agency case review meetings facilitate information sharing across agencies. The collective review of facts and perspectives regarding a particular case can result in better decision-making by child protection, law enforcement, and prosecutors (Davidson, 1997).

Professionals in the mental health, child protection, law enforcement and criminal justice fields have come to recognize the need to utilize well trained interviewers to obtain information about the maltreatment from the child victim. All three of these systems rely on the statement of the child victim to formulate decisions regarding the needs of the child, the next steps in the investigation, and the likelihood of successful prosecution. It is important for skilled interviewers to use age appropriate, focused and nonleading questions to elicit information from the child about the abuse, in a comfortable and supportive environment. Improper interviewing of sexual abuse victims has been found to be associated with false allegations and negative outcomes for children (DeVoe & Faller, 2002; Wood & Garven, 2000).

The use of trained interviewers lessens the possibility of retraumatization of the child which can occur through participation in the investigation and adjudication processes. In addition, conducting one multidisciplinary interview, involving child protection, law enforcement and the prosecutor's office, avoids the need for the victim to repeat the details of the abuse to numerous individuals.

A number of different models of multidisciplinary cooperation have been developed to respond to reports of child abuse. Sheppard and Zangrillo (1996) outline three models of interagency collaboration; joint investigation programs, multidisciplinary interview centers and children's advocacy centers. Joint investigation protocols provide an opportunity for law enforcement, child welfare, prosecutors, and medical and mental health professionals to cross report, share information and monitor case progress without added expense to the cooperating agencies. A multidisciplinary interview center builds on the basic elements of this model by creating a facility within one of the participating agencies in which the agency representatives can meet and child interview specialists can conduct forensic interviews.

Children's advocacy centers represent a more comprehensive multidisciplinary approach to minimize the trauma experienced by the child and expedite services and resources. These centers, which may be housed within a host agency or independently, support child victims by coordinating protective service and law enforcement involvement and offering health and mental health services or resources to the child and family. These agencies may be administered by one of the participating agencies or they may represent a private agency with their own board of directors and staff (Sheppard & Zangrillo, 1996). Children's advocacy center involvement typically revolves around the coordination of one multidisciplinary team interview conducted by a trained professional. Some centers may also provide medical, mental health and victim advocacy services and coordinate the collection and preservation of evidence through an on-site forensic medical examination (McCauley et al., 2001). Ideally, the offices of the investigating detectives and child protection investigators are located within the children's advocacy center (Sheppard & Zangrillo, 1996). By working together to provide a coordinated, multidisciplinary response, children's advocacy centers hope to improve the outcomes of child abuse cases in the criminal courts. The findings of two recent studies indicate that prosecution and conviction rates may be increased through the interventions of children's advocacy centers (Joa & Edelson, 2004; T. Cross, personal communication, October 3, 2004).

Child welfare policies regarding information sharing and collaboration with other agencies differ greatly from state to state. All states specify in their statutes that law enforcement can be involved in investigations relating to specific types of abuse, usually sexual abuse and/or severe abuse (U.S.D.H.H.S., 2003a). At least thirty states have authorized, but not mandated, joint investigations by protective services and law enforcement (A.P.R.I., 2004). However, case referral to law enforcement and the prosecutor's office is usually discretionary. Although coordination between systems is now considered the best method of practice, only about half of all jurisdictions have developed protocols to ensure that agencies work together on cases (Whitcomb & Hardin, 1996).

Future Focus

The National Research Council (1993) has reported that there is a dire need for more research in the field of child maltreatment. The differences between neglect and physical and sexual abuse, and the factors that contribute to each of them, need to be clarified in more depth to enhance the efficacy of intervention efforts. Data are needed on the utility of coordinated multidisciplinary responses to abuse including the effectiveness of children's advocacy centers. Researchers have also pointed out that more attention should be paid to the role of the juvenile and criminal courts in cases of child abuse (Widom, 2001). For example, it is not yet known if and how much criminal penalties serve to reduce the incidence of maltreatment. Another important question to be answered is whether criminal interventions, such as the arrest and removal of the offender from the home, can serve to protect a child victim from further abuse (Widom, 2001).

The importance of prevention of child maltreatment is also gaining recognition. Although there has always been interest in developing and implementing prevention programs, historically funding in this area has been negligible. Currently, prevention of child maltreatment is a major focus of the federal Children's Bureau and the Office on Child Abuse and Neglect (U.S.D.H.H.S., 2003c).

Professionals in child maltreatment have targeted three groups for prevention activities; the general public, populations at high-risk for child abuse, and families in which maltreatment has already occurred (U.S.D.H.H.S., 2003c). School-based child sexual abuse prevention programs, which have been in place since 1980, have been the most common type of prevention program. These programs attempt to train children to recognize appropriate and inappropriate touch (Kohl, 1993) and provide teachers and school administrators with information regarding identifying and responding to maltreatment. More recently school-based programs have been developed to teach children skills that may deter them from becoming abusers themselves. These programs have focused on peaceful conflict resolution, problem-solving, stress management, anger management and empathy training (McCauley et al, 2001). Children who participate in these programs demonstrate greater knowledge of abuse and utilize protective behaviors and strategies when threatened (Finkelhor & Dzuiba-Leatherman, 1995, as cited in U.S.D.H.H.S., 2003c)

Another promising endeavor in the area of prevention are community-based programs that reach out to families prior to involvement with child protective services. Community based child abuse prevention programs have focused on addressing family stressors associated with child maltreatment by providing parenting education and support, resources and referrals. Prevention programs that offer support to families with children under three that are at risk for child abuse and neglect have been found to be helpful in reducing the occurrence of maltreatment (Geeraert, Van Den Noortgate, Grietens & Onghena, 2004). Levanthal (1997, as cited in U.S.D.H.H.S., 2003c) suggests that the effectiveness of community based services can be increased through the provision of intensive services over time, a focus on parenting skills, child-centered practices, addressing basic needs issues, and by including fathers in the intervention. It is believed that community based programs can be more successful in reaching parents prior to abuse occurring because they are less stigmatizing and more accessible to families than public child welfare agencies (McCauley et al., 2001).

CHAPTER 3

Theoretical Perspectives on Inter-agency Collaboration

Understanding the ways in which the actions of the criminal justice and child protection systems may impact each other requires an examination of sociological theory on the nature of social systems (Bulkley, 1967). Structural-functional theory in sociology assumes that structures in our society are composed of mutually integrated parts that are always striving toward equilibrium. Contradictions within and among social systems result in adjustments within and between institutions in our society (Bulkley, 1967).

Systems theory provides a conceptual framework for understanding social structures and institutions. The theory utilizes equilibrium as one of its core elements focusing on the fluid and interactive nature of systems. The theory postulates that social systems constantly attempt to create an internal and external balance and, therefore, are best understood as dynamic and interactive organisms (Bulkley, 1967).

A social system can be defined as a set of elements that create orderly interaction in our society. Social systems are the tools by which the needs of individuals, families and society, as a whole, are addressed (Norlin & Chess, 1997). A social system is composed of "the interaction of a plurality of individual actors whose relations to each other are mutually oriented through the definition and mediation of a pattern of structured and shared symbols and expectations" (Loomis, 1960). Social systems exist at every level of interaction, from a pattern of association between two families, to ongoing communications between community organizations, to economic exchanges between nations. Social systems may be informal in nature, for example, the casual relationships that exist between individuals

35

living in an apartment complex, or formal, such as the character of the organizational structure that exists within the criminal justice system.

One of the primary propositions of systems theory is that all social systems utilize the same principles of functioning (Smelser, 1994). Loomis' (1960) Processually Articulated Structural Model (PASM) is based of this principle. The PASM model provides a framework for understanding the elements and processes of social systems. Social systems are comprised of nine types of elements and processes including (Loomis, 1960):

- goal attainment (objectives of the system)
- norms (norms characterizing the system)
- status roles (functions and roles within the system)
- rank (structure of individual and group standing within the system)
- power (systemic capacity to control)
- sanction (systemically controlled rewards and penalties)
- facility (means to attain ends utilized by system)
- knowledge (beliefs informing the system)
- sentiment (feelings about the system)

Systems can also be defined by their boundaries, which describe the relationships within and outside of a system and give the system a specific identity. Boundaries define the overall role of the system in our society (Zastrow & Kirst-Ashman, 1997). For example, one boundary surrounding the child protection system is the limitation of the organization to the specific mandate of providing adequate protection and care for children.

Systems theory postulates that all systems have a tendency to organize behavior in such a way as to maintain homeostasis, a state of balance (Zastrow & Kirst-Ashman, 1997). This is useful in that it keeps social institutions from easily disintegrating, however, it can be detrimental if the maintenance of the status quo takes precedence over the overall mission of the system (Norlin & Chess, 1997).

Systems exist in a state of constant interaction with other systems. These interactions are usually patterned, resulting in mutual exchanges and communications that create ongoing relationships between them. Relationships between systems are characterized by systemic input and output. Input is defined as information, activity or resources received by one system from another system. Ouput is the production of a system; resources, actions or communications that are the result of the internal processing of input (Zastrow & Kirst-Ashman, 1997). The output of one system is likely to become input for another system. The interface is that point (or points) of contact or communication that occurs between two or more systems in the input and output process (Zastrow & Kirst-Ashman, 1997).

For example, the criminal justice system receives input in the form of child abuse case referrals from protective services. The system then develops output in the form of the case prosecution decision, which is partly based on the information contained within and the timing related to the case referral from child protection.

Likewise, the child protection system receives input in the form of the report of child maltreatment and the information obtained through the protective service investigation. That input is utilized in the decision-making process regarding what is needed to create an adequate living environment for the child. Removal of the child from the home is one of a number of outputs that may follow as a result of this input.

Activity surrounding the prosecution decision, such as the arrest of a suspect, may also serve as input for child protection in the form of information on the current risk of abuse to the child. This information may influence the creation of output within the child protection system, namely the decision of whether or not a child should be removed from or returned to his or her home.

Systems theory clearly supports the supposition that, on a case by case basis, the output of the criminal justice system can influence the decision-making and interventions of child protection. Likewise, the actions of protective services may impact the determinations and outcomes within the judicial system for a particular case. However, it is unclear the extent to which the two institutions can work together at their points of interface to more effectively meet their distinct goals. The ability of the two systems to work together to create and maintain a coordinated pattern of mutually beneficial interaction deserves further examination.

Unfortunately, systems theory, in its current form, is unable to provide a framework for understanding the factors that stimulate and deter cooperative efforts between systems. The theory fails to identify a method by which the complex, non-linear processes that characterize the relationships between systems can be operationalized (Hudson, 2000). In addition, systems theory has yet to develop tools for identifying when points of interface between two systems occur due to the purposeful creation of collaborative processes versus exchanges that are not predicted or planned on a systemic level.

Merging the concepts of systems theory with aspects of complexity theory provides a more useful framework for understanding the factors that influence actions within and between systems (Hudson, 2000). Complexity theory conceptualizes systems as dynamic compositions of ever-changing and, at times, unpredictable transitions and events. The theory allows for the examination of a nonlinear systemic process that captures the blending of both chaotic and routine courses of action (Michaels, 1989).

The continuous process of individual and organizational adaptation is a central component of complexity theory. Under complexity theory, systems are viewed as containing internal processes that absorb and spontaneously respond to changes imposed upon the system by external forces (Michaels, 1989). Adaptation models attempt to predict behavior by capturing the fundamental processes at work both within and between systems (Axelrod & Bennett, 1997).

The adaptation approach is helpful to the question at hand because the outcomes of inter-organizational interactions are difficult to predict, even by individuals familiar with the system. The smallest forms of interaction between agencies can have large scale unexpected effects, because so many interactive processes occur simultaneously at various levels within a system.

One adaptation model that attempts to identify the elements that influence cooperation within and between systems is the landscape theory of aggregation. Aggregation refers to the "organization of elements of a system into patterns that tend to put highly compatible elements together and less compatible elements apart" (Axelrod & Bennett, 1997, p.72). Landscape theory specifically focuses on the ways in which the elements of two systems can or cannot fit together and which configurations are most likely to occur. In the context of this text, it can be used to lay a foundation for understanding the potentiality of cooperative efforts between the criminal justice and child protective systems (Axelrod & Bennett, 1997).

Landscape theory uses the size, distance and propensity of systems to estimate configurations that represent relationships between them

(Axelrod & Bennett,1997). Size may be understood as both the scope of a system and the number of agencies and individuals that belong to it. Distance refers to the ways in which two or more systems may be grouped in relation to each other. Propensity can be defined as the degree of potential conflict that exists between two systems. Landscape theory purports that systems that lack similarity in size, distance and/or have a high degree of potential conflict are less likely to join together in cooperative efforts (Axelrod & Bennett,1997)

To apply this theory to the question at hand requires an assessment of the factors that could support or limit cooperation between criminal justice and child protection agencies. The two systems in which these agencies are imbedded are roughly equal in size, both being national social institutions that utilize state or county infrastructures to deal with cases of social or criminal misconduct. The distance between the two systems is considerable. The two institutions are sub-systems of two separate and distinct supra-systems, the judicial branch of state and national government and the national and state child welfare system. In most states, statutory policy allowing for joint investigations or the formation of multidisciplinary teams between the two systems serves as the only formal structural linkage between the systems. Points of contact between the two institutions exist primarily on the lower, practice levels.

For the purpose of this study, the propensity or degree of potential conflict between the criminal justice and child protection system will be determined through an examination of the similarities and differences that exist between their functional elements, as previously described in the PASM model.

The PASM model provides a useful framework for analyzing the relational compatibility of criminal justice and child protection systems. The activities of the two social systems are clearly based upon overlapping but distinct goals and objectives. The goal of the judicial system is to protect individuals and the community and provide justice to those who have suffered harm. Criminal justice agencies accomplish this by upholding the laws of society, making decisions as to when a crime has been committed and assigning consequences to offenses (Sagatun & Edwards, 1995).

In contrast, the overarching mission of the child welfare system is to provide for the well-being of children. The system was developed to create an institutional structure that would strive to meet the physical,

Table 1: A Comparison of the Functional Elements of the Child Protection and Criminal Justice Systems

System Function	Child Protection	Criminal Justice
Goal	Ensure that children are provided with adequate care and protection.	Protect individuals and society from harm. Provide justice to victims of crime.
Norms	Agency interventions are informed by what is in the best of interest of the child. Interests of the child may outweigh rights of the parent.	Individuals who engage in criminal acts must be held accountable, however, the accused is innocent until proven guilty beyond a reasonable doubt.
Status Roles	Limited functions within a bureaucratic structure	Autonomous functions in a bureaucratic setting
Rank	Rigid hierarchical structure; clear ranking of positions	Loosely structured hierarchy; team approach to cases.
Power	Individuals are afforded decision-making power which can impact the lives of abused children and their families.	Individuals decide which cases will be prosecuted. The system has the ability to interfere with individual freedom.
Sanction	Temporary or permanent alterations in child custody.	Incarceration, restraint of movement, treatment.
Knowledge	Child maltreatment is harmful to children and children should be protected from it.	Child maltreatment is harmful to society. Abusers of children should be punished.
Sentiment	Agency intervention is justified and necessary.	Society is protected from harm by the actions taken by the agency.

psychological and social needs of children.   Child protection organizations contribute to this goal by intervening with children in danger of maltreatment and providing services or placement for children in need of assistance or protection.   The needs of the child are central to the child protection system (Costin, 1972).

It is clear that the criminal justice and child protection systems play crucial, but distinct, roles in our society.   The first focuses on upholding laws and the second on meeting the needs of children.   The separation of the two systems is necessary to ensure clarity of purpose and to allow for the most effective environment in which each can pursue their mission.

The criminal justice system was not designed to meet the needs of abused children in a holistic manner.   It is often unable to provide child victims with the social recognition and reparations they may desire in regards to the abuse they have suffered.   The abundance of rights afforded to the accused by the criminal justice system is necessary to uphold its role as the impartial purveyor of justice.   However, it often interferes with the court's ability to address criminal offenses to the satisfaction of victimized parties (Conte, 1984).

Alternatively, the child protection system is not structured to address criminal activity.   It acts as a safety net for children and, in conjunction with the juvenile courts, serves to address a broad range of issues relating to the quality of children's lives.   Protective service operations are designed to meet the best interests of the child, not the strict procedures of fairness that guide the criminal courts (Sagatun & Edwards, 1995).   This allows the child protection system to quickly intervene in children's lives which most likely saves many young people from continued abuse and neglect.   However, the system is purposefully limited in its ability to address the behavior of the maltreating offender.

Both the criminal justice and child protection systems share the protection of individuals in our society as a common theme.   Criminal justice seeks to protect the abused child by identifying and placing limitations on offenders.   Protective services attempts to ensure protection by focusing on meeting the child's needs for adequate care and safety.

The two systems also share a common set of child abuse cases in which they initiate investigation and, potentially, intervene.   However, the mandates of each are broader than the small segment of child abuse cases upon which their work intersects.

The norms of the two systems also overlap. Norms refer to the standards that inform the systemic mission and the means by which the system reaches its goal. Norms may include both written and unwritten standards influencing a particular system (Loomis, 1960). Child protection and criminal justice share the norm that the physical and sexual abuse of children is wrong and that parents are responsible for providing adequate care for their children.

However, protective service involvement is informed by the norm that actions taken by the agency should be in the best interest of the child. A child's right to safety and care can outweigh a parent's right to govern the life of a child. The state's interest in protecting the children can surpass the desires of either the parents or the child.

In contrast, the central norm of the criminal justice system is that individuals who engage in criminal acts must be held accountable. Offenders should be punished and/or rehabilitated so that individuals in our society may be protected from harmful behavior. Judicial involvement is guided by the norm that everyone should be treated equally, or without bias, under the law. An individual accused of a crime should be considered innocent until proven guilty beyond a reasonable doubt (Grosman, 1969).

Status-role can be defined as the roles that individuals play within any given system. The rank of an individual within a system is often a function of their status-role. Rank refers to an individual's standing within a system; the importance of the individual to the system and the authority they are accorded by the system (Loomis, 1960).

The roles of individuals within protective services are clearly delineated. Child protection is carried out in state-based organizations that function as bureaucracies. The characteristics of a bureaucracy include the organization of positions hierarchically, the specialization of positions, a rigid structure of operational procedures and impersonal relationships between actors (Netting, Kettner, & McMurtry, 1998; Wilson, 1989).

Child protection employees are designated a specific function within the hierarchy as a case screener, investigator, ongoing caseworker, trainer, supervisor, administrator or a member of the support staff. The activities that an employee may engage in are clearly defined for each role. Although the day to day activities of screeners, investigators and caseworkers allow for independence in terms of focus, independent decision making is limited for all employees below the supervisory or administrative level. Supervisor approval is usually required before actions can be taken on any case.

The rank, or standing of individuals within the system is high for positions at the top of the hierarchy and low for positions situated at the bottom. The authority of protective service front line workers such as support staff screeners, investigators and caseworkers is significantly less than that of supervisors and administrators.

The rationale for this tight organizational structure lies in the function of this agency within our broader society. Protective services is charged with the protection of <u>all</u> maltreated children. The seriousness of the consequences that could result from mistakes made by agency employees puts tremendous pressure on protective service administrators to adhere to procedures that will minimize errors. Detailed procedural guidelines, close supervision and extensive documentation are examples of the system's attempt to ensure quality control in the behavior of all of its employees.

In many ways, the criminal justice system also functions as a bureaucracy, however, the reliance of the system on individual knowledge and expertise does not allow for a rigid internal structure (Grosman, 1969). Positions in the criminal justice system are organized hierarchically but they also require specialized training and credentials. Operational procedures outline the adjudication process and the steps to be taken to meet systemic goals. The roles in the broader judicial system include judges, clerks, district attorneys, defense attorneys, victim advocates, administrators and support staff; each of whom has a set place in the formal hierarchy.

However, the organizational hierarchy is far less rigid than the protective service structure. Assistant district attorneys have a direct reporting link to the state's attorney but they function very independently and without close supervision. Outside of the time spent in court, the day to day work of individuals within the prosecutors office is characterized by autonomy. The education, knowledge and expertise required of prosecutors and their high standing within the criminal justice hierarchy affords them an operational role that is particularly unconstrained.

The prosecutor has the authority to represent the district attorney and make decisions about which cases to prosecute and the means by which the adjudication should be brought forward. Prosecutors are able to engage in a great deal of discretionary behavior, on both an individual and structural level (Louthan, 1985). Therefore, unlike protective service investigators, prosecutors have the autonomy to be both flexible and creative in their decision-making.

On the level of the supra-system, both the criminal justice and child welfare systems have been granted authoritative power, the right to control the behaviors of individuals in our society. Systems operationalize power through the use of sanctions; the rewards or penalties that are distributed in relation to how individual behavior concurs with or deviates from norms (Loomis, 1960). Criminal justice sanctions include incarceration, restraint of movement and court ordered treatment. Child welfare sanctions include taking a child into custody on a temporary basis and recommending the removal of a child or the termination of parental rights.

However, status-role limits the power of most individuals within both systems to grant sanctions. For example, protective service investigators can only remove children temporarily on an emergency basis. To obtain formal state custody, a juvenile court judge must sign an order. The prosecutor is limited in a similar manner. Although he or she can initiate an arrest and bring forward a criminal case against an alleged offender, only a judge or jury can find a defendant to be guilty of a charge that will result in any sanctions against the individual.

Within both systems, the decision-making of individual staff members who engage directly with the public is pivotal in the allocation of sanctions. These front line employees, who serve as 'street level bureaucrats' (Lipsky, 1980), have discretion over how the specific sanctions of their institution will be allocated.

Within child protection, the street-level bureaucrats include the case screeners and investigators who compile the facts of the case, make a substantiation decision and assess the immediate risk to the child. Protective service investigators, set policy for their agency every day through their decision-making regarding which child is and is not being provided with adequate care (Lipsky, 1980). Cases that are dropped at this point are, essentially, not at risk for negative sanctions.

The prosecutor is faced with a similar task in his or her assessment of which cases should or should not be pursued for criminal adjudication. The personal needs, attitudes, and biases of the individuals in these positions greatly influence which individuals will be considered for sanctions at a later point.

The decisions of protective service investigators are influenced by their role as the public representative of a rigidly bureaucratic organization. The media pays a great deal of attention to their work and steps taken by front line workers are regularly met with public criticism. This watchful atmosphere results in conservative decision-making and low risk behavior on the part of most caseworkers (McNamara, 1998).

Child protection investigators also have unreasonably high caseloads and limited resources. In response, they strive to find ways to accomplish their work that will both meet with the expectations of the agency and satisfy their own ideals in regards to their role. Any tasks not considered essential by either the caseworker or his or her supervisor have little chance of being completed. The record of constant turnover among front line protective service workers confirms the difficulty individuals face in these demanding and publicly unappreciated positions.

In comparison, individuals who serve as prosecutors face less pressure both publicly and within their internal organizational structure. They, too, represent the state, however, the nature of the risk-taking in which they engage does not have the same potential for public reproach. A protective service worker may be found at fault for allowing a child to remain in an abusive home but a prosecutor is less frequently critiqued for not prosecuting an offender who commits a second offense.

The discretionary ability of prosecutors affords them more independence and power in decision-making than that afforded to most protective service workers. Given their autonomy, prosecutors have more freedom to allow their personal ideals and professional self-interest to influence their decision-making (Grosman, 1969).

In regards to resource management, prosecutors are faced with the same dilemma as protective service investigators. They are obliged to address what they must do before they can address what they would like to do. Once the police make an arrest, a case is in process and the prosecutor is compelled to take action to stop the case (i.e. drop the charges). The other option is to simply allow the case to go forward. Therefore, police referred cases always monopolize the prosecutor's docket because intervention is required to halt the prosecution (D. Deakin, personal communication, August 1, 1999).

The choice of which cases to prosecute clearly involves time management. The District Attorney cannot go to court for every case that comes to the office so those cases that are perceived as having the potential for success are the ones primarily chosen for prosecution (Bucci, Wall, Suarez, Coakley, Soldati, 1998).

However, the behavior of prosecutors is also influenced by the norms of their profession (Grosman, 1969). Obtaining and maintaining the respect of judges, defense attorneys, colleagues, and the public is important to most prosecutors. Prosecutors feel pressure to succeed at trial. They want to be seen as competent attorneys and good decision-makers. Prosecutors fear that if they too often bring forward cases that prove to be unsuccessful, they will be more likely to be challenged in the future by defense attorneys at each procedural step (Grosman, 1969).

Knowledge and sentiment, the final two elements of the PASM model, are inextricably intertwined. They also inform all of the other systemic functions. Knowledge refers to the beliefs that are held by individuals within the system and sentiment is concerned with the feelings people within the system have about the system (Loomis, 1960).

Within the protective service system, individual workers are expected to believe in the overarching norms that children must be protected from maltreatment and that agency intervention is both valid and necessary. Since most protective service workers entered the field with the desire to help others, it is necessary that they believe that the work they do is important and in the best interest of children, families and society. The role of the protective service front-line worker is similar to that of many other street bureaucrats. In order to feel good about the intrusive role they must play with families, protective service investigators may choose to conceptualize their work narrowly, focusing on individual or family dysfunction, and avoid examining the limitations of the overall approach of the bureaucracy they represent (Lipsky, 1980).

Criminal justice staff members are also expected to take on the norms of their agency, particularly the importance of controlling individuals in order to protect society. Systemic structure requires that employees view individuals as victims or offenders, which may cause worker's dissonance, especially when dealing with juvenile offenders.

Overall, individuals in the judicial system appear to have more freedom than protective service employees to exhibit a range of beliefs and feelings about systemic intervention. This may be due to the primarily positive public view of the institution as the overseer of public morality and social control. In addition, the wider range of approaches that are utilized by criminal justice, such as plea bargains, probation, mandated treatment, diversionary programs, and incarceration, allows for more freedom of belief among individuals within that system.

In summary, this comparison of the functional elements of child protection and criminal justice indicates that the two systems overlap to some extent on goal attainment (i.e. protecting children) and norms (i.e. child abuse is wrong) but differ substantially in the areas of power, sanction, facility, status-role, rank, knowledge and sentiment.

Dissimilarities in these functions result in separate and distinct actions being taken by individuals within the two organizations. Confronted by each case of alleged child maltreatment, the behavior of the child protection and criminal justice systems and their employees is influenced by the unique functions and processes that frame their role in society.

To summarize, in this chapter concepts underlying both systems theory and complexity theory were used to assess the overall collaborative ability between the criminal justice and child protection systems. The theoretical model asserted that two distinct systems have opportunities to function in a manner that is beneficial to both through the exchange of inputs and outputs. However, systems that are dissimilar in size, distance and propensity may be limited in their ability to cooperate effectively.

Although criminal justice and child protection are comparable in size, they lack formal structural linkages. The response of protective services and criminal justice to the same cases of abuse is officially linked only by state statutes that authorize or mandate information sharing and that allows for the formation of joint investigative teams (American Prosecutors Research Institute, 2004). Policies regarding the timing of the case referrals and procedures outlining interagency cooperation do not exist in many jurisdictions. This distance between the two systems does not facilitate interagency collaboration.

In addition, the functional elements of child protection and criminal justice vary in a number of important areas including power, sanction, facility, status-role, rank, knowledge and sentiment. These systemic differences may create significant barriers when the two systems attempt to work cooperatively in response to incidents of child maltreatment. In the past, efforts toward cooperative behavior between these two systems were initiated by individual actors who operated within the limits of the functional elements of their agency. Despite the shared values and goals and goodwill of individuals within both agencies, differences in worker roles, status, autonomy, public standing and beliefs created barriers that interfered with the ability of the two systems to act in a mutually beneficial manner.

In recent years, professionals involved in a myriad of social problems have recognized the need for effective models for interdisciplinary collaboration (Bronstein, 2003; Howell, Kelly, Palmer, & Mangum, 2004). A number of communities have experimented with or established collaborative processes and/or interdependent, umbrella organizations (such as children's advocacy centers and fatality review teams) to facilitate multidisciplinary coordination around reports of child maltreatment. These collaborations have been supported by new federal funding that encourages cooperation between child protection and other agencies (Goldman & Salus, 2003). The guidelines identified by these groups as essential to effective collaboration reflect the elements identified in the previous theoretical formulation. First, cooperating agencies operate best when they share core values and goal. Therefore, the focus of the multidisciplinary effort should be on a common goal that overlaps with the goals of each agency. Second, the role and procedural strengths and limitations of each agency must be identified and accepted. The differences between systems in regards to power, facility and status are not amenable to change. The group should recognize that conflicts that arise from these systemic differences are inevitable. These differences, however, can be minimized through shared decision-making and accountability, and by encouraging communication that corrects misperceptions about each agency and emphasizes the positive intentions of all parties (Goldman & Salus, 2003; Stark, D.R., 1999). Finally, the development of formal policies and procedures that ensure communication and cooperation between all responding agencies from intake through adjudication is essential. Efforts to minimize the distance between protective service workers and prosecutors will result in much more effective investigations and outcomes for all involved parties.

CHAPTER 4

The Relationship Between Child Placement and Case Prosecution Decisions

Factors Influencing Child Placement

What causes some children to be removed from their home following a report of child maltreatment? Historically, child placement has been one of the primary interventions utilized by the child protection system in the United States. Therefore, those factors that influence the out-of-home placement of maltreated children have been the focus of numerous empirical and case studies. These studies, though difficult to compare due to different methods of defining child placement, and variations in samples, data collection methods, and statistical methodology[2], provide a foundation for identifying case characteristics often found to influence placement.

Empirical research indicates wide variation in removal rates for abused children. Finkelhor (1983), in an analysis of all reports of sexual abuse to the National Clearinghouse in 1978, reported that in

---

[2] For example, approximately half of the studies described in this chapter examined only sexual abuse cases while the other half focused on all forms of maltreatment. In addition, a variety of data collection methods were used including record abstraction, caseworker surveys and child and family interviews.

.

17% of the cases, children were placed in foster care. In contrast, a study (Tjaden & Thoennes, 1992) of legal intervention in child maltreatment cases found removal rates of 40%, 45% and 65%, respectively, in three different jurisdictions. Other recent studies of abused children have reported removal rates ranging from 7% to 73% (Faller, 1991; Hunter, Coulter, Runyan & Everson, 1990; McDonald & Johnson, 1993; Pellegrin & Wagner, 1990; Rittner, 1995).

This variation is primarily the result of differences in sampling frames. For example, studies on child removal have analyzed data using samples drawn from diverse sources including the child protection system, the juvenile and criminal justice systems and a national reporting clearinghouse. This variation interferes with the ability of researchers to provide an accurate estimate of child placement (Hunter et al., 1990; Faller, 1991).

Child welfare workers report that the primary factor used to assess the need for placement is the adequacy of care and current risk of further maltreatment to the child. Several variables can influence the risk assessment including the severity of the abuse, prior abuse or neglect reports, the functioning, support and cooperation of the primary caretaker, the perpetrator's current access to the child, the intent of the perpetrator (deliberate or accidental), and the age and psycho-social functioning of the child (Meddin, 1985; Rossi, Schuerman, & Budde, 1999; U.S.D.H.H.S., 2003d). These and many other case characteristics have been studied by researchers to identify which variables are most likely to actually predict placement. Table 2 summarizes the findings of the empirical studies.

The severity of the abuse has been found to be associated to child placement in a number of studies. In an analysis of 8,610 cases of all forms of child abuse reported to the North Carolina registry, severity of abuse was found to be a significantly predictor of child removal (Runyan, Gould, Trost & Loda, 1981). Two studies of substantiated cases under investigation by child protection agencies found severity of abuse, as well as the frequency of the abuse, to be significantly related to child placement (Pellegrin &Wagner, 1990; Tjaden & Thoennes, 1992). In addition, Cross, McDonald, Martell and Ahl (1999) found the duration of the abuse, which may be an indicator of severity, to be highly associated with removal.

Prior reports of abuse or neglect have been found to be associated with child removal in only one study (Tjaden & Thoennes, 1992).

Likewise, Hunter's (et al.) 1990 study of 100 sexual abuse cases is the single study to confirm a link between the relationship of child removal to perpetrator access to the child.

One study has found the presence of multiple forms of maltreatment to be clearly associated with an increased likelihood for placement. In a study of sexual abuse cases, Finkelhor (1983), found that cases that included other types of abuse or a report of both abuse and neglect were more likely to involve removal.

Several studies have verified a relationship between parental and family functioning and placement. Low familial functioning, parental substance abuse and mental health problems, and domestic violence have all been found to be associated with child removal (Cross, Martell, McDonald & Ahl, 1999; Finkelhor, 1983; Runyan et al., 1981). In addition, in three studies of sexual abuse (Cross et al., 1999; Hunter et al., 1990; Pellegrin & Wagner, 1990), two involving protective service samples and one utilizing a criminal justice sample, maternal support and cooperation were found to be significantly related to child placement.

A strong relationship between the nonabusing mother's attitude toward the child's report of sexual abuse and out-of-home placement of the child has been noted by several researchers (Cross et al., 1995; Faller, 1988; Hunter et al., 1990). The absence of maternal support has been associated with a child experiencing more severe behavioral and psychological problems as well as child placement (Everson, et al., 1989).

The age of the child victim has also been found to be associated to child placement. In two studies of sexual abuse (Cross et al., 1999; Finkelhor, 1983), older children were found to be at significantly higher risk for out-of-home placement.

The referral source of a case and the court jurisdiction in which the report is filed have also been found to be significantly associated with child removal. In a study of all forms of maltreatment, Runyan (et al., 1981) found that cases referred by the courts and police, versus a child protection agency, were most likely to result in placement even after adjusting for the severity of the abuse.

The out-of-home placement of abused children can vary greatly by region, state and county (Cross et al., 1999; Everson et al., 1989; Finkelhor, 1983). Placement decisions may be determined more by

Table 2: A Summary of Studies Examining Variables Correlated With Child Placement in Cases of Child Abuse

Author(s)	N	Sample Source (Record abstraction used unless otherwise noted.)	Results (Correlates of placement)
Runyan et al., 1981	8,610	Confirmed cases of all child maltreatment reported to a state registry.	-parental use of severe punishment -severity of abuse -single parent -parental substance abuse -lack of social supports -father in the military -court jurisdiction -cases referred by court or police
Finkelhor, 198?	6,096	National Clearinghouse data on sexual abuse reports from 31 states.	-self-report of child victim -older child (13-18) -parent as perpetrator -both a male and female perpetrator -six or more children in family -report of other abuse or neglect -inadequate housing -family substance abuse -family mental health problems -spousal abuse -geographic region
Hunter et al., 1990	100	CPS sexual abuse cases. (Caseworker survey & child/mother interviews)	-maternal support -perpetrators' residence
Jaudes and Morris, 1990	138	Hospital medical records of children who met state criteria for sexual abuse.	-initial report of sexual abuse correlated with a custody change.

Table 2: A Summary of Studies Examining Variables Correlated With Child Placement in Cases of Child Abuse (continued)

Author(s)	N	Sample Source (Record abstraction used unless otherwise noted.)	Results (Correlates of placement)
Pellegrin and Wagner, 1992	43	Substantiated CPS sexual abuse cases. (Record data and caseworker survey.)	-mother cooperative with CPS -mother's belief in child's report -frequency and severity of abuse -mother's employment status
Tjaden and Thoennes, 199?	833	CPS substantiated cases of all types of child maltreatment.	-frequency and severity of abuse -prior reports of abuse and/or neglect
Jellinick et al., 1992	206	Neglected and abused children brought to Juvenile court.	-parental noncompliance with court orders
Rittner, 1995	447	Neglected and abused children under CPS supervision.	-Ethnicity (Hispanic children at greater risk of placement.)
Cross et al., 1995	256	Sexual abuse cases referred to regional criminal justice systems (Record abstraction and mother/child interviews.)	-geographic site -child's age -duration of abuse -family disturbance -maternal support -prosecution decision

localized system factors such as juvenile and criminal court processes, protective service placement policies, the availability of foster care, and highly publicized abuse cases than by family or case characteristics. Runyan et al. (1981) speculates that variation in the training judges receive, divergent working relationships between agencies, contrasting agency views, and differing resource levels are potential explanations for the geographic and/or jurisdictional differences in child placement.

Several researchers have asserted that poverty often predicts which children are most at risk for placement (Eamon, 1994; Garbarino, 1980; Pelton, 1985). In his study of over 6,000 sexual abuse cases, Finkelhor (1983) found inadequate housing and a family with six or more children to be variables significantly associated with child placement.

Reports of child abuse and low socioeconomic status are highly correlated and poor children have been over-represented in the foster care system since its inception (Pelton, 1985). Studies of family preservation programs have found low family income to be highly correlated with higher rates of placement for maltreated children (Eamon, 1994). Child neglect is highly associated with low socioeconomic status. Bath and Haapala's (1993) study of family preservation programs found that abused children whose families were also referred for neglect were at highest risk for child placement.

Another factor that has been examined in numerous studies is the race or ethnicity of the child victim. Race or ethnicity has not typically been found to be associated with placement in multivariate analyses. However, in an analysis of 447 child protection cases, Rittner (1995) found the ethnicity of the child victim to be the only case characteristic significantly related to placement.

This summary of research findings relating to predictors of placement supports protective service claims that the child placement decision is a function of those factors by which the level of risk of future abuse is assessed. These studies confirm that the frequency and severity of the abuse, the perpetrator's access to the child, prior abuse or neglect reports, the functioning, support and cooperation of the primary caretaker, and the age and psycho-social functioning of the child and family are often critical factors in the removal decision by protective services. However, the considerable variation in findings between existing studies indicates that child placement is a complex and multifaceted process that deserves further attention. More information is needed on when each of these risk assessment factors becomes primary and how relationships between predictive variables may impact the need for placement. Additional research is needed to more adequately describe the variables that drive the placement decision for all forms of child maltreatment as well as specific forms of abuse.

The empirical data also suggest that a number of additional variables may play an important role in the placement decision. Key factors such as the age and ethnicity of the child victim, the referral source, the geographic area and the court jurisdiction have also been found to be significantly related to removal. Research on the influence of structural factors external to the case including local child protection protocols as well as the statutory requirements regarding mandated reporting, record disclosure and cooperative practices between protective services, law enforcement and the juvenile and criminal courts are needed.

Factors Influencing Criminal Prosecution

Much of the research relating to the criminal prosecution of child abuse cases has focused on the progress of cases through the judicial system, the investigative and criminal court processes, the child-witness experience in the courtroom, and the dispensation of cases (Berliner & Conte, 1995; Brannon, 1994; Bulkley, 1988; Cheit & Goldschmidt, 1997; Goodman et al., 1992; Henry, 1997; Lipovsky et al., 1992; Lipovsky, 1994; & Lipovsky & Stern, 1997). Many child abuse cases, however, are declined for prosecution and involve no arraignment, grand jury investigation or trial. The case prosecution decision is the piviotal point in the criminal justice process that determines which offenders will be held accountable for their actions and which victims will receive the benefits of the justice system (Cross et al., 1995). In recent years, a small but growing number of studies have begun to focus their attention on the factors that influence the acceptance or rejection of child abuse cases for prosecution.

Currently, reliable national data on the number of child abuse cases that are prosecuted is lacking (Hashima and Finkelhor, 1999). Empirical research studies report varying rates of criminal prosecution for child abuse. In 1978, the National Center on Child Abuse and Neglect reported that less than 5% of substantiated child abuse cases were prosecuted in criminal court (National Center on Child Abuse and Neglect, 1978). Similarly, Tjaden and Thoennes (1992) found a 4% criminal prosecution rate in their study of physical and sexual child abuse cases in a protective service sample. Likewise, an examination of National Clearinghouse data by Finkelhor (1983) revealed that criminal charges were filed for only 5% of all reports of abuse. This study, however, great variation was found between states. An analysis of only sexual abuse cases in this sample revealed a 24% prosecution rate.

In contrast, Chapman and Smith (1987), MacMurray (1989) and Cross (et al., 1994) found prosecution rates of 63%, 55% and 61% respectively, in their studies of the criminal justice handling of sexual abuse cases. Faller and Henry (2000) found a similar charging rate of 69% in their study of 323 cases of child sexual abuse. However, in a national telephone survey of 600 prosecutors in counties with a population of 50,000 or more, 85% reported prosecuting 100 or fewer sexual abuse cases the previous year with a combined average of 62 cases prosecuted (Smith & Goretsky, 1994). This research mirrors the great variation in rates of prosecution found in a recent analysis of criminal justice decisions made in 21 studies of child abuse (Cross, Walsh, Simone, & Jones, 2003).

Low prosecution rates tend to be reported for samples drawn from statewide registries of all reports of abuse to protective services. The accuracy of these estimates is undermined by the wide variation in severity and type of abuse within the sample and the lack of information regarding whether or not the abuse incident met requirements for criminal behavior.

Alternatively, the higher rates of prosecution revealed in samples drawn from criminal justice agencies may be biased by the selective sample of cases that ever reach the prosecutor. In many states, less severe cases of abuse are not forwarded to the criminal justice agency. They are investigated solely by protective services.

The reported variation between studies is very likely due to more than just differences in the sampling frames utilized (Cross et al., 2003). The reasons for the variation in prosecution rates are complex. Differences in practice between jurisdictions appears to be a likely determinant. There is considerable variation in the referral rates to prosecutors by region and agency. State and county policy vary greatly in terms of which cases must be referred by child protection for prosecutorial consideration (Cross et al., 2003). States mandating referrals of all or a portion of child protection cases are likely to have lower prosecution rates due to the wider range of cases that will be examined by the district attorney. In addition, differences relating to how reports become cases in the prosecutor's office will influence the charging rate. For example, in regions in which informal discussion between the prosecutor and child welfare agency influences referral, a pre-screening process naturally occurs. Therefore, fewer cases are referred that are unlikely to result in prosecution (Cross et al., 2003).

Prosecutors may also differ in their preparation and willingness to prosecute different types of child abuse cases. Some prosecutors may incorporate the wishes of the child and family to influence the prosecution decision. Others will want to consider the impact of the criminal court process on the emotional well-being of the child victim or weigh the desire and ability of the victim's family to support the child through a court proceedings (Davis & Wells, 1996).

In addition, charging rates can be influenced by the knowledge and outlook of both prosecutors and judges. Prosecutors may vary in their training on child abuse and/or their willingness to prosecute these cases. The perspectives of judges on child abuse may influence district attorneys decision-making regarding which cases to bring forward (Cross et al., 2003). Finally, staff turnover within the judicial system can impact which cases are chosen for prosecution (Davis & Wells, 1996).

Given the multiple factors that influence prosecution decision-making process, an accurate assessment of national and regional charging rates is not available at the present time. Research samples that include all substantiated abuse cases reported to law enforcement, child protection and the district attorney within one region can provide a useful baseline. In addition, qualitative data on the decision-making process are needed to gain a better understanding of the intricacies that influence whether or not a case of child abuse is prosecuted.

Empirical studies on the characteristics that are significantly associated with the prosecution of child abuse cases have uncovered a number of additional factors that influence prosecution. Table 3 provides a summary of the studies that have examined the predictors of prosecution.

Type of abuse is often found to be correlated with case prosecution. To date, most studies of child abuse have focused exclusively on sexual abuse and these samples have typically had higher rates of prosecution than studies of all types of maltreatment. The few studies that have examined all forms of maltreatment have all found higher rates of prosecution for cases of sexual abuse (Tjaden & Thoennes, 1992; Tjaden & Anhalt, 1994). Only one recent study (Mennerich, Cross, Martell & White, 2001) has documented higher rates of prosecution for physical versus sexual abuse cases.

Victim age has also proven to be an important predictor of case prosecution. In many studies of both sexual abuse and all types of maltreatment victims over the age of 7 or between 7 and 12 are more likely to have their cases chosen for prosecution (Brewer, Rowe & Brewer, 1997; Cross, DeVos & Whitcomb, 1994; Finkelhor, 1983; MacMurray, 1989; Mennerich et al., 2001; Tjaden & Thoennes, 1992; Straud, Martens, and Barker, 2000). The severity of the abuse has also been found to be highly associated with case prosecution. Cases involving more serious types of abuse or abuse of a longer duration have typically been found to be correlated with case prosecution (Brewer et al, 1997; Cross et al., 1994; MacMurray, 1989; Tjaden & Thoennes, 1992). However, this relationship needs to be examined in more depth as Stroud (et al., 2000) found cases involving child victims without serious injuries to be most likely to be prosecuted.

The importance of child victim gender as a predictor of case prosecution is less clear. MacMurray (1989) found cases of male victims of sexual abuse more likely to be prosecuted than the cases of female victims. However, other studies of both sexual and physical maltreatment found higher prosecution rates for cases involving female victims (Tjaden & Thoennes, 1992; Stroud et al., 2001).

Perpetrator characteristics have also been found to be associated with case prosecution. Finkelhor (1983) found that sexual abuse perpetrators with a prior criminal record, substance abuse problem, or history of spousal abuse were most likely to be prosecuted. In Tjaden and Thoennes' (1992) sample of all types of maltreatment, cases involving a perpetrator of an ethnic minority had higher rates of prosecution. Cross (et al., 1994) found a relationship between race and prosecution in initial bivariate analyses, however, the relationship did not remain significant in a multivariate analysis. Non-parent and non-familial offenders have been found to be more likely to have their cases prosecuted (Brewer et al., 1997; Chapman & Smith, 1987; Stroud et al., 2000; Tjaden & Thoennes, 1992). However, one sexual abuse study (MacMurray, 1989) found higher rates of prosecution for cases involving parent and step-parent perpetrators versus all other perpetrators. In Bradshaw and Marks (1990) study of sexual abuse, the relationship of the child victim and the offender was not found to be a significant predictor of prosecution.

Research findings also indicate that the source of the report to the criminal justice system may be associated with which cases are chosen for prosecution. Two studies have found that cases that are first reported to the police versus a social service agency are more likely to be prosecuted (Finkelhor, 1983; Mennerich et al., 2001).

A few additional predictive factors relating to prosecution have been found in two other studies. Oral-genital abuse, the use or threat of force, and the presence of physical or eyewitness testimony was found by Cross (et al., 1994) to be significantly related to prosecution. In an interview sub-sample drawn from the same study, maternal support of the child victim and the complaint of abuse and low levels of child psychopathology were also found to be associated with cases being chosen for prosecution. Bradshaw and Marks (1990) found medical evidence and a shorter interval between the abuse incident and the report to significantly predict prosecution. In addition, in this study, the presence of an offender statement in the prosecutor's case file was found to be correlated with case prosecution.

Reports from District Attorneys in the field concur in part with the research findings and clarify the numerous barriers that exist in the prosecution of physical and sexual abuse cases (Bucci et al., 1998; Davis & Wells, 1996). Prosecutors report that the decision of whether or not to prosecute a case of child abuse is influenced by a number of factors. These include the legal sufficiency of the case, time and resource limitations faced by the prosecutor, the availability of diversionary alternatives and the probability of trial success (American Prosecutors Research Institute, 2004). District Attorneys must weigh the type of evidence available and the child's age and ability to testify effectively against the level of proof they know will be required by a jury and judge to secure a conviction. Prosecutors also take into account numerous factors when considering prosecution including the impact of testifying on the child, familial support for prosecution, the prior criminal record of the accused and the media attention being focused on the case (American Prosecutors Research Institute, 2004; Davis and Wells, 1996).

Prosecutors also report that it can be particularly difficult to prosecute sexual abuse cases because many people, including jurors, have difficulty believing the details of the sex crimes perpetrated against children. Public stereotyping of sexual abusers as easily-identified deviant members of society makes successful prosecution challenging when the typical perpetrator is a professional, white male who is married with children (Bucci, et al., 1998).

Even though corroboration is not legally required, most jurors still want it before they will find an alleged perpetrator guilty beyond a reasonable doubt (Davis & Wells, 1996). The prosecution of child

Table 3: A Summary of Studies Examining Variables Correlated With Prosecution in Cases of Child Abuse

Author(s)	N	Sample Source (Data collected via record abstraction unless otherwise noted.)	Results (Correlates of prosecution)
Finkelhor, 1983	6,096	National Clearinghouse data on substantiated sexual abuse cases submitted by 31 states	-victim aged 7-12 -male offender -non-familial offender -offender with prior police record -offender with substance problem -offender with history spousal abuse -police referral
Chapman and Smith, 1987	388	Sexual abuse cases under investigation by either social services or law enforcement	-non-parental perpetrator
MacMurray, 1989	87	Random sample of sexual abuse cases from one District Attorney's office	-male child victim -victim aged 5-13 -father or step-father perpetrator -longer duration of abuse
Bradshaw and Marks 1990	350	Sexual abuse cases from one District Attorney's office	-medical evidence -shorter interval between incident and report -offender statement in case file
Tjaden and Thoennes 1992	833	Physical and sexual abuse cases CPS substantiated in three counties	-sexual abuse -victim 7-12 -female victim -severe maltreatment -non-parent perpetrator -ethnic minority offender

Table 3: A Summary of Studies Examining Variables Correlated With Prosecution in Cases of Child Abuse (continued)

Author(s)	N	Sample Source (Data collected via record abstraction unless otherwise noted.)	Results (Correlates of prosecution)
Cross, DeVoss and Whitcomb, 1994	431	Sexual abuse cases referred for prosecution in four urban jurisdictions.	-victim aged 7 and up -oral-genital abuse -use or threat of force -duration of abuse > 1 month -physcial or eyewitness evidence -higher level of maternal support -lower level of child psychopathology
Brewer, Rowe and Brewer, 1997	200	Substantiated sexual abuse cases referred for services to a nonprofit agency by the police, DSS or a medical facility	-older child victim -multiple victims -serious abuse (when medical evidence was present) -offender outside family -victim's mother is married -no custody dispute
Stroud, Marten and Barker, 2001	1043	Sexual abuse cases referred to child advocacy center for a forensic interview	-female victim -victim 5-17 -victim race/ethnicity -age of perpetrator -non-parent offender -male perpetrator

sexual abuse without medical or physical evidence or a confession is difficult. These types of cases are less likely to be chosen for prosecution (Bucci, et al., 1998).

Prosecutors agree that it can be easier to successfully prosecute the case of a 7 to 12 year old sexual abuse victim because jurors question the validity of reports by both adolescents and very young children

The ability of young children to separate reality from fiction and their vulnerability to suggestion causes jurors to doubt the accuracy of their statements.   In addition, the statements of teenage victims of sexual abuse are questioned because of both the voluntary sexual activity of adolescents and the belief that adolescents can lie and be vindictive (Bucci, et al., 1998).   The fact that the disclosure of sexual abuse often occurs some time after the onset of the abuse can also be problematic (Bucci, et al., 1998).

A national survey of prosecutors in 600 counties (Smith & Goretsky, 1994) confirms these suppositions. Prosecutors reported that sexual abuse cases were most often rejected due to the youth of the child victim, a lack of medical evidence and insufficient evidence. In addition, a secondary reason for rejecting a case was the perception that reports from teenagers may not be credible. In this same study, child victims as problematic witnesses and child victims not being supported by their families were reported by prosecutors as factors hindering successful prosecution (Smith & Goretsky, 1994).   In contrast, a study by Faller and Henry (2000) suggests that working in close collaboration with law enforcement and child protection can enable prosecutors to be effective in their prosecution of sexual abuse. Early referral between agencies and swift, effective investigations can support successful prosecution.   Faller and Henry assert that investigative professionals should rely less on the capacity of the child witness and more on securing confessions and plea-bargains through improved coordination.

The prosecution of physical abuse cases involves other types of challenges. It may be easier to support a case of physical abuse in the judicial system because there is often medical or physical proof, such as a fracture, bruise or the instrument with which the child was beaten. However, when the physical abuse case involves a parent as a perpetrator it can be very difficult to bring a case to trial. When a child remains in the home or with relatives following a report of physical abuse by a parent, the child is very likely to recant his or her statements due to pressure from family members.   Therefore, the successful prosecution of physical abuse cases often rests on whether or not the investigation was swift and involved both law enforcement and child protection (Bucci, et al., 1998).

Public perceptions regarding the nature of physical abuse cases can also impede successful prosecution.   Many jurors do not take physical abuse seriously and believe that parents do not intentionally harm their children. Injuries are sometimes regarded as the accidental result of attempts by parents to discipline their children (National Institute of Justice Update, 1995).

Prosecutors state that the working with a child as a victim and or witness can result in unique barriers to prosecution. For child victims of both sexual and physical abuse, it may be too difficult for the victim to face the perpetrator at trial. Children also may refuse to incriminate the offender, change their account of the incident, or recant their testimony. When the child is an infant or has multiple caretakers it is often difficult to definitively identify the perpetrator. Cases that involve very young children or children who are not competent to speak in court for reasons other than age are also less likely to be prosecuted. In addition, cases involving juvenile perpetrators may be considered best addressed by a juvenile court versus a criminal court (Bucci, et al., 1998).

In summary, research findings support criminal justice assertions that considerations such as the age and functioning of the child, the availability of evidence, and the support of the family are all important factors that must be weighed in the case prosecution decision. The ability of the child to serve as a credible witness and the availability of direct evidence are central elements that provide support to the state's case.

Criminal Prosecution and Child Placement

The ways in which the responses of the criminal justice system and the child protection system may influence each other has not been investigated in previous research. Butler, Atkinson, Magnatta and Hood's (1995) study on the collaboration of child welfare, mental health and juvenile justice systems found placement decisions to be highly correlated among the three systems. However, previous research has not examined the ways in which the interventions of one system may influence the responses of another for the same report of child abuse.

Systems theory and complexity theory provide models by which the relationship between criminal justice and protective services interventions may be conceptualized. The involvement and case decisions of the prosecutor can be viewed as the output of the criminal justice system. This activity becomes input for other systems, including the family of the abused child and the protective service system. These systems digest this information and respond to it, resulting in their own output.

The protective service investigation and removal decision can also be seen as output that is received in the form of input by the family of the victim and criminal justice. These systems absorb this information which, in turn, influences their output. This exchange of output and processing of input may occur concurrently or simultaneously. The result is a non-linear, highly interactive and dynamic process of mutual exchange and influence.

The forms by which this interactive exchange may occur are quite varied and not mutually exclusive. For example, the primary function of the criminal justice system is to identify and punish those who violate the law; however, in child abuse cases, the decision to prosecute and the outcome of prosecution may unintentionally alter the risk of further abuse to the child. The assessment of risk is one of the primary factors used in determining the need for placement, therefore, in some cases, the prosecution decision may strongly influence the need for removal.

The actions of the criminal justice system such as arrest, investigation, prosecution, restraining orders, mandated treatment, and incarceration can potentially protect abused children from or minimize the risk of future maltreatment. These actions can limit the access of the perpetrator to the child by physically removing the alleged perpetrator from the home or prohibiting contact between the alleged perpetrator and the child victim (Cross et al., 1999). A criminal investigation can also alter the behavior of the alleged perpetrator and/or nonoffending parent by influencing their perception of the seriousness of the event or raising concerns regarding how the investigation may impact their life. Alleged perpetrators can voluntarily seek treatment for substance abuse, battering or sexually abusive behavior. Others may opt to avoid criminal prosecution by fleeing the state. Nonoffending parents may find criminal justice involvement to be compelling evidence of the serious nature of the offense and deny the perpetrator access to the child (Cross et al., 1999). Therefore, it is likely that criminal justice interventions can sometimes have a direct or indirect impact on the necessity to remove a child from the home.

Professionals involved in the child protection field have called for more efforts to be taken to remove offenders versus children from homes in which abuse is occurring (Faller, 1990). Whether by voluntary agreement, court order, arrest or incarceration, the removal of an offender from the home allows the child to remain within the family unit and is likely to protect a victim from further abuse. However, in some situations the removal of the offender may not shield the child from further harm. For example, if other forms of maltreatment are occurring in the family, the child may still be at risk. In addition, if an offender is arrested, other family members may blame and inflict emotional abuse on the child for bringing emotional or financial distress to the family (Faller, 1990).

It is also possible that the interventions of the child protection system can influence the case prosecution decision. The primary function of child protection is the safeguarding of children, however, the initiation of a protective service investigation and/or the removal of a child victim may inadvertently assist or hinder the ability of the prosecutor to move forward on a case. For example, a protective service investigation that is prior to or concurrent with a criminal justice investigation may directly compromise the ability of the prosecutor to build a strong case. If an alleged offender becomes aware of child abuse charges through the child protection investigation, he or she may destroy evidence or pressure the child victim to deny the abuse (Pence & Wilson, 1994).

In addition, it is possible that the initiation of a protective service investigation may influence the perceptions and behavior of a nonoffending parent or caretaker (Meddin, 1985). The primary caretaker may take concrete steps to support the prosecution of the case in order to influence the risk assessment and, therefore, the removal decision, by child protection. For example, the nonoffending parent may support the child's involvement by bringing the child to interviews or providing the prosecutor with information regarding the whereabouts of the offender.

The placement of a child victim outside of the home may also influence the case prosecution decision. The removal of a child from their home, with the concurrent loss of a support network of family and friends, may weaken their ability to negotiate the criminal court processes or serve as a witness (Cross et al., 1999). Alternatively, in those cases in which child victims may suffer from maltreatment due to their report of abuse and/or face serious pressure to recant their accusation, out-of-home placement could be both in the best interest of the child and support the prosecutor's case.

In an examination of all child sexual abuse cases referred to prosecutors in four urban jurisdictions, Cross (et al., 1999) uncovered a significant relationship between child placement and case prosecution. Utilizing data collected through the Child Victim as Witness research project (Whitcomb et al., 1994), Cross found the decision of whether or not to prosecute a case to have the strongest association with parental report of child placement over all other variables in the study including the relationship of the child to the perpetrator, the duration of and frequency of abuse, and the level of maternal support. This finding offers strong evidence for a relationship between the interventions of two distinct systems, criminal justice and child protection.

The nature of this association is not readily apparent. The prosecution decision may influence the placement decision, the placement decision may influence whether or not a case is prosecuted or a third variable (or variables) may impact the responses of both systems. Unfortunately, the original purpose of data collection for Cross' (et al., 1999) research was not to identify predictors of placement. Therefore, necessary information was not collected on important variables relating to child placement and case prosecution, such as the timing of the two decisions, the factors that led to the placement and whether or not protective services was involved in the placement. This prevented a more in depth analysis of the ways in which case prosecution and child placement may be related.

Several explanations can be put forth to explain the relationship between a case being declined for prosecution and a child being placed outside the home, all of which require further exploration. First, criminal justice intervention may assist protective service efforts to protect a child primarily by decreasing the risk to the child. By eliminating or limiting the perpetrator's access to the child or influencing the behavior of the perpetrator and/or nonoffending parent, the risk of future abuse may be lessened.

It is also possible that child placement may make the act of prosecution more difficult by impacting the child's ability to participate in the criminal justice system. Child victims may have difficulty negotiating the demands of the system without the help of their support systems.

Alternatively, there may be a third explanatory factor that is associated with both the child placement and case prosecution decisions. The cooperation and participation of nonoffending family members with both the criminal justice and protective service systems may provide support for the prosecution of the case while simultaneously reflecting a safe and healthy home environment to protective services (Cross et al., 1999). Conversely, prosecution may be declined and placement may be utilized more frequently in cases in which families are experiencing both internal and external stressors that impede healthy family functioning (Cross et al., 1999). Family functioning difficulties may both interfere with successful prosecution and indicate a need for placement.

Finally, it is also possible, given the rising number of offenses overloading the judicial system, that the cases of children already in placement when they reach the District Attorney are given less attention. These may cases may be perceived as having a less urgent need for criminal justice intervention, as they are already being serviced under the protective service system.

Each of the explanations is plausible and they are not mutually exclusive. Each has distinct policy implications. The study described in the following two chapters attempts to clarify the relationship between the prosecution and child placement decisions.

CHAPTER 5

Systemic Interventions in Child Abuse in Suffolk County, Massachusetts: A Study

The purpose of this chapter is to describe a study that explored how the prosecution decision by the criminal justice system and the removal decision by protective services may be related to one another. Specifically, this study sought to identify those factors that predict child placement by protective services and those factors that predict criminal prosecution, in cases of child abuse.

Two hypotheses were tested. The study first examined what case characteristics, child and family characteristics, protective service assessment characteristics and criminal justice interventions are associated with the child placement decision following a report of child abuse. It was hypothesized that the decision by the District Attorney to prosecute a case would be positively associated with child victims not being removed from their home by protective services. Next, the study examined what case characteristics, child and family characteristics, and child protection interventions and outcomes are associated with the prosecution decision following a report of child abuse. The study tested the hypothesis that removal of the child from the home by protective services would be positively associated with cases not being chosen for prosecution by the criminal justice system.

This study provides an opportunity to look for answers to many of the questions raised in preceding chapters regarding the relationship between the prosecution decision and child placement. Specifically, it serves as a follow-up examination of the relationship found by Cross' (et al., 1999) between child placement and the decision to decline prosecution and tests whether this prior finding can be both reproduced in another jurisdiction and applied to all types of child maltreatment.

Context of the Study

The study involved both the Massachusetts Department of Social Services and the Child Abuse Unit of the Suffolk County District Attorney's Office. These two agencies represent the protective service and criminal justice systems responding to reports of child abuse in the Boston region.

The Massachusetts Department of Social Services (DSS) was created in 1978 to protect abused or neglected children and provide a range of preventative services to support and strengthen families (Massachusetts Department of Social Services, 2000.) The Boston regional office of DSS is comprised of five area offices, Jamaica Plain, Roxbury, Dorchester, Boston, and Chelsea/Revere. Each of these offices, under the direction of an area director, is responsible for the implementation of DSS policy in a specific geographic area.

Cases of child maltreatment typically come to a DSS area office in one of three ways: an allegation that a child has been abused or neglected by a caretaker or is at risk for abuse or neglect (known as a 51 A report), a court order that DSS provide services, or through a voluntary request for services from a family (J. Lynch, personal communication, May 22, 1997). Cases determined to fall within the mandate of the agency are referred for an investigation. Two types of investigation are possible, a DSS initiated investigation (51 B investigation) or a Sexual Abuse Intervention Network (SAIN) investigation jointly conducted by DSS, law enforcement and the District Attorney's office. Table 4 provides a case flow chart detailing the screening, investigation and case referral process of DSS.

The purpose of both of these investigations is to determine if there is reasonable cause to believe that the child has suffered maltreatment by a caretaker or family member. Departmental regulations require that DSS investigations be completed and a report written within 10 days. However, the importance of completing a thorough review of the case and the heavy workload of DSS investigators can often interfere

Table 4: Case Flow of the Massachusetts Department of Social Services (DSS)

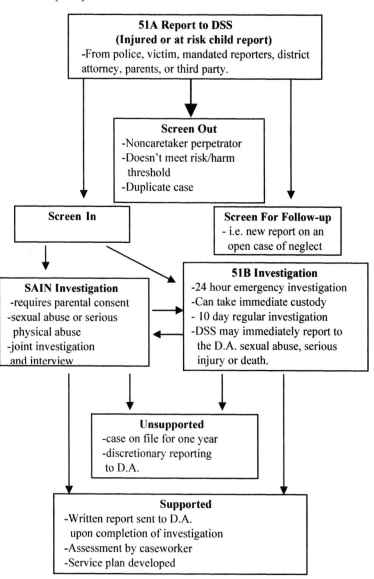

with a caseworker's ability to meet this deadline. Therefore, cases are not always completed by the ten day deadline and they are sometimes backdated (Wong, 1998).

Although the 51B investigation is conducted by protective services, Massachusetts state law allows DSS to immediately report to the District Attorney cases of child sexual assault or serious physical abuse prior to the substantiation of maltreatment. This early reporting can result in the initiation of a joint investigation in which DSS, the District Attorney and other agencies join together to engage in a joint interview of the child victim (J. Fine, personal communication, May 22, 2001). In practice, however, team meetings typically follow DSS substantiation thereby limiting the ability of child protection, law enforcement and the district attorney to engage in joint decision-making in the initial phases of the case.

In contrast, a SAIN (Sexual Abuse Investigation Network) investigation refers to a special type of joint investigation by a team comprised of a member of the Child Abuse Unit of the District Attorney's Office, law enforcement, DSS and other agencies involved in a particular child abuse case (Cross & Spath, 1998). A SAIN investigation is initiated when a DSS investigator refers a case to the SAIN unit. Any sexual abuse cases or serious physical abuse cases can be referred at the discretion of the protective service investigator. The purpose of the SAIN investigation is to allow protective services, law enforcement and the District Attorney to work cooperatively in their initial investigation of the report of abuse.

In Massachusetts, SAIN teams are not utilized frequently or consistently across areas (Cross & Spath, 1998). Only a small percentage of DSS cases are referred for SAIN investigation. The initiation of a SAIN team for a case requires a proactive and swift response on the part of the DSS investigator. Permission from a parent or guardian must be obtained. This limits the ability of the SAIN program to investigate cases in which the alleged perpetrator is a parent of the child victim or those cases in which the non-offending parent is not cooperative.

Massachusetts statutes mandate that DSS share all substantiated reports of abuse with the criminal justice system (Wilber, 1987). Child protection agencies are required to send copies of all substantiated reports of abuse to the District Attorney's office.

Investigations that result, either through the traditional DSS investigation or SAIN processes, in a finding of plausible abuse are considered substantiated by DSS. Substantiated cases are assigned to a caseworker to assess whether the child is currently safe or at risk and to provide social services to the child and family when necessary. Agency personnel must develop a service plan to ensure a safe living environment for any child determined to be at risk. Within 45 days of the referral to the prosecutor, the caseworker is required to forward to the District Attorney's office a copy of the DSS service plan (J. Lynch, personal communication, May 22, 1997).

Children are removed from the home and placed in alternative settings when it is determined that the child is unable to receive adequate care or protection in their current living environment. In 1997, Massachusetts DSS had on their caseload more than 11,000 children who had been placed in foster homes, residential care facilities or with relatives providing kinship care (Massachusetts Department of Social Services, 2000). When DSS temporarily removes a child determined to be in imminent danger, the caseworker must file a juvenile court petition within 24 hours. In Massachusetts, the juvenile courts often follow the recommendations of the protective service agency regarding the need for placement.

For both 51B and SAIN investigations, Massachusetts DSS has instituted additional procedures in cases in which domestic violence and child abuse co-occur. The initial screening questions utilized in both DSS and SAIN investigations include questions designed to uncover indicators of domestic violence in the family (Spath, 2001). If domestic violence is revealed in the initial report or investigation, a special protocol is used to assess the family and environmental risk factors. Investigators are encouraged to protect the well-being of the child by acting as an ally to the non-offending parent, assisting them with the development of a family safety plan and providing them with information regarding shelters for battered women and possible judicial interventions and supports. In addition, the protective service investigator is encouraged to assist in the filing of a criminal report and/or application for a restraining order (Spath, 2001).

In Massachusetts, the District Attorney's Office of each county is responsible for the prosecution of all reported criminal activity. The Suffolk County District Attorney's Office is the largest district attorney's office in New England, handling over 50,000 criminal cases a year. The jurisdiction of the office includes the Boston metropolitan area as well as the Chelsea, Revere and Winthrop areas. The prosecutorial staff is composed of the District Attorney, Assistant District Attorneys, Victim Witness Advocates, and legal and administrative assistants.

The Child Abuse Unit of the office handles all cases involving victims under the age of 18. The Unit operates on the fundamental premise that children have the right to be protected from harm and that offenders against children should be prosecuted (Suffolk County District Attorney's Office, 1996.) The Unit is committed to utilizing a multidisciplinary approach in investigating reports of child abuse. To this end, the Unit works in conjunction with protective service staff and mental health professionals whenever possible to minimize the number of times a child is interviewed, decrease the number of people involved in questioning the child, and streamline the child's involvement in the judicial process and the services provided to the child and his or her family (Suffolk County District Attorney's Office, 1996).

The criminal acts of child abuse identified in Massachusetts' statutes include assault and battery, assault and battery with a deadly weapon, rape, indecent assault and battery, and sexual exploitation (National Center for the Prosecution of Child Abuse, 1999). In Massachusetts, the most serious forms of child abuse are typically adjudicated in Superior Court and lesser offenses are handled by a District Court. In Suffolk County, the majority of physical abuse charges and approximately half of the sexual abuse charges are District Court indictments. The Superior Court manages all of the serious felony cases, for example, all rape cases. The Assistant District Attorney that reviews the case will determine the most appropriate court venue for the prosecution of each case (D. Deakin, personal communication, August 9, 1998). All incoming reports of child abuse are sent to the Child Abuse Unit and are assigned within 48 hours to both an Assistant District Attorney and a Victim Witness Advocate (Suffolk County District Attorney's Office, 1996). The Assistant District Attorneys are primarily responsible for the formal prosecution of cases. Victim Witness Advocates collect information on cases, interview victims and assist victims and their families with court policies and procedures (Harshbarger, 1987).

Reports of child abuse arrive at the District Attorney's Office in one of three ways: a DSS referral, a police referral or referral from a

District Court. Due to the overlapping practices of these referring agencies, the District Attorney can receive the same report of abuse from more than one source. As previously explained, DSS is required to send reports on all substantiated cases of child abuse to the District Attorney following the ten day investigation. If a case is referred for a SAIN investigation, the report will be sent over immediately to insure a joint investigation. Table 5 provides a chart outlining the flow of child abuse cases through the Suffolk County District Attorney's Office.

Although the swift referral of cases from DSS to the DA is encouraged internally in both organizations, under-referral and late referral of cases is a matter of concern. DSS caseworkers abide by no firm deadline for the initial referral of substantiated cases to the DA.

Some child abuse cases begin with police notification instead of a mandated report to DSS. Law enforcement officers investigate reports of child abuse to determine if there is probable cause that a crime has been committed. If the police determine that there is not enough evidence to support that a crime has been committed, they will usually make no arrest and simply keep the complaint on file. However, police officers are mandated reporters and, therefore, must file a report of suspicion of abuse to DSS within 24 hours. Therefore, abuse cases involving perpetrators who are caretakers that are first investigated by the police but involve no arrest essentially become DSS cases. These case reports are eventually received by the DA from DSS following the protective service investigation. The District Attorney has asked that the police directly notify the Child Abuse Unit of all child abuse investigations undertaken, however, this does not always occur.

There are two ways in which the police may initiate an arrest in cases of child abuse. If there appears to be sufficient evidence supporting the crime, the police may make an immediate arrest and send the case to the appropriate District Court for charging. An immediate arrest is always the most appropriate course of action when a child's life is in danger. Alternatively, law enforcement may write a report on a criminal act and, at a later date, seek a complaint at the District Court. All complaints of child abuse received by the District Court are immediately faxed to the Child Abuse Unit within the District Attorney's Office. The Suffolk County Child Abuse Unit tries to make the prosecution decision within thirty days following intake. However, depending on the circumstances, case prosecution decisions long as three months. Therefore, the protective service investigation

Table 5: Child Abuse Case Flow Chart, District Attorney's Office, Suffolk County, Massachusetts

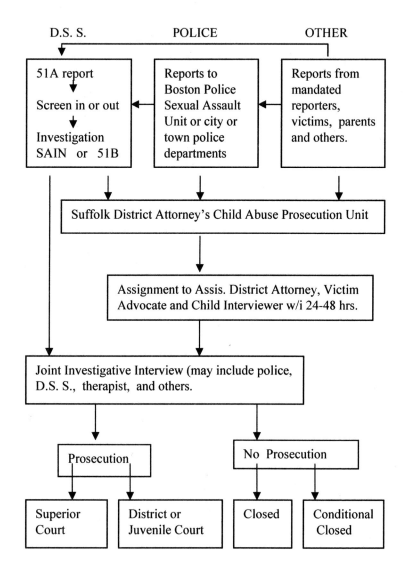

initiated by DSS often occurs prior to the criminal investigation undertaken by the District Attorney. This lack of coordination between initial investigations can impact the ability of the District Attorney to successfully prosecute cases. It is very helpful for the District Attorney to collect testimony and evidence from the child victim prior to the alleged perpetrator becoming aware of the complaint. When a perpetrator becomes aware that a case is pending against him, he may take steps to undermine the investigation (D. Deakin, personal communication, August 9, 1998).

Study Sample

The study sample included all children abused by a family member or caretaker whose cases were referred to the Child Abuse Unit of the Suffolk County District Attorney's Office from June 1, 1997 to August 15, 1998. In order to qualify for the sample, cases had to have the following characteristics:

1. The case involved a report of maltreatment that was identified by the Suffolk County District Attorney's Office as constituting a criminal act
2. The case fell under the jurisdiction of the Suffolk County District Attorney's Office or a Boston area District Court.
3. The case was also under investigation by the Massachusetts Department of Social Services.

Data Collection Procedures

This study was part of a research project entitled *Studies of the Impact of Criminal Justice and Child Welfare System Involvement on Child Survivors of Abuse* which was headed by Dr. Theodore Cross, Senior Research Associate with the Family and Children's Policy Center at Brandeis University. The research project was funded by the National Center on Child Abuse and Neglect.

Data were collected from three sources. The case records of the Child Abuse Unit of the Suffolk County District Attorney's Office served as the primary data source. Information on case characteristics and criminal justice interventions and outcomes was abstracted from intake, case status and disposition forms by the Child Abuse Unit. These forms contained information on case characteristics, disposition and processing including: alleged victim's name; alleged perpetrator's name; intake date; case referral source; child's sex, age and ethnicity; defendant's sex, age and ethnicity; perpetrator's relationship to child; type of abuse; allegations; charge, arrest, disposition and sentencing information; and the prosecution decision. (See Appendix A).

An important variable absent in the lotus files of the Child Abuse Unit was the income level for the family of each child victim. National incidence studies consistently report a strong relationship between family income and aspects of child maltreatment (Sedlack, & Broadhurst, 1996). To obtain an estimate of socioeconomic status for each family, census data on median income by zip code were collected.

The second method of data collection was a survey that was sent to staff members of the Boston regional offices of the Massachusetts Department of Social Services regarding each case. The survey was designed to obtain information on protective service involvement and assessment in each case. The survey for this study was combined with the survey of another member of the research group relating to domestic violence in child abuse cases. References to the survey hereafter refer only to survey questions relating to the current study (questions 1-15). The survey instrument consisted of questions regarding the intake date, referral source, case and family characteristics not found in the criminal justice files, prior child maltreatment and placement, and the protective service assessment of and response to the current abuse report. In addition, a section of the survey included questions regarding protective service caseworker perceptions of the impact of criminal justice interventions on the placement decision for each case. Specifically, for every case in which DSS was able to keep the child within the home or return a removed child to the home, caseworkers were asked to provide information as to whether or not criminal justice actions were helpful in regards to these outcomes and how judicial interventions may have assisted in these outcomes. (See Appendix B).

To test the validity of the survey, a pilot test was conducted with social workers from a nonprofit child and family services agency. The survey was pre-tested on child abuse cases received during April and May of 1997 by the Suffolk County Child Abuse Unit. This allowed for the detection and correction of minor problems relating to the data collection process and a final revision of the survey instrument.

The case intake forms of the Child Abuse Unit were utilized to collect information regarding the name and date of birth of the child victim, the names of the child's parents and the alleged perpetrator; and the DSS office associated with each case. This information was provided to the Program Manager of the Boston Regional Office of DSS, who confirmed whether cases had been screened in by DSS. The program manager then provided the name of the DSS caseworker last assigned to the case and identified the area office associated with the case.

Approximately sixty days after each case was referred to the Child Abuse Unit of the District Attorney's office, DSS staff members received a survey for completion.[3] Some DSS staff members had been informed of the study by their area directors; however, an explanatory letter was sent with each survey to ensure their understanding of the study. A cover note was attached to each survey which provided case identifying information for the DSS staff member including the name and date of birth of the child, the names of the parents, the name of the alleged perpetrator, the date of the abuse incident, and the case number.[4] The DSS worker was asked to complete the survey, remove the attachment and return the survey to the researcher in an enclosed, stamped and addressed envelope. To protect the confidentiality of the child, cases were only identified on each survey by only an identification number assigned by the Child Abuse Unit.

To increase the return rate for the surveys, follow-up phone calls were conducted 4 to 5 weeks after the mailing to ask DSS staff members to complete unanswered surveys. In addition, the researcher visited each of the DSS area offices with the Boston Region Program Manager to answer caseworkers' questions regarding the study. To increase the survey return rate, in April of 1998 caseworkers were informed that each completed and returned survey would result in a $10 donation to the Children's Activity Fund associated with the branch office involved with the case.[5] This resulted in a final survey return rate of 49%.

---

[3] When cases involved more than one perpetrator, the DSS caseworkers were asked to answer the survey in relation to only one perpetrator; the individual who would be regarded as the primary perpetrator.

[4] One year into the study, DSS changed the case identification system being utilized, from a consumer number (which was assigned to each child), to a case number (which was assigned to each family).

[5] The Children's Activity Fund is a special resource available to DSS caseworkers who need additional funds to provide for the special needs of

The third source of data was informational interviews conducted by the researcher with key informants, two staff members of the Child Abuse Unit of the District Attorney's Office and two staff members of the Boston region of Massachusetts DSS. Information regarding factors that influence the prosecution and placement decision were obtained through interviews with the Coordinator of Child Victim Services and an Assistant District Attorney associated with the Suffolk County Child Abuse Unit, the DSS Boston Region Program Manager and a DSS Area Director.

The fourth source of data involved an analysis of Boston area newspaper coverage of child maltreatment during the case data collection time period. The influence of the media is an important domain often omitted from studies examining decision-making by agencies that respond to cases of child abuse. Although a comprehensive analysis of media impact was beyond the scope of this study, a content analysis of the Boston Globe and Boston Herald was conducted from January 1, 1997 until the end of data collection to control for this variable. For the content analysis, information was collected regarding the number of stories about child abuse including general news stories, incident reports, editorials and legislative initiatives that appeared in the Globe and Herald during the specified time period. Information regarding the tone of each newspaper story toward DSS, be it negative, positive, or neutral, was also collected.

News stories relating to child abuse that referred to the interventions of protective services or the criminal justice system were examined to assess the representation of each agency as negative, positive or neutral. Finally, data were collected on the ways in which the interventions of each of these agencies was represented in these same news stories. Interventions were grouped in four categories; pro-arrest/prosecution, anti-arrest/prosecution; pro-placement, and anti-placement.

Data Preparation

The data file was converted into a system file for data analysis using the Statistical Package for Social Sciences (SPSS). Quantitative information received from the surveys were first entered into an excel

---

children on their caseload, for example, birthday presents.

file, transferred into an SPSS system file and then merged with the DA data. Qualitative data from the surveys was typed into a word processing file. A written data dictionary was created as a guide to the data files.

The data obtained from the media content analysis were coded according to date, number, content and tone of articles. Time periods with numerous news stories regarding child abuse and/or portraying negative coverage of the agencies or agency interventions were identified and used to create several new variables. These variables provided information as to whether or not negative media coverage of the general child protection system, the Suffolk County District Attorney's office or Massachusetts DSS, as well as the interventions of case prosecution, child removal, or the lack of child removal in child abuse cases, had occurred in the thirty days prior to each report of abuse. In addition, a variable was included that identified whether high media coverage of child maltreatment in general had occurred in the thirty days prior to each report of abuse. Those child abuse cases for which an investigation was initiated by the DA or DSS in the thirty days following potentially influential media coverage were identified utilizing these variables.

Human Subjects Protection

Two of the primary principles that must be incorporated into all studies involving human beings are a respect for all persons and an obligation to minimize harm to individuals (Office of Human Research Protections, 2001). These principles are especially important in any study relating to subject matter of a personal and/or sensitive nature, such as the abuse of children.

In the present study of maltreatment, the protection of the child victims, alleged offenders and family members of victims was of primary importance to the researcher. The chosen methodology of case abstraction and interviews with agency staff members allowed for a study of the subject matter without the direct involvement of the parties mentioned above. Therefore, the main concern of the researcher was protection of the identity of the individuals involved in the cases under examination.

After obtaining approval of the study from the Deputy Commissioner of the Massachusetts Department of Social Services and the Suffolk County District Attorney, processes to provide human subjects with protection were reviewed by key individuals within each agency. The comments of the primary contact people from the two agencies were incorporated into the final data collection procedures. In addition, a human subjects protection procedure was submitted to and approved by the Brandeis University Institutional Review Board.

To protect the confidentiality of the child victims and defendants, the names of the child victims and alleged perpetrators were removed from the SPSS files after they were copied at the District Attorney's office. Only members of the research group and staff members at DSS and the District Attorney's office had access to the names of the individuals involved. Subject identification numbers were used on all data files in lieu of names.

For identification purposes, the name of the child victim, primary caretaker and alleged offender were only recorded on a cover sheet that was attached to each survey sent to a DSS caseworker.   DSS caseworkers removed these cover sheets prior to returning the surveys. The returned surveys identified each case of abuse solely by the subject identification number.

Data Analysis

A data dictionary was created and examined to correct for inputting errors, inconsistencies and inappropriate coding. Frequency tables were then created to double check for coding errors and identify cases and variables with many missing values.

Formal data analysis began with descriptive, univariate analyses of all variables including child victim, family and abuse characteristics, case characteristics, prior protective service involvement, characteristics of the child's primary caretaker and family, protective service assessment and interventions, perpetrator characteristics and criminal justice interventions and outcomes.

Those variables with missing values for more than 30% of the cases were excluded from the further analysis. Variables with 10-30% missing values were analyzed to determine whether or not there was a significant correlation with either of the dependent variables when the group of cases with unknown values were included in the variable as a separate value. [6] For example, in those cases with missing values for

---

[6] For quantitative variables, the mean was utilized as the value for the group with missing values.

the ethnicity of the perpetrator, the ethnicity variable was recoded to include the group with missing values as 'unknown'. The variable was then tested for a significant association with both case prosecution and child removal in both forms, one without an 'unknown' category and one with an 'unknown' category. In the test of the variable without the 'unknown' category, the cases with missing values were simply excluded from the analysis.

In the case of perpetrator ethnicity, the variable was not found to be significantly related to child removal in either form. However, when tested for an association with case prosecution, perpetrator ethnicity was found to be significantly associated with case prosecution when the missing values were included in the analysis. Therefore, the perpetrator ethnicity variable with the missing values coded as 'unknown' was kept for inclusion in the data analysis.

Bivariate analyses of predictors of case prosecution and predictors of child placement were then conducted for the entire sample and for the sexual and physical abuse sub-samples. The significant associations found in the bivariate analyses provided the information needed to employ two multivariate analyses of the data.

The nature of the questions under study posed some potential difficulties at this step of the analysis. It was postulated that the dependent variables identified in the two hypotheses would serve as significant explanatory variables for each other. In other words, it was hypothesized that case prosecution would be a significant independent variable in the model predicting child placement and that child placement would be a significant explanatory variable in the model predicting case prosecution.

The inclusion of these two variables, first as the dependent variable in one equation, and then as an explanatory variable in the other, raises the potential problem of simultaneity between the two equations. If simultaneity is ignored and the two models are estimated separately, the estimates in the equations will be both biased and inconsistent (Ramanathan, 1995).

Therefore, the form of the multivariate analysis utilized in this study was dependent on the outcome of the bivariate analyses. If child removal and case prosecution were found to be significantly associated, the mulitvariate analysis would have to take the form of two reduced form equations. In the model estimating child removal, the independent variable of prosecution would be replaced by a new independent variable representing the probability of prosecution. Likewise, in the model estimating case prosecution, the independent variable of child removal would be replaced by a new independent variable representing the probability of child removal. These new independent variables would be created by obtaining reduced form estimates of the likelihood of prosecution and the likelihood of removal.

On the other hand, if the two hypotheses were not supported by the bivariate tests of association, then reduced form estimates would not be necessary. If evidence of a significant association between child removal and case prosecution was not found, the multivariate analysis could take the form of two logistic regressions, one predicting case prosecution and one predicting child removal.

Limitations of the Study

In terms of the application of this research to areas outside of Massachusetts, the findings can be generalized to other regions only through careful comparison of the policies of the Massachusetts criminal justice and child protection systems to those of other states. The Commonwealth of Massachusetts is typical of most states in that it uses, in its statutes and regulations, a standard of inflicted harm or substantial risk of harm to the health or welfare of a child to determine the acts that constitute child abuse (National Clearinghouse on Child Abuse and Neglect Information, 2003). Specifically, Massachusetts protective service regulations define abuse as the "non-accidental commission of any act by a caretaker upon a children under eighteen which causes, or creates a substantial risk of, physical or emotional injury, or constitutes a sexual offense under the laws of the Commonwealth, or any sexual contact between a caretaker and a child under the care of that individual" (Massachusetts Department of Social Services, 2000). The regulations define neglect as the "failure by a caretaker, either deliberately or through negligence or inability, to take those actions necessary to provide a child with minimally adequate food, clothing, shelter, medical care, supervision, emotional stability and growth, or other essential care; provided, however, that such inability is not due solely to inadequate economic resources or solely to the existence of a handicapping condition" (Massachusetts Department of Social Services, 2000). In Massachusetts, protective services is mandated by statute to investigate all reported cases of potential or actual physical or emotional injury or neglect.

The Commonwealth of Massachusetts is very similar to the majority of states in that the public child welfare agency is administered by the state and the agency has primary responsibility for coordination of the 24 hour reporting hotline, report screening, and case investigation (U.S.D.H.H.S., 2003d). The identification of health, mental health and education professionals as mandated reporters in Massachusetts statutes also mirrors other states, however, additional groups are included that are unique to the Commonwealth (USDHHS, 2003d). In Massachusetts, drug and alcohol counselors, probation and parole officers, court clerks, firefighters and clergy are also legally mandated to report child abuse (National Clearinghouse on Child Abuse and Neglect Information, 2003). In the screening and investigation process, Massachusetts is similar to many other states in that the determination of maltreatment and risk of further abuse or neglect is the primary focus. However, twenty other states have also established alternative responses that allow the agency to provide services without a determination of maltreatment or risk (U.S.D.H.H.S., 2003d).

Nationally, there is significant variation in the time allowed by different jurisdictions to complete investigations, however, Massachusetts has mandated the fastest time period for this task compared to all other states. Non-emergency investigations must begin within two working days and be completed within 10 days (Kopels, Chariton & Wells, 2003). Most states allow child protective services more than four weeks to complete the inquiry (U.S.D.H.H.S., 2003d).

In addition, Massachusetts is one of a very few number of states that mandates that all cases substantiated by protective services be forwarded to the district attorney's office for review following investigation (Wilber, 1987). This policy provides an opportunity for all criminal acts of child abuse to be considered for prosecution. However, although case data is forwarded, this information is often received after the child protection investigation is completed and agency decisions are implemented. Although child protection is allowed by statute to conduct joint investigations and collaborate with other agencies, there is no law that requires the agency to work collaboratively on cases.

Therefore, in comparison to other states the child protection system in Massachusetts has two distinct characteristics. The state mandates the completion of case investigation in ten days and child protection must forward all substantiated cases to the criminal prosecutor.

As with all research endeavors, this study is also impacted by data limitations. Although 406 of the District Attorney's cases were identified as having DSS involvement during the time period of the study, it is probable that dual system case identification was not completely accurate. A small number of DA cases may not have been identified as DSS cases due to the misspelling of names, inadequate identifying information, and a child victim having a common name. However, it is likely that these errors occurred randomly.

Some of the data provided on each case by the District Attorney's Victim/Witness Advocates and DSS staff members were necessarily subjective. The nature of the study did not allow for the collection of information regarding child and family characteristics directly from the child or family. Subjective assessments were made by DSS staff members in a number of areas (i.e. indications of parental substance abuse, parental support of the complaint and cooperation with DSS, etc). The findings regarding the influence of these subjective indicators on the prosecution and placement decision should, therefore, be understood as the relationship of the perceptions of the actors of this system to prosecution and placement.

The study was also limited by missing data regarding the socioeconomic status of the families of the victims, which has previously been found to be correlated with child removal and the exclusion of relevant criminal justice data. Information from the 1990 census regarding the median incomes of the geographic areas involved in this study was collected and is presented in Appendix C in an attempt to consider the impact of socio-economic status. Information on two variables important to the prosecution decision in prior studies (i.e. type of evidence available and prior criminal record of the alleged perpetrator) was not available to the researcher.

Finally, response bias may also have influenced the findings of this research project. The final sample included 198 cases of child abuse that had both protective service and criminal justice involvement. The study had a return rate of 49% for the DSS surveys. To ascertain whether or not the final sample differed significantly from the overall population of dual system child abuse cases, several case factors (i.e. DSS office, type of abuse, child's age, town of residence and victim and perpetrator ethnicity) were compared between cases with returned surveys and cases without returned surveys to determine if bias existed.

The sample is impacted by the differential return rates of surveys from the DSS area offices. The DSS area office assigned to the case was found to be significantly related to whether or not a survey was returned. The return rates for the five area offices were as follows: Jamaica Plain, 55%; Roxbury, 62%; Boston, 35%; Dorchester, 30%; and Chelsea, 56%. Area offices outside of the Boston area had a cumulative return rate of 77%. The varying return rates from the area offices is believed to be primarily the result of the different levels of priority given the study by the senior managers of each area.

Two demographic variables were found to be significantly related to both DSS area and whether or not a survey was returned: victim ethnicity and alleged perpetrator ethnicity. Sixty-three percent of surveys relating to white child victims were returned, 36% of the African-American child surveys were returned, 50% of the Latino child surveys were returned and 51% of the surveys relating to child victims of other races were returned. In the overall sample, 43% of the white child victims were from Chelsea, which had the highest survey return rate and 51% of African-American child victims were from Dorchester and Boston, which had the lowest return rates. This resulted in an overrepresentation of White children and an under-representation of African-American children in the final sample. The same bias occurred regarding perpetrators. Forty-five percent of the white perpetrators were associated to child victims connected to the Chelsea office and 48% of the African-American perpetrators were associated with child victims connected to the Boston and Dorchester offices.

This bias places limitations on the ability of this study to truly describe the sample it was designed to represent. In terms of finite numbers, children and perpetrators of color are adequately represented, however, the overall sample does not reflect the population from which it was drawn. The similarities, however, in the case characteristics between the white and non-white children and perpetrators provides some assurance that the bias is primarily related to differences in the populations served by the area offices versus differences in the cases themselves. However, any findings relating to differences in interventions by area offices are complicated by the correlation of victim and perpetrator ethnicity with these offices.

Sample Description

The following section outlines the characteristics of the overall sample as well as three important sub-samples. The overall sample, or the dual system case sample, includes all cases of child abuse that were under investigation by both the Massachusetts Department of Social Services and the Suffolk County District Attorney's Office for which a completed DSS survey was received. The three sub-samples to be discussed include the sub-sample of cases that were substantiated by DSS, the sexual abuse case sub-sample and the physical abuse case sub-sample.

The Dual System Case Sample

Table 6 provides a descriptive overview of the characteristics of the dual system case sample and a breakdown of prosecution and removal rates for sub-categories of variables. In this table, information regarding the distribution of case characteristics are displayed for each variable. For example, the table indicates that child victims ages 0-6 comprise 30% of the sample, whereas victims ages 7-12 constitute 36% of the sample. In addition, the table provides information regarding the removal and prosecution rates for each value of each variable. For example, the table indicates that 22% of the child victims ages 0-6 were removed from their home and that 15% of the cases involving children between the ages of 0 and 6 were prosecuted.

Approximately two-thirds of the child victims were female and 77% of alleged perpetrators were male. The average age of the child victims was 10 and the average age of the perpetrators was 34. Many of the perpetrators were related to the child victim; 36% were the parent of the child victim and 17% were relatives. Most of the children had biological mothers as their primary caretakers (78%), however, in 9% of the cases the primary caretaker was the biological father.

Sixty-seven percent of the cases involved reports of sexual abuse. The majority of case reports (77%) were first received by DSS versus the District Attorney's office and 58% of the case intakes at the two agencies occurred within 15 days of each other. DSS was the source of 43% of the reports received by the District Attorney, however, the District Attorney was the source of report to DSS in only 10% of the cases.

Table 6. Characteristics of Child Abuse Cases Under Investigation by Protective Service and Criminal Justice

The dual system case sample (N=198) includes child abuse cases in the Suffolk County District Attorney's Office that were also under investigation by Massachusetts DSS. The prosecution rates were estimated from the entire dual system case sample. However, since only those cases substantiated by protective services can result in a placement by DSS, the removal rates were calculated from the substantiated case sample (N=138).

Case Characteristics	% of Dual system sample (N=198)	% Removed	% Prosecuted
Child characteristics			
Age of child victims			
0-6	30	22	15
7-12	36	24	37
13-17	32	48	30
18+	.8	-	100
Unknown	.8	-	-
Age at onset of abuse			
0-6	41	30	16
7-12	36	26	42
13-17	23	55	32
Male	32	27	27
Female	68	35	30
English-speaking	93	33	30
Race/Ethnicity			
Caucasian	36	25	30
African-American	37	35	35
Latino	16	32	13
Haitian	5	75	38
Other	6	67	50
Residence at time of abuse			
Prim. caretaker	89	34	31
With relative	5	33	14
Foster home	4	0	0
Other	2	0	0

Table 6. Characteristics of Child Abuse Cases Under Investigation by Protective Service and Criminal Justice (continued)

Case Characteristics	% of Dual system sample (N=198)	% Removed	% Prosecuted
Perpetrator Characteristics			
Male	77	26	27
Female	23	42	46
Age			
0-17	9	11	13
18-27	12	14	28
28-37	28	37	43
38-47	19	23	36
48-57	9	14	44
58-67	2	25	-
68-77	.3	-	-
Unknown	20	59	-
Race/Ethnicity			
Caucasian	24	24	24
African-American	30	23	45
Latino	11	33	26
Other	6	38	18
Unknown	28	47	21
Relationship to child victim			
Biological or step-parent	36	40	40
Mother's boyfriend	8	6	44
Other relatives	17	27	13
Non-familial	33	24	19
Unknown	6	86	14
Perpetrator known/unknown			
Known	94	30	30
Unknown	6	83	0
Primary Caretaker Characteristics			
Type of primary caretaker			
Biological mother	78	31	32
Biological father	9	36	24

Case Characteristics	% of Dual system sample (N=198)	% Removed	% Prosecuted
Foster parent	1	-	-
Other relative	10	40	16
Other	2	50	-
Race/Ethnicity			
Caucasian	29	30	38
African-American	30	33	33
Latino	23	10	19
Haitian	7	62	33
Other	11	54	10
Type of Abuse			
Sexual	67	27	20
Physical	33	42	49
Systemic Characteristics			
First agency to receive report			
DSS	54	33	19
DA	7	36	62
Police	30	10	39
DSS/DA received report on same day	9	0	24
DSS received report prior to DA	77	37	27
DA received report prior to DSS	6	14	57
15 or less days between intakes	52	31	43
16 to 34 days between intakes	19	31	25
Criminal Justice Variables			
Source of report to DA			

Table 6. Characteristics of Child Abuse Cases Under Investigation by Protective Service and Criminal Justice (continued)

Case Characteristics	% of Dual system sample (N=198)	% Removed	% Prosecuted
DSS	43	44	18
District Court	18	21	56
Police	26	27	29
Other	12	26	30
Jurisdiction of incident			
Boston	4	0	0
Brighton	3	50	17
Chelsea	14	25	25
Dorchester	17	39	52
East Boston	3	33	33
Hyde Park	7	50	11
Jamaica Plain	7	22	46
Mattapan	4	100	14
Revere	6	50	33
Roslindale	3	50	20
Roxbury	12	26	30
South Boston	3	0	40
Other	16	22	20
Initial arrest (prior to District Attorney intake)	22	26	51
District Court			
District Court involvement	34	22	56
No District Court involvement	66	35	15
Criminal charges			
Rape	34	25	23
Indecent assault and battery	40	30	23
Assault & battery	25	30	53
Assault & battery w/ deadly weapon	15	35	63

Case Characteristics	% of Dual system sample (N=198)	% Removed	% Prosecuted
Sexual Abuse Intervention Network (SAIN)	17	44	24
Case status			
Cases chosen for prosecution	26	28	-
Closed without prosecution	65	31	-
Prosecution status pending	9		62
Protective Service Characteristics			
DSS investigating office			
Jamaica Plain	14	41	25
Roxbury	19	32	22
Boston	11	35	28
Dorchester	12	39	58
Chelsea/Revere	24	28	24
DSS internal unit/Contract agency	5	0	0
DSS office outside Boston region	16	32	39
Prior case characteristics			
Prior substantiated abuse report	29	32	30
Prior substantiated neglect report	39	50	27
Prior removal	19	62	11
Source of report to DSS			
Mandated reporter	48	33	23
Police	26	33	44
District Attorney	10	18	29

Table 6. Characteristics of Child Abuse Cases Under Investigation by Protective Service and Criminal Justice (continued)

Case Characteristics	% of Dual system sample (N=198)	% Removed	% Prosecuted
Other (i.e. child self-report)	16	39	8
DSS substantiated report	77	33	35
Media Variables			
High media coverage prior to report to DA	15	20	45
High media coverage prior to report to DSS	20	31	48
Negative coverage of criminal justice prior to DA report	5	38	25
Negative coverage of protective services prior to DSS report	22	16	42

An initial arrest prior to a report occurred in only 22% of the cases. The District Attorney chose only 26% of the cases for prosecution. A SAIN investigation was initiated for only 17 percent of the cases.

For 86 percent of the cases, a protective service investigation was undertaken by a Boston region DSS office or a Boston agency under contract with DSS. Fifteen percent of the cases in the sample were investigated by a DSS office outside of the Boston region. DSS substantiated 77% of the reports of abuse in the sample.

Information regarding the differential rates of child removal and case prosecution within and between variables is provided in the second and third column of Table 6. In this sample, removal rates increased with the age of the child and varied greatly by child ethnicity. Physical abuse cases were more likely to result in removal than sexual abuse cases; with a 42% versus a 27% removal rate.

The removal rates rose as the number of days increased between the District Attorney and DSS intakes. Cases that were reported to the District Attorney and DSS on the same day had the lowest removal rate of 14%. Cases with 15 to 34 days between agency intakes had a 31% rate of removal and cases in which there were 35 or more days between intakes had a 42% removal rate. In those cases involving removal, 68% of the placements occurred prior to the DA intake date. In 24% of the cases involving removal, the placement occurred after the DA intake date and in 8% of these cases, children were removed on the same day as the DA intake.

Cases chosen by the District Attorney for criminal prosecution had a removal rate similar to those not chosen (28% versus 31%), however, the few cases that were still pending a decision regarding prosecution at the end of the data collection period had a high removal rate of 62%. Child victims who had previously been removed from their homes by DSS or had on record a prior substantiated neglect report had removal rates of 62% and 50% respectively.

Variation is also apparent in the prosecution rates presented in Table 6. The prosecution rate for physical abuse cases was 49% and the rate for sexual abuse cases was 20%. Cases referred to the District Attorney by a District Court were prosecuted at the highest rate (56%) whereas cases referred by DSS were prosecuted at the lowest rate (18%). Thirty-seven percent of the cases of child victims between ages 7 and 12 were prosecuted versus 15% of the children ages 0 to 6 and 30% of the children ages 13 to 17.

African-American perpetrators were prosecuted more frequently than all other perpetrator ethnic groups (45%). Perpetrators who were the parent of the child victim or the boyfriend of the mother of the child were prosecuted more frequently than perpetrators with any other type of relationship to the child victim.

Data from the dual system sample were also analyzed to determine if local print media coverage of child abuse had a significant impact on child removal or case prosecution. A search of the Boston Globe and Boston Herald for 1997-1998 revealed 248 articles relating to child maltreatment. The percentage of cases following periods of high media coverage of child abuse (30 days preceding the report) are reported in Table 6. High media coverage was defined as more than two articles on one day, more than five in a week and/or more than thirteen in a month. In addition, the proportion of case intakes that closely followed negative coverage of the criminal justice system or the child protection system is provided in the table. Negative coverage of the criminal justice system focused primarily on the inappropriate investigation and prosecution of some reports of child abuse. No articles were found that provided negative coverage of the judicial system for neglecting to prosecute cases.

Negative coverage of protective services included criticism relating to both the inappropriate removal and the lack of removal of children. In addition, protective services was criticized for not meeting agency deadlines for investigations and not providing adequate support services to families in crisis. As Table 6 makes apparent, negative coverage relating to protective services occurred much more frequently in the press than negative coverage of the criminal justice system.

In conclusion, the dual system case sample provides an overview of the characteristics of abuse cases in which protective service and criminal justice involvement overlaps. In a number of ways, the pattern of removal rates and prosecution rates in this sample mirrors results of previous studies and supports field reports from protective services and criminal justice. For example, the higher rate of older children experiencing removal and the increased rate of prosecution for cases with child victims between 7-12 supports previous findings.

The data also point to correlates to removal and prosecution not previously discussed in the literature. For example, a greater number of days between agency intakes on a case is clearly associated with two difficult outcomes for child victims. Cases that take more than one month to be referred from one agency to the other have both higher rates of child removal from the home and lower rates of criminal case prosecution.

The Substantiated Case Sample

Tables 7 and 8 provide information on the sub-sample of cases that were substantiated by DSS. The substantiated cases represent those reports in which the occurrence of abuse was verified through the DSS investigation resulting in an open case file with the department. Table 7 provides an overview of the case characteristics of the substantiated sample and Table 8 provides information on the substantiated cases in which child removal occurred.

An analysis of the demographic and case characteristics of the dual systems sample and the substantiated case sub-sample was conducted to determine how the characteristics of the substantiated cases varied from the overall sample. A comparison of the characteristics of non-substantiated cases with substantiated cases revealed only two significant differences. The substantiated case sample included far fewer cases involving Caucasian perpetrators than the dual systems sample. Cases in which the perpetrator was Caucasian versus any other race were found to be significantly less likely to be substantiated by protective services (χ^2=4.824, p<.02). In addition, cases that involved alleged offenders who were the parent of the child victim or the boyfriend of the child victim's mother were over-represented in the substantiated case sample. These cases were significantly more likely to be substantiated by DSS than any other type of child victim/perpetrator relationship (χ^2=18.184, p<.001).

The substantiated case sample (N=138) displayed in Table 7 provides an overview of case characteristics relating to DSS assessment and intervention. The DSS case findings category represents the child and family characteristics reported by DSS caseworkers for each of the cases. None of the assessment variables are mutually exclusive. Forty-six percent of the cases were found by DSS to involve physical abuse and 51% involved sexual abuse. There were indications of neglect in 25% of the cases and it was reported that the primary caretaker lacked parenting skills in 30% of the cases. Domestic violence was found to be present in the home in 24% of the cases. The perpetrator had lived with or had access to the child's home in 32% of the cases. In 26% of the cases, the primary caretaker was alleged to be the perpetrator of the abuse. In the majority of cases it was determined through the DSS investigation that the primary caretaker was able to protect the child from further abuse and able to

**Table 7: Characteristics of Substantiated Child Abuse Cases
Under Investigation by Protective Service and Criminal Justice**

The substantiated case sample (N=138) includes only those dual system cases that were substantiated by DSS. The case findings reflect the conclusions of the DSS case investigations. The abbreviation of PC refers to the primary caretaker of child victim.

Case Characteristics	% of Substantiated case sample (N=138)	% Removed	% Prosecuted
DSS case findings			
Physical abuse	46	25	28
Sexual abuse	51	26	27
Child with serious physical or mental health problems	12	50	21
Indications of neglect	25	56	15
Child emotionally abused	15	62	28
Other abused children in home	27	33	42
Child abandoned	4	80	25
PC lacks parenting skills	30	50	27
Inadequate family income	13	31	23
Domestic violence	24	29	35
Adult substance abuser in home	19	23	42
Adult with psychological problems in home	15	35	17
PC is alleged perpetrator	26	63	40
Perpetrator lived with or had access to child's home	32	33	32
PC not cooperating with DSS	14	26	7
PC no support abuse complaint	26	54	35

Table 7: Characteristics of Substantiated Child Abuse Cases Under Investigations by Protective Service and Criminal Justice

Case Characteristics	% of Substantiated case sample (N=138)	% Removed	% Prosecuted
PC does not support prosecution	19	52	33
PC can provide adequate protection	75	17	36
PC can provide adequate care	72	14	36
Child removed from home	30	-	32

provide adequate care for the child. Thirty-three percent of the children (N=45) were removed from their homes. Table 8 refers to case characteristics of the sub-sample in which removal occurred. Most of the removals (60%) were initiated by DSS. However, 13% were voluntary placements by parents and 10% were ordered by Juvenile Court. The majority of the removed children were placed in foster homes (57%). Thirty-one percent of the removed children were returned to their home within two months of DSS intake.

Comparison of Sexual and Physical Abuse Cases

Turning now to a comparison of sexual versus physical abuse cases, Tables 9 and 10 provide separate overviews of the characteristics of these two distinct sub-samples. A comprehensive analysis of how sexual abuse and physical abuse cases differ is beyond the scope of this study, therefore, discussion will be limited to the most important similarities and differences between the two types of abuse. In the sexual abuse sample, the majority of child victims were female (81%). In contrast, males comprised almost half of the child victims in the physical abuse sample (47%). Ninety-six percent of the sexual abuse perpetrators and 58% of the physical abuse perpetrators were male. Sexual abuse victims were most often Caucasian (42%) and child victims of physical abuse were most often African-American (40%).

Most of the sexual abuse perpetrators in the sample were not related to the child victims. Ten percent were the boyfriends of the mother of the child victim and forty-two percent were other non-family members. In contrast, a biological or step-parent comprised 80% of the perpetrators in the physical abuse cases.

The two types of abuse cases also varied in terms of systemic characteristics. Only 68% of the reports of sexual abuse were received by DSS prior to the DA however, 87% of the physical abuse cases were reported first to DSS. Similarly, an arrest prior to DA intake characterized 60% of the physical abuse cases but only 9% of the sexual abuse cases. Forty-five percent of the physical abuse cases were chosen for prosecution. In contrast, this occurred in only 25% of the sexual abuse cases.

DSS substantiated 71% of the sexual abuse cases and 89% of the physical abuse cases. The physical abuse cases had a higher removal rate than sexual abuse cases. Children were removed from the home in 36% of the substantiated physical abuse cases versus 26% of the sexual abuse cases. The DSS case findings for sexual and physical abuse reports varied in only a few areas. Most significantly, a primary caretaker being the alleged perpetrator was found to be much more common in the physical abuse sample (43%) than the sexual abuse sample (13%).

In conclusion, it is clear that a number of differences exist in the case characteristics of sexual and physical abuse cases in this study. Unlike the sexual abuse sub-sample, physical abuse cases were found to be more likely to involve either a male or female victim, an African-American victim and a parent as the perpetrator. Typical systemic entry for a physical abuse case would involve an immediate arrest by police, an emergency placement by DSS followed by a case being chosen for criminal prosecution.

In contrast, a typical sexual abuse case in this sample would be more likely to involve a Caucasian female victim who had been sexually assaulted by someone outside of her immediate family, such as the mother's boyfriend. The incident would have been first reported to DSS by a mandated reporter sometime after the onset of the abuse. The child would be less likely to have their case criminally prosecuted or face out of home placement than the physically abused child.

Table 8: Characteristics of Substantiated Child Abuse Cases Involving Removal Under Investigation by Protective Services and Criminal Justice

This sub-sample of substantiated cases that involved removal (N=45) includes only those dual system cases that were substantiated by DSS in which a child was placed outside the home.

Case Characteristics	% of Cases Involving Removal	% Removed	% Prosecuted
Type of first removal			
DSS	60	-	28
Voluntary by parent/guardian	13	-	25
Juvenile Court	10	-	25
Other (i.e. temporary custody or guardianship change, child initiated removals)	17	-	33
Type of first placement			
Foster home	57	-	24
Relative	21	-	63
Other (i.e. health or mental health facility, youth shelter)	12	-	16
Returned to home within two months of DSS intake	31	-	9

These findings typify the differences between physical and sexual abuse cases. Incidents of physical abuse often lend themselves to a more immediate response by law enforcement due to the observable and/or public nature of the offenses. This immediate response often allows for the collection of physical and medical evidence that support case prosecution. Both an immediate arrest and the availability of evidence can lay the groundwork for successful prosecution.

Table 9: Characteristics of Child Sexual Abuse Cases Under Investigation by Protective Services and Criminal Justice

The sexual abuse case sample includes all dual system cases involving sexual abuse offenses reported to the District Attorney (N=132). The prosecution rates were estimated from the entire sexual abuse sample. The removal rates and DSS case findings were calculated from the sub-sample of sexual abuse cases that were substantiated by DSS (N=85). Removal characteristics were calculated from the sub-sample of sexual abuse cases in which removal occurred (N=23).

Case Characteristics	% of Sample	% Removed	% Prosecuted
Child characteristics			
Age of child victims			
0-6	31	12	6
7-12	38	29	31
13-17	31	44	19
Age at onset of abuse			
0-6	43	16	7
7-12	36	31	36
13-17	21	57	13
Male	19	7	9
Female	81	31	22
Race/Ethnicity			
Caucasian	42	21	26
African-American	32	38	16
Latino	18	27	6
Haitian	4	75	25
Other	3	0	33
English-speaking	93	29	21
Residence at time of abuse			
With primary caretaker	84	30	20
With relative	7	0	17
Foster home	7	0	0
Other	2	0	0

Table 9: Characteristics of Child Sexual Abuse Cases Under Investigation by Protective Services and Criminal Justice

Case Characteristics	% of Sample	% Removed	% Prosecuted
Perpetrator Characteristics			
Male	96	28	21
Female	4	0	0
Age			
0-17	13	11	13
18-27	12	13	15
28-37	22	30	28
38-47	20	27	35
48-57	7	20	29
58-67	4	0	0
68-77	0	-	-
Unknown	23	43	8
Race/Ethnicity			
Caucasian	41	38	19
African-American	33	28	24
Latino	19	29	21
Other	7	20	20
Unknown perpetrator	5	0	0
Known perpetrator	95	27	20
Relationship to child victim			
Biological or step-parent	20	46	21
Mother's boyfriend	10	8	33
Other relatives	22	28	12
Non-familial	42	17	20
Unknown	5	67	17
System Characteristics			
First agency to receive report			
DSS	57	32	12
DA	7	17	44
DA/DSS same day	12	0	14
Police	24	19	30

Table 9: Characteristics of Child Sexual Abuse Cases Under Investigation by Protective Services and Criminal Justice (cont.)

Case Characteristics	% of Sample	% Removed	% Prosecuted
DSS intake prior to DA intake	68	29	15
DA and DSS intake on same day	8	17	44
15 or less days between intakes	44	27	19
16 to 34 days between intakes	19	21	15
35 or more days between intakes	29	35	13
Criminal Justice Variables			
Source of report to DA			
DSS	44	29	8
District Court	5	33	17
Police	34	25	30
Other	17	26	30
Jurisdiction of incident			
Boston	2	0	0
Brighton	3	50	25
Chelsea	14	25	6
Dorchester	14	43	33
East Boston	4	33	20
Hyde Park	9	43	11
Jamaica Plain	6	25	50
Mattapan	5	100	14
Revere	6	20	13
Roslindale	3	33	0
Roxbury	7	13	10
South Boston	4	0	40

Table 9: Characteristics of Child Sexual Abuse Cases Under Investigation by Protective Services and Criminal Justice

Case Characteristics	% of Sample	% Removed	% Prosecuted
Other	5	20	25
Unknown	18	15	19
District Court involvement	15	13	14
Sexual Abuse Intervention Network (SAIN)	30	35	23
Arrest prior to DA intake	9	27	30
Criminal allegations			
Rape	50	25	23
Indecent assault and battery	41	27	23
Assault & battery	1	0	100
Assault & battery w/ deadly weapon	0	-	-
Case status			
Cases chosen for prosecution	23	21	-
Closed without prosecution	69	28	-
Pending prosecution status	8	43	-
Protective Services Variables			
Prior case characteristics			
Prior substantiated abuse report	29	36	16
Prior substantiated neglect report	37	18	10
Prior removal	24	56	8

Table 9: Characteristics of Child Sexual Abuse Cases Under Investigation by Protective Services and Criminal Justice (cont.)

Case Characteristics	% of Sample	% Removed	% Prosecuted
Source of report to DSS			
Mandated reporter	54	29	16
Police	16	19	33
District Attorney	9	25	20
Other	21	33	9
DSS investigating office			
Jamaica Plain	17	38	16
Roxbury	17	23	10
Boston	11	37	23
Dorchester	10	40	46
Chelsea/Revere	23	19	8
DSS internal unit/Contract agency	5	0	0
DSS office outside Boston region	18	27	37
Report substantiated by DSS	71	27	25
Primary Caretaker Characteristics			
Type of primary caretaker			
Biological mother	72	25	23
Biological father	9	38	0
Foster parent	4	0	0
Other relative	13	38	14
Other	3	0	0
Race/Ethnicity			
Caucasian	35	25	24
African-American	22	33	13
Latino	27	8	17

Table 9: Characteristics of Child Sexual Abuse Cases Under Investigation by Protective Services and Criminal Justice

Case Characteristics	% of Sample	% Removed	% Prosecuted
Haitian	6	67	33
Other	9	50	10
Media Variables			
High media coverage in 30 days prior to report to DA	15	13	26
High media coverage in 30 days prior to report to DSS	22	25	27
Negative coverage of criminal justice 30 days prior to DA report	7	29	29
Negative coverage of protective services 30 days prior to DSS report	20	6	25
DSS case findings **(Substantiated sexual abuse cases only. N=85)**			
Physical abuse	18	40	23
Sexual abuse	81	27	26
Child with serious physical or mental health problems	16	42	8
Indications of neglect	24	55	0
Child emotionally abused	9	57	0
Other abused children in home	23	20	17

Table 9: Characteristics of Child Sexual Abuse Cases Under Investigation by Protective Services and Criminal Justice (cont.)

Case Characteristics	% of Sample	% Removed	% Prosecuted
Child abandoned	3	50	0
PC lacks parenting skills	25	24	11
Inadequate family income	13	25	10
Domestic violence	24	28	22
Adult substance abuser in home	9	50	14
Adult with psychological problems in home	19	14	14
PC is alleged perpetrator	13	50	10
Perpetrator has lived with or has had access to child's home	28	33	19
PC not cooperating with DSS	17	7	8
PC does not support abuse complaint	20	35	7
PC does not support prosecution	20	47	13
Finding that PC can provide adequate protection	81	19	27
Finding that PC can provide adequate care	77	16	26
Child removed from home	26	-	20

Table 9: Characteristics of Child Sexual Abuse Cases Under Investigation by Protective Services and Criminal Justice

Case Characteristics	% of Sample	% Removed	% Prosecuted
Removal case characteristics			
(Includes only sexual abuse cases involving removal. N=23)			
Type of first removal			
DSS	47	-	0
Voluntary by parent/guardian	21	-	25
Juvenile Court	11	-	50
Other (i.e. temporary custody or guardianship change, child initiated removals)	21	-	50
Type of first placement			
Foster home	63	-	8
Relative	16	-	33
Other (i.e. health or mental health facility, youth shelter)	20	-	25
Returned to home within two months of DSS intake	37	-	0

In comparison, the hidden nature of sexual offenses often does not lend support to the prosecutor's case. In fact, an immediate arrest in a sexual abuse case can hamper the successful prosecution of a criminal case by prematurely informing the accused of the pending charges, placing the victim at further risk, and rushing the investigative process.

Table 10: Characteristics of Physical Child Abuse Cases Under Investigation by Protective Services and Criminal Justice

The sample of physical abuse cases includes all dual system cases involving physical abuse offenses reported to the District Attorney (N=61). The prosecution rates were estimated from the entire physical abuse sample. The removal rates were calculated from the sample of physical abuse cases that were substantiated by protective services (N=53). Removal characteristics were calculated from sub-sample of physical abuse cases in which removal occurred (N=23).

Case Characteristics	% of Sample (N=61)	% Removed	% Prosecuted
Child Characteristics			
Age of child victims			
0-6	24	46	42
7-12	40	17	50
13-17	34	53	56
Age at onset of abuse			
0-6	39	59	39
7-12	34	19	56
13-17	27	53	64
Male	47	39	42
Female	53	43	55
Race/Ethnicity			
Caucasian	27	33	43
African-American	40	32	62
Latino	12	50	33
Haitian	8	75	50
Other	14	50	29
Child's residence at time of abuse			
With primary caretaker	98	41	49
With relative	2	100	0
Perpetrator Characteristics			
Male	58	21	47
Female	42	48	54
Age			
0-17	0	-	-
18-27	10	17	20

Table 10: Characteristics of Physical Child Abuse Cases Under Investigation by Protective Services and Criminal Justice (cont.)

Case Characteristics	% of Sample (N=61)	% Removed	% Prosecuted
28-37	53	42	55
38-47	19	13	40
48-57	4	0	100
58-67	2	0	0
68-77	0	-	-
Unknown	11	88	17
Race/Ethnicity			
Caucasian	23	0	40
African-American	51	19	68
Latino	12	50	40
Other	14	68	17
Unknown perpetrator	8	100	0
Known perpetrator	92	35	51
Relationship to child victim			
Biological or step-parent	80	36	51
Mother's boyfriend	7	0	75
Other relatives	7	25	25
Non-familial	4	75	0
Unknown	2	100	0
System Characteristics			
First agency to receive report			
DSS	48	45	38
DA	7	0	100
DSS/DA same day	5	0	67
Police	41	47	50
DSS intake prior to DA intake	87	48	46
DA and DSS intake on same day	2	0	0
15 or less days between intakes	60	36	59
16 to 34 days between intakes	23	42	33

Table 9: Characteristics of Child Sexual Abuse Cases Under Investigation by Protective Services and Criminal Justice (cont.)

Case Characteristics	% of Sample (N=61)	% Removed	% Prosecuted
35 or more days between intakes	29	35	13
Criminal Justice Variables			
Initial arrest (prior to DA intake)	60	25	0
Source of report to DA			
DSS	48	64	39
District Court	48	20	65
Police	4	50	0
Other	0	-	-
District Court Involvement	68	24	61
Jurisdiction of incident			
Boston	8	0	0
Brighton	3	50	0
Chelsea	13	25	63
Dorchester	23	36	75
East Boston	2	0	100
Hyde Park	2	100	0
Jamaica Plain	8	0	40
Revere	7	100	75
Roslindale	1	100	100
Roxbury	20	36	50
Other	5	100	0
Unknown	8	40	25
Sexual Abuse Inter. Network (SAIN)	8	100	25
Criminal allegations			
Rape	0	-	-
Indecent assault and battery	2	100	0
Assault & battery	80	31	53
Assault & battery w/ deadly weapon	49	35	63
Case status			
Cases chosen for prosecution	45	33	-
Closed without	43	39	-

Table 10: Characteristics of Physical Child Abuse Cases Under Investigation by Protective Services and Criminal Justice (cont.)

Case Characteristics	% of Sample (N=61)	% Removed	% Prosecuted
prosecution			
Pending prosecution status	11	83	-
Protective Services Variables			
DSS investigating office			
Jamaica Plain	10	50	60
Roxbury	23	42	42
Boston	12	50	40
Dorchester	15	38	75
Chelsea/Revere	25	39	53
DSS internal unit/Contract agency	5	0	0
DSS office outside Boston region	12	43	43
Prior case characteristics			
Prior substantiated abuse report	28	25	60
Prior substantiated neglect report	36	52	63
Prior removal from home	6	80	33
Source of report to DSS			
Mandated reporter	33	43	47
Police	50	43	50
District Attorney	14	14	43
Other	4	67	0
Report substantiated by DSS	89	42	51
Primary Caretaker Characteristics			
Type of primary caretaker			
Biological mother	77	41	49
Biological father	13	33	57
Foster parent	0	-	-

Table 9: Characteristics of Child Sexual Abuse Cases Under Investigation by Protective Services and Criminal Justice (cont.)

Case Characteristics	% of Sample (N=61)	% Removed	% Prosecuted
Other relative	9	43	20
Race/Ethnicity			
Caucasian	21	42	81
African-American	35	33	61
Latino	14	20	29
Haitian	12	57	33
Other	19	57	10
Media Variables			
High media coverage in 30 days prior to report to DA	16	30	80
High media coverage in 30 days prior to report to DSS	15	44	100
Negative coverage of criminal justice 30 days prior to DA report	2	100	0
Negative coverage of protective services 30 days prior to DSS report	25	27	71
DSS case findings (Substantiated physical abuse cases only. N=53)			
Physical abuse	89	44	52
Sexual abuse	2	0	100
Child with serious physical or mental health problems	4	75	100
Indications of neglect	19	58	44
Child emotionally abused	23	64	46
Other abused children in home	34	50	69
Child abandoned	4	100	50

Table 10: Characteristics of Physical Child Abuse Cases Under Investigation by Protective Services and Criminal Justice (cont.)

Case Characteristics	% of Sample (N=61)	% Removed	% Prosecuted
PC lacks parenting skills	32	65	47
Inadequate family income	6	50	67
Domestic violence	24	31	55
Adult substance abuser in home	26	33	58
Adult with psychological problems in home	9	83	25
PC is alleged perpetrator	43	68	46
Perpetrator has lived with or has had access to child's home	35	32	50
PC not cooperating with DSS	4	100	0
PC no support abuse complaint	30	72	64
PC does not support prosecution	13	63	83
PC can provide adequate protection	70	11	52
PC can provide adequate care	70	9	52
Child removed from home	36	-	67
Removal case characteristics (Includes only substantiated physical abuse cases involving removal. N=22)			
Type of first removal			
DSS	69	-	56
Voluntary by parent/guardian	0	-	80

Table 9: Characteristics of Child Sexual Abuse Cases Under Investigation by Protective Services and Criminal Justice (cont.)

Case Characteristics	% of Sample (N=61)	% Removed	% Prosecuted
Juvenile Court	15	-	0
Other (i.e. temporary custody or guardianship change, child initiated removals)	15	-	0
Type of first placement			
Foster home	53	-	44
Relative	29	-	80
Other (i.e. health or mental health facility, youth shelter)	18	-	0
Returned to home within two months of DSS intake		31	-

In terms of the child removal decision, protective services must make this determination based on the current level of safety provided for the child and the ability of the primary caretaker to provide adequate care for the child. Child removal may be more likely in cases of physical abuse due to the perception of immediate physical risk to the child. It is also possible that some of the difference in removal rates between the physical and sexual abuse cases in this sample may be the result of the higher proportion of physical abuse cases involving primary caretakers as perpetrators. The data also make clear that similarities exist in the characteristics of physical and sexual abuse cases. For example, DSS usually received the report prior to the DA for both physical and sexual abuse cases and there was little variation in the number of days between the agency intakes for the two types of cases. In addition, a high rate of removal was found for both physical and sexual abuse offenses when the child victim was Haitian.

Another interesting similarity is the presence of prior reports of abuse and/or neglect and of current domestic violence in both sexual and physical abuse cases. Domestic violence was reported in 24% of both the sexual and physical abuse cases. In previous research, domestic violence has been commonly associated with child physical abuse as a natural extension of a violent home. However, the presence of domestic violence in sexual abuse cases may be indicative of home environments that allow for its occurrence by interfering with the ability of the mother of the child victim to provide protection for the child.

Predictors of Child Removal

To address the first research question, data were analyzed on both bivariate and multivariate levels to determine what case characteristics, child and family characteristics, protective service assessment characteristics and criminal justice interventions and outcomes are associated with the child removal decision. The hypothesis that the decision by the District Attorney to prosecute a case would be positively associated with child victims not being placed outside of their home was tested. This association was tested for the entire substantiated sample as well as the sexual abuse sub-sample and the physical abuse sub-sample.

All independent variables were first examined individually to test their significance in influencing child placement. (See Appendix D for a listing of all independent variables included in the tests of association with removal.) Cases not substantiated by DSS were not included in bivariate analyses with placement because formal removal by DSS or the Juvenile Court could only occur in the 138 substantiated cases. Information regarding child placements initiated solely by parents in unsubstantiated cases was not available.

Table 11 provides a summary of those factors that were found to be significantly associated with child placement outside the home in bivariate statistical analyses of the substantiated sample. [7] Older child victims, prior reports of neglect and child victims who had experienced

---

[7] All statistical tests were based on an alpha value of .05. The odds ratio indicated refers to the relative odds of removal under one condition versus the other.

prior removal were all found to be significantly related to placement outside the home.

Significant variations in placement rates were also found in an examination of primary caretaker ethnicity. Children whose primary caretaker was Latino were the least likely to be removed (10%). Thirty percent of the children who had Caucasian primary caretakers were removed and 33% of the children who had African-American primary caretakers were removed. Child victims whose primary caretaker was Haitian or classified as 'Other' were most likely to be removed (61% and 53% respectively).

The rate of removal for each primary caretaker ethnic group was tested against the average rate of removal for all other ethnic groups combined. Table 11 provides information on the rate of removal for children whose primary caretakers were Haitian in contrast to the average rate of removal for all other ethnicities combined.

Cases substantiated for physical abuse versus sexual abuse by DSS were found to be significantly associated with child placement. In addition, current neglect of the child victim was also a predictor of removal. Cases that involved primary caretakers neglecting, emotionally abusing or abandoning a child were found to be significantly associated with child placement. Primary caretakers who lacked parenting skills or did not support the prosecution of the case were also significantly more likely to have the child victim removed. Cases in which the primary caretaker was identified as the alleged perpetrator were also found to be significantly correlated to placement. As might be expected, the primary caretaker's lack of support of the complaint was also found to be highly associated with the primary caretaker being the alleged perpetrator (Chi-Square=16.278, p<001).

The relationship of the perpetrator to the child was found to be significantly related to placement in two additional ways. Cases that involved a perpetrator who was the biological or step-parent of the child victim were more likely to result in child removal than any other relationship category. Cases in which the perpetrator's identity was unknown versus known were also found to be significantly associated with child placement. Only one media variable was found to be significantly associated with the removal of child victims. Cases that were preceded by time periods in which there was no negative coverage of protective services were found to be significantly associated with more child placemnts.

Table 11: Factors Significantly Associated With Removal in Cases of Child Abuse
Bivariate Analysis

Sample includes only child abuse cases in the Suffolk County District Attorney's Office that were also substantiated by the Massachusetts Department of Social Services. N=138. PC refers to primary caretaker of child victim. The symbol ° signifies the use of a Fisher's Exact Test to calculate probability.

Variable	n	% Removed	t	χ²	P value	Odds Ratio
Child Characteristics						
Older child	132	-	-2.361		.02	-
Ethnicity of child						
Haitian	13	61			.01°	4.00
All other ethnicities	122	30				
Prior removal of child	21	62		8.956	.003	4.15
No prior removal	113	28				
Prior neglect report	48	50		9.856	.002	3.33
No prior neglect report	89	24				
Primary Caretaker Characteristics						
Ethnicity of Primary Caretaker						
Haitian	13	62			.01°	4.00
All other ethnicities	122	29				
PC neglects child	34	56		10.398	.001	3.70

Table 11: Factors Significantly Associated With Removal in Cases of Child Abuse (continued)

Variable	n	% Removed	t	χ^2	P value	Odds Ratio
No report of neglect	101	26				
PC emotionally abuses child	21	62		9.135	.003	4.15
No report of emotional abuse	114	28				
PC abandoned child	5	80			.04°	8.69
No report of abandonment	130	31				
PC lacks parenting skills	40	50		7.105	.008	3.03
Adequate parenting skills	95	26				
PC is alleged perpetrator	35	63		18.534	.000	5.82
PC is not alleged perpetrator	100	23				
PC no support abuse complaint	35	54		9.334	.002	3.37
PC supports abuse complaint	100	26				
PC no support prosecution	25	52		4.538	.03	2.57
PC supports prosecution	108	30				
PC not able provide	34	82		52.214	.000	24.52

Table 11: Factors Significantly Associated With Removal in Cases of Child Abuse (continued)

Variable	n	% Removed	t	χ^2	P value	Odds Ratio
protection						
PC able to provide protection	101	16				
PC not able to provide adequate care	38	84		62.330	.000	35.53
PC able to provide adequate care	97	13				
Perpetrator Characteristics						
Unknown perpetrator	6	83			.01°	11.62
Known perpetrator	132	30				
Biological/step parent perpetrator	58	40		3.569	.05	2.03
All other types of perpetrators	74	24				
Case Characteristics						
Substantiated physical abuse	62	42		4.332	.03	2.18
No substantiated physical abuse	72	25				
Allegation of serious injury	15	67		8.586	.003	5.00

Table 11: Factors Significantly Associated With Removal in Cases of Child Abuse (continued)

Variable	n	% Removed	t	χ^2	P value	Odds Ratio
No allegation of serious injury	121	29				
Case pending prosecution decision	13	62			.02°	3.80
Case closed or chosen for prosecution	124	30				
Media Characteristics						
No negative coverage of DSS 30 days prior to DSS intake	107	37		4.941	.02	3.22
Negative coverage of DSS 30 days prior to DSS intake	31	16				

Neither the arrest of the perpetrator nor the decision to prosecute a case were found to be associated with placement. However, when the prosecution variable was recoded to represent cases pending a prosecution decision versus cases in which a decision had been made (a case being chosen for prosecution or closed), the high percentage of pending-decision cases involving child placement resulted in a significant finding of association.

The Sexual Abuse Sub-sample

The variables that were found to be significantly related to removal on a bivariate level in the sexual abuse sub-sample mirrored the findings of the overall sample. Table 12 provides bivariate analyses relating to removal for the sub-sample of substantiated sexual abuse cases (N=85).

Older child victims, an older age at the onset of the abuse, the child's relationship to the perpetrator, prior or current reports of neglect and child victims who had experienced prior removal were found to be significantly related to placement. Children with primary caretakers who were Haitian versus any other ethnicity, were also found to be more likely to be removed from the home. Cases that were preceded by no negative coverage of protective services were more likely to result in removal.

Having a primary caretaker who was cooperating with DSS was found to be significantly related to placement in only the sexual abuse sample. Primary caretakers who were reported to be cooperating with the DSS were more likely to have the child victim removed.

No interventions by the criminal justice system, including the arrest of the perpetrator and the prosecution decision, were found to be significantly related to child placement in the sexual abuse sample. This finding is in direct contrast to Cross' (et al., 1999) finding of an association between child placement and cases being declined for prosecution in a sample of sexual abuse cases. Since the Cross (et al., 1999) study collected data on placements that occurred only after referral to the criminal justice system, it is possible that the lack of association between prosecution and placement in the present study could be the result of differences in the timing of placement. The sub-sample of cases in which the removal decision occurred following referral to the District Attorney was, therefore, examined. No relationship was found between the placement and prosecution decisions in the overall post-referral sub-sample or the sexual abuse post-referral sub-sample.

Another significant difference between the prior research (Cross et al., 1999) and the present one is the composition of the samples. In Massachusetts, all cases of sexual abuse and serious physical abuse must be forwarded by DSS to the District Attorney. This contrasts with referral policies in the CVAW states which allow protective service to refer cases that they consider most serious to criminal justice on a discretionary basis. It is possible, therefore, that the lack of a significant finding in the present study signifies a difference in the types of cases involved in the two samples. The present study may be comprised of many more cases of a less serious nature than the CVAW sample.

To test for this possibility, it was necessary to create a sub-sample of cases that could reasonably be considered serious. Sexual abuse cases involving child rape were tested for an association between child placement and non-prosecution, however, no relationship was found.

The Physical Abuse Sub-sample

Next, the data were analyzed to determine the factors associated with removal in the sub-sample of physical abuse cases. Only physical abuse cases substantiated by DSS (N=53) were included in these analyses. Table 12 summarizes those factors that were found to be statistically associated with child removal on a bivariate level.

The correlates of removal in the physical abuse sample varied somewhat from the overall sample and the sexual abuse sub-sample. Physical abuse cases that had no District Court involvement, were investigated by SAIN, or did not involve an immediate arrest were found to be significantly associated with child removal. In addition, cases that involved female perpetrators were significantly associated with removal in the physical abuse sample.

The correlates of removal in the physical abuse sub-sample that duplicated those in the overall sample included having a primary caretaker who was emotionally abusive, not supporting the complaint of abuse or lacked parenting skills. Cases involving primary caretakers who were the alleged perpetrators of the abuse were found to be associated with removal in both this sub-sample and the overall sample. The prosecution decision was not found to be significantly related to removal in the physical abuse sub-sample.

Table 12: Factors Significantly Associated With Removal in Cases of Child Sexual Abuse
Bivariate Analysis

Sample includes only child sexual abuse cases in the Suffolk County District Attorney's Office that were substantiated by the Mass. Department of Social Services. N=85. PC refers to primary caretaker of child victim. The symbol ° signifies the use of a Fisher's Exact Test to calculate probability.

Variable	n	% Removed	t	χ^2	P value	Odds Ratio
Older child	82	-	-3.171		.002	-
Older age at onset of abuse	70	-	-2.572		.01	-
Biological/step parent perpetrator	22	46		5.998	.01	3.77
All other types of perpetrators	59	19				
Prior removal of child	16	66			.009°	4.74
No prior removal of child	65	22				
Prior neglect report	27	48		8.630	.003	4.38
No prior neglect report	57	18				
Haitian primary caretaker	6	67			.04°	1.42
All other primary caretakers	77	23				

Variable	n	% Removed	t	χ^2	P value	Odds Ratio
Primary caretaker neglects child	22	55		10.460	.001	5.45
No report of PC neglect	60	18				
Primary caretaker not able to provide protection	16	63		15.983	.000	6.95
Primary caretaker able to provide protection	69	19				
Primary caretaker not able to provide adequate care	19	68		21.743	.000	12.00
Primary caretaker able to provide adequate care	63	16				
No negative coverage of DSS	69	32			.03°	7.66
30 days prior to DSS intake						
Negative coverage of DSS	16	6				
30 days prior to DSS intake						

Table 13: Factors Significantly Associated With Removal in Cases of Physical Child Abuse (continued)

Table 13: Factors Significantly Associated With Removal in Cases of Physical Child Abuse
Bivariate Analysis

Sample includes physical abuse cases in the Suffolk County District Attorney's Office that were substantiated by the DSS. N=53. PC refers to primary caretaker of child victim. The symbol [a] signifies the use of a Fisher's Exact Test to calculate probability. PC refers to the primary caretaker of the child victim.

Variable	n	% Removed (N=53)	χ^2	P value	Odds Ratio
District Court involvement	33	69	8.991	.003	6.87
No District Court involvement	16	24			
SAIN investigation	4	100		.03	[a]
No SAIN investigation	39	41			
Female perpetrator	23	48	3.811	.05	3.50
Male perpetrator	24	21			
Unknown perpetrator	5	100		.009°	[a]
Known perpetrator	48	35			
PC emotionally abuses child	14	64	4.065	.04	3.60
No report of emotional abuse	39	33			
PC is alleged perpetrator	25	68	13.678	.000	10.00
PC is not alleged perpetrator	28	18			
PC not cooperating w/ DSS	4	100		.02°	[a]
PC cooperating with DSS	49	37			

Variable	n	% Removed (N=53)	χ^2	P value	Odds Ratio
PC does not support complaint of abuse	18	72	10.590	.001	7.64
PC supports complaint of abuse	35	26			
PC lacks parenting skills	17	65	5.547	.01	4.09
PC has adequate parenting skills	36	31			
PC not able to provide adequate protection	18	100	38.422	.000	___a
PC able to provide adequate protection	35	11			
PC not able to provide adequate care	19	100	41.745	.000	___a
PC able to provide adequate care	34	9			
Perpetrator not arrested prior to DA intake	25	60	6.766	.009	4.54
Perpetrator arrested prior to DA intake	28	25			

a. Odds ratio was not calculated due to a zero cell count.

To summarize, the case prosecution decision was not found to be significantly associated with child removal in bivariate analyses of the sexual abuse sub-sample, the physical abuse sub-sample or the overall substantiated sample. The analyses did, however, reveal a number of case, child and protective service assessment characteristics that are significantly associated with child removal in the substantiated sample. Two criminal justice variables, an allegation of serious injury and a case pending the prosecution decision, were found to be significant factors in regards to child removal in this sample. A number of the significant factors, such as age of child, child ethnicity and perpetrator relationship to child, replicated findings of previous studies. However, significant correlates not examined in previous research, such as prior removal, prior or current neglect, primary caretaker ethnicity and primary caretaker as perpetrator were also uncovered.

Multivariate Analysis: Child Removal

The final step undertaken to more accurately identify the factors influencing child removal was a multivariate analysis of the data. The potential problem of simultaneity that was previously discussed was negated by the finding of no association between child removal and case prosecution in the bivariate analysis. Therefore, given the dichotomous form of the dependent variable, logistic regression, was chosen as the best estimator for the equation. Logistic regression analysis, which is estimated by methods of maximum likelihood, provides an assessment of how multiple variables, examined together, predict the dependent variable. The findings provide an estimate of the independent contribution of each independent variable to the dependent variable.

Understanding a logistic regression model can be difficult because of the complex form of the dependent variable. The dependent variable represents the logarithm of the probability of the dependent variable occurring divided by the probability of it not occurring.

Backwards stepwise logistic regression was utilized to ensure that no significant variables were being eliminated due to suppressor effects. Variables found to be significantly related to the dependent variable in the bivariate analysis were entered into the logistic equation in sets, grouped as case characteristics, child characteristics, primary caretaker characteristics, perpetrator characteristics, and media characteristics. To guard against family-wise error, individual variables were then introduced into the model only if the entire set of variables significantly contributed to the prediction of the dependent variable (Cohen and Cohen, 1983).

Bivariate predictors of child removal were entered into a logistic equation to provide an estimate of the independent contribution of child, family and case variables, perpetrator variables, protective service history and assessment variables, criminal justice intervention and outcome variables, and other variables to child placement.

Following the estimation of the model, diagnostics were run to ensure that the assumptions of logistic regression analysis were not violated.   The model was tested for interaction effects and multicollinearity.   Residuals were created and case outliers were identified and examined regarding their influence on model specification.   Standardized, studentized and deviance residuals were plotted to test for adherence to a logistic distribution.   Leverage and d-beta values were examined to identify cases that had a strong influence on model parameters.

Only cases that were substantiated by DSS were included in the multivariate analysis.   The following independent variables were entered into the logistic equation: age of child victim, ethnicity of victim, prior neglect, prior removal, current neglect, current emotional abuse, child abandoned, lack of parenting skills, primary caretaker as perpetrator, primary caretaker support of complaint, primary caretaker support of prosecution, ethnicity of primary caretaker, substantiated physical abuse, allegation of serious injury, prosecution status and negative media coverage of protective services.

Two independent variables that captured the DSS caseworker's appraisal of the primary caretakers' ability to care for and protect the child from further abuse were excluded from the analysis because they represented the overall protective service assessment of more specific case and family characteristics.   Perpetrator characteristics, as a set, were not found to contribute significantly to the model; therefore, they also were excluded.

The final model (Model A), displayed in Table 14 included age of child, the presence of current neglect, primary caretaker as perpetrator, primary caretaker support of complaint, prior removal and ethnicity of primary caretaker.   The variables in the final model represent the factors that serve as the most efficient independent estimators for child removal.

Two interaction terms, representing the interaction between current neglect and prior neglect, and the interaction between a complaint not being supported by a primary caretaker and a case involving a primary caretaker as a perpetrator were added to the final model to test for their significance; however, neither resulted in a significant change in the model chi-square statistic.

In addition, to test for the possibility that the case prosecution variable might significantly impact removal in combination with other factors, prosecution was added to the model. This comparison model (Model B), which is also displayed in Table 14, portrays the predictors of removal when all of the significant independent variables, plus the prosecution variable, are included. No significant relationship between removal and prosecution was revealed. This negated the need to address any potential simultaneity bias.

Case residuals for the final model were examined for normality and six outliers were identified. The impact of these outliers on the coefficients was not substantial and none of the cases were removed from the sample. The independent variables in the model were also tested for multicollinearity. Six variables found to have a tolerance level of less than .60 were examined. Having a primary caretaker as a perpetrator had the lowest tolerance score of .44. This variable was found to be correlated with the primary caretaker not supporting the complaint, a substantiated report of physical abuse, current neglect and concurrent emotional abuse. In addition, current neglect was found to be correlated with prior neglect. Although the presence of multicollinearity weakens the efficiency of the coefficients, these independent variables were still included in the final model. Given the complex relationship that characterizes these variables, it is not possible to address the research question without accepting the presence of some multicollinearity. In this multivariate analysis, the variables of primary caretaker as perpetrator and primary caretaker not supporting the complaint show themselves to be rather robust despite the presence of multicollinearity by still emerging as independent predictors of placement. Likewise, current neglect also proves to be a final predictor of placement despite its correlation with prior neglect.

Table 14: Comparison of Estimated Models Describing Factors Influencing Child Removal in Cases of Child Abuse
Logistic Regression Analysis

Independent Variable	Model A B (p-value)	Model A Exp (B)	Model B B (p-value)	Model B Exp (B)
Age of child	.1165 (.06)	-----	.1513 (.01)	-----
Current neglect	1.7747 (.005)	5.8985	1.7627 (.004)	5.8280
PC is perpetrator	1.5776 (.02)	4.8435	1.521 (.01)	4.5769
PC does not support complaint	1.3627 (.04)	3.9068	1.7567 (.18) NS	-----
Prior removal	2.1881 (.003)	8.9180	.8911 (.34) NS	-----
PC ethnicity	----- (.04)	-----	----- (.02)	-----
Caucasian	-.9547 (.08)	.3849	-.3659 (.42) NS	-----
African-American	-.2523 (.59) NS	-----	-.6093 (.20) NS	-----
Latino	-1.4903 (.04)	.2253	-1.4716 (.02)	.2296
Haitian	1.5761 (.02)	4.8361	1.5128 (.01)	4.5395
Emotional abuse	.3386 (.56) NS	-----	.0179 (.89) NS	-----
PC lacks parenting skills	.0266 (.87) NS	-----	.7435 (.38) NS	-----

Independent Variable	B (p-value)	Exp (B)	B (p-value)	Exp (B)
PC does not support prosecution	.0832 (.77) NS	-----	.9813 (.32) NS	-----
Case chosen for prosecution			.0530 (.81) NS	-----
Intercept	-3.4223 (.000)	-----	-3.1370 (.000)	-----

N=105

Model Chi-square	47.928	(p<.0000)	56.848	(p<.000)
-2 Log Likelihood	84.311		93.388	
Pseudo R-squared	.37		.29	

The significance of the model chi-square statistic indicates that including information about the independent variables in the final model allows us to make better predictions regarding which cases will and will not result in removal. The inclusion of any additional variables would not improve prediction. The pseudo R-squared statistic is a goodness of fit statistic that provides an estimation of how much variation is explained by the final logistic regression model.[8]

A comparison of Models A and B in Table 14 reveals important differences between the two estimations. The inclusion of the prosecution variable in Model B resulted in the loss of three significant variables; prior removal, complaint unsupported and Caucasian ethnicity. In addition, the higher goodness of fit statistic for Model A informs us that more variation in the model can be explained when prosecution is excluded from the estimation.

---

[8] This statistic was estimated by the following equation: 1 - (-2 log likelihood / Initial -2 log likelihood)

The unstandardized logistic coefficient is identified by the heading Exp (B). S.E. refers to the standard error for each variable. Exp (B) indicates the odds ratio or the probability of the event occurring over the probability that it will not, given other variables being equal. This provides information regarding the relationship between the odds that a child will be removed when the independent variable is present versus the odds that removal will occur when it is not. For example, in Model A, the odds ratio of 5.89 for current neglect indicates that the odds of placement when neglect is present is almost 6 times the odds of removal when neglect is not present, while holding constant the other variables. Similarly, the odds of placement in cases involving primary caretakers as perpetrators is 9 times the odds of placement when the primary caretaker is not the perpetrator. Likewise, the odds of placement when there has been a prior removal are almost 9 times the odds of placement when removal has not previously occurred. Also the odds of removal when the complaint is not supported by the primary caretaker is almost 4 times the odds of removal when the opposite is true.

The odds of placement for a case involving a Haitian primary caretaker is almost 5 times the odds of removal for all other ethnicities, grouped together. In contrast, the odds of removal when there is a Latino primary caretaker is 22% of the odds of removal for all other ethnicities. Likewise, the odds of placement for cases in which there is a Caucasian primary caretaker is 38% of the odds of removal across all ethnicities.

Another manner in which to discuss these results is to identify the probability of child placement occurring in varying case examples. Examining the probability of placement under specified conditions allows us to understand the influence of combinations of independent variables on child placement. The case examples provided on the following pages allow for a comparison of removal rates based on cases with varying characteristics. The probability estimates for each example are calculated by including or excluding each factor in a probability equation.[9]

---

[9] Probability of child placement formula:

$P = 1 / 1 + e^{-z}$

Z = constant + b(neglect) + b (PC perpetrator) + b(complaint unsupported by P.C.) + (prior removal) + b(PC ethnicity) + b(age of child)

The first set of case examples provides an estimation of the probability of removal for a five year old child victim when the ethnicity of the primary caretaker varies. Case example 1A provides an estimated probability for the child victim when none of the dichotomous independent variables are present. Case examples 1B through 1E provide estimations of the cumulative probabilities of removal as each independent variable is added to the equation. The increasing rates of removal associated with the addition of each independent variable provides an indication of the impact of each independent variable on the probability of removal. Using the same format, the second and third sets of case examples provide estimations of the probability of removal for a ten year old and fifteen year old, respectively.

Case Examples-Probability of Removal

I: Probability of Removal for Five-Year-Old Victim by Primary Caretaker Ethnicity

A. All other independent variables weighted zero.

Primary Caretaker Ethnicity	Probability of removal
Caucasian	.02
African-American	.04
Latino	.01
Haitian	.22

B.   Prior removal present. All other independent variables
     weighted zero.

Primary Caretaker Ethnicity	Probability of Removal
Caucasian	.16
African-American	.29
Latino	.11
Haitian	.72

C.   Prior removal and current neglect present. All other
     independent variables weighted zero.

Primary Caretaker Ethnicity	Probability of Removal
Caucasian	.54
African-American	.70
Latino	.41
Haitian	.94

D. Prior removal, current neglect and a primary caretaker as the perpetrator present. All other independent variables weighted zero.

Primary Caretaker Ethnicity	Probability of Removal
Caucasian	.85
African-American	.94
Latino	.77
Haitian	.99

E. Prior removal, current neglect, primary caretaker as perpetrator and complaint unsupported by primary caretaker present.

Primary Caretaker Ethnicity	Probability of Removal
Caucasian	.96
African-American	.98
Latino	.93
Haitian	.99

II: Probability of Removal for Ten Year Old Victim by Primary Caretaker Ethnicity

    A. All other independent variables weighted zero.

Primary Caretaker Ethnicity	Probability of removal
Caucasian	.04
African-American	.08
Latino	.02
Haitian	.33

    B. Prior removal present. All other independent variables weighted zero.

Primary Caretaker Ethnicity	Probability of Removal
Caucasian	.26
African-American	.42
Latino	.17
Haitian	.81

C. Prior removal and current neglect present. All other independent variables weighted zero.

Primary Caretaker Ethnicity	Probability of Removal
Caucasian	.68
African-American	.82
Latino	.55
Haitian	.96

D. Prior removal, current neglect and a primary caretaker as the perpetrator present. All other independent variables weighted zero.

Primary Caretaker Ethnicity	Probability of Removal
Caucasian	.91
African-American	.95
Latino	.85
Haitian	.99

E. Prior removal, current neglect, primary caretaker as perpetrator and complaint unsupported by primary caretaker present.

Primary Caretaker Ethnicity	Probability of Removal
Caucasian	.97
African-American	.99
Latino	.96
Haitian	.99

III: Probability of Removal for Fifteen Year Old by Primary Caretaker Ethnicity

A. All other independent variables weighted zero.

Primary Caretaker Ethnicity	Probability of Removal
Caucasian	.07
African-American	.12
Latino	.04
Haitian	.47

B. Prior removal present. All other independent variables
weighted zero.

Primary Caretaker Ethnicity	Probability of Removal
Caucasian	.39
African-American	.56
Latino	.27
Haitian	.89

C. Prior removal and current neglect present. All other
independent variables weighted zero.

Primary Caretaker Ethnicity	Probability of Removal
Caucasian	.85
African-American	.92
Latino	.77
Haitian	.99

D. Prior removal, current neglect and a primary caretaker as the perpetrator present. All other independent variables weighted zero.

Primary Caretaker Ethnicity	Probability of Removal
Caucasian	.97
African-American	.98
Latino	.94
Haitian	.99

E. Prior removal, current neglect, primary caretaker as perpetrator and complaint unsupported by primary caretaker present.

Primary Caretaker Ethnicity	Probability of Removal
Caucasian	.99
African-American	.99
Latino	.99
Haitian	.99

In conclusion, the multivariate analysis indicates that the primary predictors of removal in this sample are the age of the child victim, the presence of neglect, prior removal, primary caretaker ethnicity, nonsupport of the complaint by the primary caretaker and a perpetrator who is the primary caretaker. The results support the supposition that the child removal decision is most impacted by protective service perceptions of the ability of the primary caretaker to safeguard and adequately provide for the emotional and physical needs of the child.

The hypothesis that the decision by the District Attorney to prosecute a case would be positively associated with child victims not being placed outside of their home was not supported by the bivariate or multivariate analyses. No significant relationship was found between case prosecution and child removal for the substantiated sample, the sexual abuse sub-sample or the physical abuse sub-sample.

Predictors of Prosecution

Next, to test the second research question regarding predictors of prosecution, bivariate analyses of the relationship between each of the independent variables and case prosecution were conducted with all substantiated cases. Only the 185 cases that had been either chosen for prosecution or closed without further action were included in the analysis. Cases in which the prosecution decision was still pending at the end of the data collection period (N=13) were excluded from the analysis. See Appendix D for a list of the independent variables tested for an association with case prosecution.

A number of factors were found to be significantly associated with case prosecution. All statistical tests were based on an alpha value of .05. The results are provided in Table 15. Reports received first by the District Attorney or police were much more likely to be prosecuted than cases first reported to DSS. The referral source to the District Attorney was also found to be significantly related to prosecution. Cases referred by DSS were much less likely to be prosecuted than cases referred by a District Court or the police. Cases assigned to the Dorchester area DSS office were much more likely to be prosecuted than cases assigned to any other DSS offices. This is very likely a reflection of the jurisdiction in which the incident occurred as abuse incidents that took place in Dorchester were significantly more likely to be prosecuted than incidents that occurred in all of the other towns combined. Case involvement with a District Court was found to be significantly associated with case prosecution.

The age of the child at case intake and at the onset of the abuse was also found to be significantly related to prosecution. For prosecuted cases, the average age of the child victim was 10.9 at intake and 9.6 at the onset of the abuse. For cases closed without prosecution, the average age of the child at intake was 9.3 and 7.7 at the time of onset.

Since prior studies had found an association between certain age groupings of child victims and the probability of case prosecution; categorical age variables were examined to test their relationship to the dependent variable. Previous research has reported that child victims age 0-6 and age 13-17 are less likely to experience case prosecution than child victims age 7-12. However, as Table 15 indicates, the present study found a significant difference in prosecution only between victims age 0-6 and all other child victims. The prosecution rate for children age 13-17 was very similar to the prosecution rate for children age 7-12, 30% and 37%, respectively. In comparison, only 15% of the children age 0-6 were prosecuted. This finding is a result of the inclusion of both physical and sexual abuse cases in the dual system sample. Later discussion of the bivariate predictors of prosecution for the sexual abuse sub-sample reveals significantly higher prosecution rates for children age 7-12 versus children age 0-6 or 13-17.

Cases involving physical abuse, parents as perpetrators, child victims who had experienced prior removal and child victims who were residing with their primary caretaker at the time of the abuse were found to be significantly associated with prosecution. The perpetrator's sex and a female perpetrator were also found to be associated with prosecution. Perpetrator ethnicity was also found to be significantly associated with prosecution. Ethnicity was first examined as a group with five categories (Caucasian, African-American, Latino, Other and Unknown) and then examined separately, with prosecution rates for each ethnic group being compared to the average removal rate for the remaining groups combined. Only one group of offenders were found to be more likely to prosecuted. Perpetrators who were African-American had a higher rate of prosecution (45%) than any of the offender ethnic groupings. As Table 15 indicates, African-Americans were significantly more likely to experience case prosecution in comparison to all other offenders, grouped as a whole.

Case substantiation by DSS was significantly associated with prosecution. Also related to prosecution was a DSS substantiated report of physical abuse. Cases that did not involve a report of neglect and cases in which the primary caretaker was cooperating with DSS were more likely to result in prosecution.

Table 15: Factors Associated With Prosecution in Cases of Child Abuse Under Investigation by Protective Services and Criminal Justice

Overall sample includes all child abuse cases in the Suffolk County District Attorney's Office that were also under investigation by the Massachusetts Department of Social Services. N=185. DSS case findings include only those cases substantiated by DSS. N=138. PC refers to primary caretaker of child victim. The symbol ° signifies the use of a Fisher's Exact Test to calculate probability.

Variable	n	% Prosecuted	t	χ^2	P value	Odds Ratio
Child Characteristics						
Age of child at onset	166	-	2.172		.03	-
Age of child at intake						
7 - 17 years old	118	34		6.272	.01	9.60
0 - 6 years old	48	15				
No prior removal of child	129	33		5.063	.02	3.88
Prior removal of child	28	11				
Child residence with PC	144	31			.03°	7.33
Other type of child residence	6					
Perpetrator Characteristics						
African-American perpetrator	47	45		7.892	.005	2.66
All other ethnicities	125	23				
Female perpetrator	26	46		3.907	.04	2.36

Table 15: Factors Associated With Prosecution in Cases of Child Abuse Under Investigation by Protective Services and Criminal Justice (continued)

Variable	n	% Prosecuted	t	χ^2	P value	Odds Ratio
Male perpetrator	138	27				
Relationship to child						
Biological or step parent	67	40		7.082	.008	2.57
All other types	99	21				
Primary Caretaker						
PC is biological or step parent	136	31		4.071	.04	3.38
PC is not bio or step parent	26	12				
Case Characteristics						
First agency to receive report						
DA and police	53	43		10.751	.001	3.30
DSS	119	19				
DA referral source						
District Court and police	95	38		8.293	.001	2.90
DSS	78	18				
Jurisdiction of incident						
Dorchester	27	52		8.062	.005	3.24

Table 15: Factors Associated With Prosecution in Cases of Child Abuse Under Investigation by Protective Services and Criminal Justice (continued)

Variable	n	% Prosecuted	t	χ^2	P value	Odds Ratio
All other areas	145	22				
DSS area office						
Dorchester	19	58		8.685	.003	4.15
All other offices	150	25				
District Court involvement	2	56		26.085	.000	7.03
No District Court involvement	92	15				
Report substantiated by DSS	124	35		12.125	.000	10.60
Report not substantiated	37	5				
Physical abuse	55	49		15.995	.000	4.00
Sexual abuse	118	20				
Allegation of assault and battery	27	53		18.193	.000	4.75
No assault and battery allegation	144	20				
Allegation of assault and battery with a deadly weapon	43	63		18.460	.000	6.07
No assault and battery with a deadly weapon allegation	177	22				
Initial arrest occurred	43	51		13.800	.000	3.85

Table 15: Factors Associated With Prosecution in Cases of Child Abuse Under Investigation by Protective Services and Criminal Justice (continued)

Variable	n	% Prosecuted	t	χ^2	P value	Odds Ratio
No initial arrest	130	22				
Media Characteristics						
High media coverage	29	45		4.300	.03	2.38
30 days prior to DA intake						
Low media coverage	144	26				
30 days prior to DA intake						
DSS Case Findings (N=138)						
No report of PC neglecting child	95	41		6.342	.01	4.05
PC neglects child	27	15				
Substantiated report of physical abuse	55	46		4.329	.03	2.24
No substantiated report of physical abuse	66	27				
PC cooperating with DSS	107	36		6.121	.01	9.14
PC not cooperating with DSS	15	7				

Time periods in which there was high media coverage of child abuse were found to be significantly associated with more case prosecution. The criminal allegations of assault and battery and assault and battery with a deadly weapon were found to be significantly correlated with prosecution. An initial arrest of the perpetrator prior to case intake at the District Attorney's office was also found to be significantly related to case prosecution.

Sexual Abuse Sub-sample

A number of factors were found to be significantly associated with case prosecution in bivariate analyses of the sexual abuse cases.   Table 16 provides information on those variables found to be significantly related to prosecution in the sexual abuse sub-sample. Variables found to be related to case prosecution in the sexual abuse sub-sample were generally similar to those in the overall sample.

For example, the first report of the incident being filed with the District Attorney versus DSS was significantly associated with case prosecution. A case being referred to the DA's office by DSS was significantly less likely to be prosecuted than any other referral source. Cases that were assigned to the Dorchester area office of DSS were more likely to be prosecuted. Cases in which a District Court was involved were also more likely to be prosecuted.   In addition, a significant relationship was found between cases being substantiated by DSS and case prosecution. As with the overall sample, cases in the sexual abuse sub-sample that involved older children were more likely to be prosecuted. Cases that involved a primary caretaker neglecting a child were less likely to be prosecuted.

Three variables were found to be significantly related to the prosecution decision in the sexual abuse sub-sample but not in the overall sample. Having a primary caretaker who did not support the complaint of abuse was found to be significantly associated with case prosecution. Cases in which the alleged perpetrator had access to the residence of the child were less likely to be prosecuted. Cases involving primary caretakers who were able to provide adequate protection for the child were more likely to result in prosecution.

Table 16: Factors Associated With Prosecution in Cases of Child Sexual Abuse Under Investigation by Protective Services and Criminal Justice

The primary sample includes cases of child sexual abuse in the Suffolk County District Attorney's Office that were also under investigation by the Massachusetts Department of Social Services. N=132. DSS case findings include only substantiated cases N=77. PC refers to primary caretaker of child. The symbol ° signifies the use of a Fisher's Exact Test to calculate probability.

Variable	n	% Prosecuted	t	χ^2	P value	Odds Ratio
Child Characteristics						
Age of child at intake						
7 - 17 years	82	26		6.411	.01	5.86
0 - 6 years	36	6				
Case Characteristics						
First agency to receive report						
DA/police	73	33		6.687	.01	3.57
DSS	44	12				
DSS referral to DA	66	29		8.248	.0048	5.00
Other referrals to DA	52	8				
DSS area office						
Dorchester	11	46		5.348	.02	4.36
All other offices	103	17				
District Crt involvement	14	43			.02°	4.41

Table 16: Factors Associated With Prosecution in Cases of Child Sexual Abuse Under Investigation by Protective Services and Criminal Justice

Variable	n	% Prosecuted	t	χ^2	P value	Odds Ratio
No District Court involvement	79	15				
Report substantiated by DSS	77	25		6.739	.009	10.66
Report not substantiated	31	3				
DSS Case Findings (N=77)						
No report of neglect	57	33		8.036	.005	a
PC neglects child	18	0				
PC supports complaint	60	30			.05°	6.00
PC no support complaint	15	7				
PC can provide adequate protection	63	27		6.437	.04	2.40
PC cannot provide adequate protection	15	13				
Perpetrator does not have access to residence of child	60	30			.05°	6.12
Perpetrator has access to residence of child	15	7				

a. Odds ratio was not calculated due to a zero cell count.

Physical Abuse Sub-sample

In bivariate analyses of only physical abuse cases, the factors found to be significantly associated with case prosecution also reflected the findings from the overall sample. Table 17 provides information regarding the variables found to be statistically related to prosecution.

Cases involving perpetrators who were African-American were also found to be significantly associated with prosecution. As with the sexual abuse sub-sample, physical abuse incidents that occurred in the jurisdiction of Dorchester were more likely to be prosecuted as were cases in which there was District Court involvement. Cases involving allegations of assault and battery with a deadly weapon were found to be significantly associated with prosecution. Cases that were preceded by high media coverage of child abuse were also more likely to be prosecuted.

The only variable found to be significantly related to the prosecution decision in the physical abuse sub-sample but not in the overall sample was the ethnicity of the primary caretaker. Primary caretaker was tested for an association with prosecution as one categorical variable, including a value for each ethnic grouping, and as dichotomous variables, comparing the prosecution rate for each ethnic group against the average of all of the rest. The physical abuse cases that involved Caucasian primary caretakers had a much higher rate of prosecution (82%) than any of the other primary caretaker ethnic groups. As Table 17 indicates, cases with Caucasian primary caretakers were significantly more likely to be prosecuted in comparison to the primary caretakers of all other ethnic groups

In contrast to the sexual abuse sub-sample, no association was found between current neglect and case prosecution in the physical abuse sample. In both of the overall sample and the sexual abuse sample, current neglect was found to be negatively associated with case prosecution. In addition, unlike the sexual abuse sample, the agency to receive the first report of abuse was not found to be associated with prosecution in the sexual abuse sub-sample. Likewise, the age of the child, though significantly associated to prosecution in the sexual abuse sub-sample, was not found to be a correlate to physical abuse.

Table 17: Factors Associated With Prosecution in Cases of Physical Child Abuse Under Investigation by Protective Services and Criminal Justice

The sample includes physical child abuse cases in the Suffolk County District Attorney's Office that were also under investigation by the Mass. Department of Social Services. N=61. A ° symbol signifies the use of a Fisher's Exact Test to calculate probability.

Variable	n	% Prosecuted	t	χ^2	P value	Odds Ratio
African-American perpetrator	22	68		5.347	.02	3.75
All other ethnicities	33	36				
Caucasian primary caretaker	11	82		6.363	.01	7.03
All other ethnicities	41	39				
Jurisdiction of incident						
Dorchester	12	75		4.123	.04	4.16
All other areas	43	42				
District court involvement	38	61		7.898	.005	8.05
No District court involvement	13	15				
High media coverage	10	80			.02°	5.47

Table 17: Factors Associated With Prosecution in Cases of Physical Child Abuse Under Investigation by Protective Services and Criminal Justice

Variable	n	% Prosecuted	t	χ^2	P value	Odds Ratio
30 days prior to DA report						
Low media coverage 30 days prior to DA report	45	42				
Allegation of assault and battery with a deadly weapon	27	63		4.084	.04	3.09
No allegation of assault and battery with a deadly weapon	28	36				

Multivariate Analysis: Case Prosecution

Logistic regression was again chosen as the best method to identify predictors of prosecution on a multivariate level. This method of analysis allowed for an assessment of how each of the variables found to be related to prosecution on the bivariate level would fare in predicting prosecution when examined in conjunction with all of the other variables.

The method of backwards stepwise logistic regression was again used to estimate the model. Significant bivariate predictors of case prosecution were introduced into the logistic model only if the entire set of variables significantly contributed to the prediction of the dependent variable. The final model calculated the independent contribution of child, family, perpetrator and case variables, protective service history and assessment variables, criminal justice assessment and intervention variables, and other variables to case prosecution.

Following model estimation, tests were run to determine whether the assumptions of a logistic regression analysis were met. The model was tested for interaction effects and multicollinearity and case outliers were examined to determine whether or not they substantially influenced model specification. Standardized, studentized and deviance residuals were plotted to determine conformity to a logistic distribution. Leverage and d-beta values were also examined to see if any cases were overly influential in determining model parameters.

Because three bivariate predictors of prosecution involved DSS case findings, only cases that were substantiated by DSS were included in the multivariate analysis. The following independent variables were entered into the logistic equation: first agency to receive the report, DSS area office, perpetrator ethnicity, case referral source, jurisdiction of incident, type of abuse, age of child at case intake, perpetrator relationship to child, prior removal of child, primary caretaker, child's residence, arrest of perpetrator prior to intake, neglect of child, and primary caretaker not cooperating with DSS.

Six independent variables found to be significantly correlated to prosecution on a bivariate level were omitted from the multivariate analysis. Age at onset of abuse was dropped due to high multicollinearity with the current age of child variable. The substantiation of physical abuse by DSS was excluded from the analysis because it closely replicated the independent variable, type of abuse, recorded by the District Attorney's office. The allegations of assault and battery and assault and battery with a deadly weapon were excluded due to their high multicollinearity with the type of abuse. None of the sexual abuse cases were associated with the allegation of assault and battery with a deadly weapon and only one was assigned the charge of assault and battery.

The gender of the perpetrator was also found to be highly correlated with the type of abuse. Only four percent of the sexual abuse perpetrators were female, however, 44% of the physical abuse perpetrators were female. Separate analyses of physical abuse cases and sexual abuse cases did not provide any evidence that gender was in and of itself a predictor of prosecution, therefore, this independent variable was dropped from the model.[10]

An initial arrest prior to intake at the District Attorney's office was also not included in the model despite it's significance on the bivariate level. Initial arrest is highly correlated with referral source to the DA (a police versus DSS referral) and type of abuse (physical abuse). An initial arrest can only occur when the police are the first investigators on the scene as only the police have the power to initiate an arrest. For this reason, initial arrest was dropped from the model.

One interaction term, representing the interaction between current neglect and type of abuse, was added to the model to test for level of association. On a bivariate level, neglect was found to be highly associated with cases not being prosecuted in the sexual abuse sample, however, no relationship was revealed in the physical abuse sample. This suggests that the presence of sexual abuse cases and current neglect may create a special type of case that has a very low likelihood of prosecution. The interaction term was created to test for this possibility, however, it did not result in a significant change in the model chi-square statistic. As with the prior multivariate analysis, child placement was added to the model to test for an association with prosecution in the presence of other predictors, however, no significant association was found.

---

[10] Physical abuse cases with male versus female perpetrators had almost the same likelihood of prosecution. The small number of female perpetrators in the sexual abuse sample did not allow for a test of correlation between gender and the prosecution decision.

The final logistic model, Model A, which included the age of the child at intake, the presence of neglect, the type of abuse and the referral source to the District Attorney's office, is portrayed in Table 18. Case residuals were examined for normality and three outliers were identified. The impact of these outliers on the coefficients was not substantial and, since their deviation from the norm could be logically understood, none of them were removed from the sample.

Although it was not significantly related to case prosecution in the bivariate analyses, child removal was included in the comparison model, Model B, estimation to determine if it might significantly impact prosecution in combination with other factors. This second model, also displayed in Table 18, provides an estimation of the predictors of case prosecution when all of the significant independent variables, plus the removal variable, are included. Again, no significant relationship between removal and prosecution was revealed.

The model chi-square statistic is significant indicating that the inclusion of the independent variables does improve our ability to predict which cases will or will not be prosecuted. The pseudo R-squared statistic informs us that 26% of the variation in the dependent variable is explained by the independent variables in the final model.[11]
A comparison of Model A and Model B in Table 18 reveals only minor differences between the two estimations. Both estimations result in the same significant predictors of prosecution with only slight changes in significance. The goodness of fit statistics are almost identical.

As explained earlier, Exp (B) in Model A provides the odds that a case will be prosecuted when the independent variable is present versus the odds it will be prosecuted when it is not present. For example, the odds ratio of 5.88 for type of abuse indicates that the odds of prosecution in cases of physical abuse are almost six times the odds of prosecution in cases of sexual abuse cases. Similarly, the odds of prosecution when the case is referred to the DA from DSS are almost 20% the odds of prosecution for all other referral sources.

---

[11]This statistic was estimated by the following equation: 1 - (-2 log likelihood / Initial -2 log likelihood)

Table 18: Comparison of Estimated Models Describing Factors influencing Case Prosecution in Child Abuse Cases Under Investigation by Dual Systems – *LogisticRegression Analysis*

Independent Variable	Model A		Model B	
	B (p-value)	Exp (B)	B (p-value)	Exp (B)
Child age 7 or older	1.3290 (.02)	3.7771	1.1774 (.05)	.6071
Current neglect	-1.5175 (.02)	.2197	-1.6345 (.01)	.1950
Type of abuse	1.7719 (.02)	5.8822	1.1774 (.04)	4.994
Referral source to D.A.	----- (.006)	-----	----- (.004)	-----
DSS	-1.6284 (.000)	.1962	-1.6301 (.004)	.1959
District Court	.1012 (.84) NS	-----	.3705 (.50) NS	-----
Police	.6951 (.16) NS	-----	.5819 (.25) NS	
First report agency	----- (.23) NS	-----	----- (.15) NS	-----
DSS	1.4392 (.23) NS	-----	1.8476 (.17) NS	-----
District Attorney	1.5374 (.21) NS	-----	.0069 (.93) NS	-----
African-American offender	1.1297 (.28) NS	-----	.7707 (.38) NS	-----
PC not cooperating with DSS	1.0142 (.31) NS	-----	.9334 (.33) NS	-----
Parental offender	.3004 (.58)	-----	.2369 (.62) NS	-----

Table 18: Comparison of Estimated Models Describing Factors influencing Case Prosecution in Child Abuse Cases Under Investigation by Dual Systems (continued)

	Model A		Model B	
Independent Variable	B (p-value)	Exp (B)	B (p-value)	Exp (B)
Child removed from home			.0029 (.95) NS	-----
Intercept	-1.7435 (.003)	-----	-3.1370 (.000)	-----
N=109				
Model Chi-square	36.605 (p<.000)		56.848	(p<.000)
-2 Log Likelihood	105.772		93.388	
Pseudo R-squared	.26		.29	

Another manner in which to discuss these results is to identify the probability of prosecution occurring in cases examples.[12] Case examples are provided on the next three pages that specify the probability of case prosecution under varying conditions. The first set of case examples provides basic information regarding the probability of prosecution by type of abuse, sexual or physical, and the age of the child. The second and third sets of examples provide separate estimates of the probability of prosecution for physical and sexual abuse cases by child age, examining variations in referral source to the District Attorney and the presence or absence of neglect.

---

[12] Probability of case prosecution formula:

$P = 1 / 1 + e^{-z}$

Z = constant + b(neglect) + b(age of child) + b(type of abuse) + b(referral source to DA)

<u>Case Examples-Probability of Prosecution</u>

I: Probability of Prosecution by Type of Abuse and Child Age

    A. Physical abuse present. All other independent variables weighted zero.

Age of Child	Probability of Prosecution
Child under seven	.51
Child seven or older	.79

    B. Sexual abuse present. All other independent variables weighted zero.

Age of Child	Probability of Prosecution
Child under seven	.15
Child seven or older	.40

II: Probability of Prosecution of Physical Abuse Cases by Referral Source to DA

    A. Child victim seven or older. Neglect not present.

Referral Source	Probability of Prosecution
DSS	.43
District Court	.81
Police	.88

B.   Child victim seven or older. Neglect is present.

Referral Source	Probability of Prosecution
DSS	.14
District Court	.48
Police	.63

C.   Child victim under seven. Neglect not present.

Referral Source	Probability of Prosecution
DSS	.17
District Court	.53
Police	.67

D.   Child victim under seven. Neglect is present.

Referral Source	Probability of Prosecution
DSS	.04
District Court	.20
Police	.31

III: Probability of Prosecution of Sexual Abuse Cases by Referral Source to DA

    A. Child victim seven or older. Neglect not present.

Referral Source	Probability of Prosecution
DSS	.11
District Court	.42
Police	.57

    B. Child victim seven or older. Neglect is present.

Referral Source	Probability of Prosecution
DSS	.03
District Court	.17
Police	.23

    C. Child victim under seven. Neglect not present.

Referral Source	Probability of Prosecution
DSS	.03
District Court	.16
Police	.26

D. Child victim under seven. Neglect is present.

Referral Source	Probability of Prosecution
DSS	.007
District Court	.04
Police	.07

To summarize, the results indicate that the primary predictors of case prosecution in this sample are the age of the child victim, no finding of neglect, physical versus sexual abuse, and a referral to the District Attorney by the police or a District Court versus DSS. These were the case characteristics found to be independently associated with case prosecution in the final multivariate analysis. These findings support the theory that case prosecution is influenced by both the characteristics of each case of abuse and the initial systemic response to each report of abuse.

The initial hypothesis that child removal would be significantly associated with cases not being chosen for prosecution was not proven by either bivariate or multivariate tests of association. Analyses of the substantiated sample, the sexual abuse sub-sample and the physical abuse sub-sample did not reveal a statistical relationship between the prosecution and removal variables.

The Impact of Criminal Justice Interventions on Protective Service Decision-Making

Although a statistically significant relationship between child removal and case prosecution was not revealed in bivariate or multivariate tests relating to either prosecution or removal, reports by DSS caseworkers did provide support for an association between these two interventions. For each case of child abuse in which the child was not removed from the home, DSS caseworkers were asked to assess how helpful criminal justice interventions were in negating the need for placement. Likewise, for cases in which the child was removed and then returned to the home, DSS caseworkers were asked to assess the helpfulness of judicial activity in enabling children to be returned.

In 67% of the substantiated cases (N=93), the child victim was not removed from the home. Forty-seven percent (N=44) of the non-removal cases involved criminal justice activity. Criminal justice activity was defined as a case involving an arrest, a case being chosen for prosecution, and/or a case pending the prosecution decision[13]. In 70% of the no-removal cases in which judicial interventions occurred (N=28), DSS caseworkers reported that criminal justice actions were helpful in keeping the child victim in the home.

Table 19 provides a descriptive overview of the characteristics of the non-removal cases in which criminal justice interventions were found to have a positive effect. An examination of this table reveals that the Chelsea/Revere DSS investigative office was over-represented in this sub-sample comprising 37% of the cases. The majority of the cases in which judicial actions had a positive effect involved mainly Caucasian child victims whose perpetrators were primarily a parent of the child or their mother's boyfriend. Very few of these cases involved primary caretakers as perpetrators (14%). Sexual abuse cases (64%) were highly represented in the sub-sample. A number of the cases in the sample involved prior reports of abuse or neglect, 50% and 31% respectively. However, only 8% of the cases involved concurrent neglect. In only 5% of these cases had a child victim been previously removed from the home. Although the positive effect cases varied substantially in terms of the first agency to receive the report, in 81% of the cases the DA and DSS intake dates were less than 15 days apart. In addition, almost half of the cases involved an initial arrest by the police
prior to intake at the DA's office.

---

[13] Cases pending the prosecution decision were cases that the DA wanted to prosecute and were still being investigated by that office. These cases were compelling but lacked substantial physical evidence or involved a child victim who might have difficulty testifying. Therefore, they were included as involving criminal justice activity.

Table 19: Characteristics of all Child Abuse Cases in Which Criminal Justice Activity Helped to Keep Children in the Home

The positive effect sub-sample (N=28) includes all child abuse cases in which criminal justice activity by the Suffolk County District Attorney's Office occurred and was reported by DSS to be helpful in negating the need for child removal.

Case Characteristics	% of Positive effect sub-sample (N=28)
Child Characteristics	
Age of child victims	
0-6	19
7-12	42
13-17	38
18+	1
Male	28
Female	72
Race/Ethnicity	
Caucasian	50
African-American	32
Latino	0
Haitian	0
Other	11
Perpetrator Characteristics	
Male	82
Female	18
Race/Ethnicity	
Caucasian	42
African-American	46
Latino	4
Haitian	0
Other	8
Relationship to child victim	
Biological or step-parent	59
Mother's boyfriend	22
Other relatives	0
Non-familial	19

Table 19: Characteristics of all Child Abuse Cases in Which Criminal Justice Activity Helped to Keep Children in the Home

Case Characteristics	% of Positive effect sub-sample (N=28)
Primary Caretaker Characteristics	
Race/Ethnicity	
Caucasian	42
African-American	46
Latino	4
Haitian	0
Other	8
Type of Abuse	
Sexual	64
Physical	36
System Characteristics	
First agency to receive report	
DSS	35
DA	23
Police	42
DSS intake prior to DA intake	70
15 or fewer days between DA and DSS intakes	81
Criminal Justice Variables	
Criminal allegations	
Rape	19
Indecent assault and battery	30
Assault & battery	67
Assault & battery with a deadly weapon	37
Sexual Abuse Investigation Network (SAIN investigation)	10
Initial arrest (prior to DA intake)	57
Protective Services Variables	
DSS investigating office	
Jamaica Plain	3
Roxbury	15
Boston	4
Dorchester	15

Table 19: Characteristics of all Child Abuse Cases in Which Criminal Justice Activity Helped to Keep Children in the Home

Case Characteristics	% of Positive effect sub-sample (N=28)
Chelsea/Revere	37
DSS internal unit/Contract agency	4
DSS office outside Boston region	22
Prior case characteristics	
Prior substantiated abuse report	50
Prior substantiated neglect report	31
Prior removal from home	8
DSS Case Findings	
Indications of neglect	7
Child emotionally abused	15
Other abused children in home	30
PC lacks parenting skills	19
Inadequate family income	15
Domestic violence	37
Adult substance abuser in home	37
Adult with psychological problems in home	12
PC is alleged perpetrator	22
Perpetrator has lived with or has had access to child's home	30
PC not cooperating with DSS	4
PC no support complaint	15
PC no support prosecution	12
PC can provide adequate care for child victim	100
PC can provide adequate protection for child victim	100

The DSS case findings revealed that domestic violence and adult substance abuse were common characteristics in this sample of cases and in a high percentage of the cases the primary caretaker was cooperating with DSS (96%) and supporting the complaint of abuse (85%). In all of the positive effect cases, DSS found the primary caretaker able to provide adequate care and protection to the child victim.

The primary criminal justice interventions reported as helping to keep the child in the home were the arrest of the alleged perpetrator immediately following the report, the jailing of the perpetrator immediately following the report, the prosecution of the case and/or the issuance of a restraining order. Other outcomes found to be helpful in a few cases were the perpetrator being convicted, put on probation, going to prison or receiving a court order for treatment. No caseworker reported that a case not being prosecuted was helpful in keeping the child in the home or returning the child to the home.

In addition, in six cases in which criminal justice interventions did not occur, DSS caseworkers reported that criminal justice involvement helped to keep the child in the home. Three of the caseworkers indicated that the perpetrator fleeing potential prosecution helped to keep the child in the home and in another case other, unspecified, actions were reported as helpful. In two cases, restraining orders were reported as helping to keep the child in the home. These no contact orders may have been the result of a domestic violence complaint or juvenile court action separate from the allegation of child abuse.

The overall sample of cases in which there was no removal and criminal justice activity occurred was also analyzed to identify any significant differences between the cases in which DSS workers found criminal justice involvement helpful in keeping the child in the home and cases in which criminal justice interventions were not found to be helpful. The factors found to be significantly related to criminal justice actions being helpful are noted in Table 20.

The presence of domestic violence was one of the notable factors that differentiated those cases in which judicial action was helpful from those in which it was not. For all cases in which domestic violence was present (N=13), criminal justice activity was reported to be helpful in keeping the child victim in the home. In addition, in 92% of the cases investigated by the DSS Chelsea/Revere area office (N=12), judicial intervention was reported to be helpful. In contrast, criminal justice actions were perceived as helpful in only 62% of the cases investigated by all of the other area offices (N=29). No differences were found in the impact of judicial activity on physical versus sexual abuse cases. However, a positive effect occurred in 82% of the cases that involved allegations of assault and battery (N=23) versus 56% of the cases that did not involve this allegation (N=18).

Table 20: Factors Associated With Judicial Involvement Being Perceived As Helpful In Preventing Child Removal - Bivariate Analysis

Sample includes only child abuse cases in which there was no removal of the child victim and for which criminal justice interventions occurred. N=44. The % positive effect column refers to the percentage of cases for which judicial interventions were found helpful in preventing child removal. The symbol ° signifies the use of Fisher's Exact Test to calculate probability.

Case Characteristics	n	% Positive effect	χ	P value	Odds Ratio
Report of domestic violence	12	100		.005°	__ a
No report of domestic violence	28	57			
Chelsea/Revere DSS area office	11	92		.05°	6.25
All other DSS offices	29	62			
Allegation of assault and battery	22	82	3.252	.05	4.00
No allegation of assault and battery	17	56			
Biological or stepparent perpetrator	22	82	2.819	.09	3.60
All other types of perpetrators	18	58			
No report of neglect	33	77		.09°	4.16
Report of neglect	7	43			

a. Odds ratio was not calculated due to a zero cell count.

The small sample size of this subset of cases made it difficult to accurately determine statistical significance in these comparisons. An examination of differential trends that were close to, but not quite, statistically significant (p < .05) revealed an association between the relationship of the perpetrator and the perceived helpfulness of criminal justice activity. In 82% of the cases in which the perpetrator was a biological or stepparent (N=22), judicial interventions were reported to be helpful. In contrast, this positive effect occurred in only 58% of the cases involving other types of perpetrators (N=19). Judicial involvement was also found to be helpful in most of the cases in which there was no DSS case finding of neglect. Criminal justice actions were found to be helpful in 77% of the cases in which there was no report of neglect (N=34). Comparatively, judicial involvement was found to be helpful in only 43% of the cases that involved child neglect (N=7). DSS caseworkers were also asked to assess the helpfulness of criminal justice interventions in returning removed children to their home. In 33% of the substantiated cases (N=45), child victims were removed from the home. At the time of survey completion, two months following the date of the DA intake, 31% or 13 of the placed children had been returned to their home. DSS caseworkers reported that in only four of these cases (21% of the returned children) did actions taken by the criminal justice system help to return the child to the home.

Separate examination of the sexual abuse and physical abuse sub-samples revealed findings similar to the overall sample. The primary criminal justice interventions reported as helping to keep the child in the home were identical to those reported for the overall sample: the arrest of the alleged perpetrator immediately following the report, the jailing of the perpetrator immediately following the report, the prosecution of the case and/or the issuance of a no contact order.

In conclusion, the reports of DSS caseworkers support the theory that criminal justice activity can be helpful in negating the need for placement in some child abuse cases. The confinement of the perpetrator through immediate detainment or a restraining order can help some child victims to stay in the home by removing the immediate threat of abuse. However, the data suggest that criminal justice influence on the removal decision also has limitations.

The findings indicate that this positive influence occurs primarily in cases in which the primary caretaker is not the perpetrator and supports the complaint of abuse. Since the removal decision is based upon the primary caretaker's ability to protect and care for the child, it seems logical that the arrest and prosecution of perpetrators would be most helpful in negating removal when those conditions exist.

In addition, the helpfulness of the criminal justice system in removing the need for removal increases when cases are quickly referred between agencies. Although bivariate tests of association were not significant due to the small sample size, cases that were referred to the DA in 15 or fewer days were much more likely to be positively influenced by criminal justice involvement.

Of interest, also, is the finding that criminal justice activity is most helpful in cases in which neglect is not present. This corresponds to findings reported in earlier in this chapter relating to the importance of neglect in the removal decision as well as the case prosecution decision.

Finally, the relationship of a report of domestic violence, a particular DSS area office and an assault and battery allegation with the positive effect suggests that specific types of abuse cases and area office policies and practices can also impact the protective service child removal decision. The presence of domestic violence in cases of child abuse allows for more interagency collaboration and the utilization of interventions across systems, which can prove helpful in negating the need for removal.

Almost all of the positive effect cases that involved domestic violence were associated with an assault and battery allegation. However, two-thirds of the assault and battery cases did not involve a report of domestic violence. Therefore, the findings indicate that the helpfulness of judicial involvement is associated with both child physical assault cases that also involve domestic violence and cases that only involve a child abuse allegation of assault and battery.

CHAPTER 6

Implications of the Suffolk County Study

The purpose of the Suffolk County study was to examine the relationship between the interventions of two systems in cases of child abuse. The study did not find a direct relationship between the placement of children outside of the home and cases not being selected for prosecution. However, descriptive data gathered in the study did reveal evidence that, for a subset of cases, the interventions of the criminal justice system can help protective services to keep children in their home following a report of child abuse. The study also succeeded further specifying the primary predictors of child removal and case prosecution and identifying factors associated with each dependent variable that had not been uncovered in previous research. In addition, the study found evidence that an intervening variable, neglect, may be an important link between the child placement and case prosecution decisions.

Comparison with Child Victim As Witness Study

The results of the Suffolk County study conflict with those of the prior Child Victim as Witness study. It is likely that the dissimilarity in findings between the Suffolk County study and the findings of the prior Child Victim as Witness (CVAW) study is partly result of differences in sampling, case referral, and child placement definitions.

The samples collected for the two studies differed in three distinct ways. The CVAW study examined child sexual abuse cases, collecting child placement data from families six to nine months after their referral to a judicial system. In Suffolk County, the data on child placement was collected prior to and up to two months following case referral to the criminal justice system. No relationship was found between child removal and case prosecution for the overall Suffolk County sample or cases involving only sexual abuse. However, the Suffolk County study did not collect placement data after two months following referral, therefore, the possibility of an association between child placement and prosecution over a longer time period cannot be ruled out.

In regards to case referral, another reason why the Suffolk County study did not support the finding that the non-prosecution of cases is related to child removal may be that the cases referred to the Suffolk County district attorney differ significantly from the cases referred for prosecution in the four counties participating in the CVAW study. Protective services in the state of Massachusetts is unique in that all substantiated case reports must be referred to the DA (Protection and Care of Children, 1993).

In Massachusetts, the groups of individuals required to report child abuse and the circumstances under which they must report are very similar to mandated reporting policies in the states involved in the CVAW study (U.S.D.H.H.S., 2003a). However, Massachusetts has a much higher substantiation rate than any of the CVAW states. More than half of all cases investigated in Massachusetts in 2002 were substantiated (U.S.D.H.H.S., 2003b). Therefore, it is likely that the Suffolk County study includes cases that may have gone unsubstantiated by protective service agencies in the CVAW states.

In addition, in the states involved in the CVAW study, protective services uses discretion in its case referral. How the case referral decision is made is unclear, but many within protective service agencies indicate that only the most serious reports of abuse are referred to the judicial system. It is also possible that, in states that allow discretion, protective services chooses to not refer cases which they believe would benefit more by child welfare versus the criminal justice system.

Prosecution rates will tend to be higher in states in which only the most serious abuse cases are referred. This difference is apparent in a comparison of the prosecution rates in the CVAW study versus the Suffolk County study.. Sixty percent of the cases referred to the judicial system in the CVAW study were chosen for prosecution (Cross et al., 1999). Only 26% of the cases in Suffolk County were prosecuted. Therefore, the difference in the composition of the CVAW sample and the present study sample may explain why child removal and case prosecution were not found to be correlated. The relationship between child removal and case prosecution may have been dimiNIShed by the presence of many more cases that were unlikely to be chosen for prosecution.

Finally, another important difference between the prior and present study relates to the definition of child placement. The Suffolk County study defined child placement as any protective service placement that had occurred in relation to the specific incident of abuse that was under investigation by the criminal justice system. In contrast, the CVAW study defined child placement as any out-of-the-home living arrangement reported by the parents that occurred between the referral for case prosecution and the follow up interview with the criminal justice system. The CVAW study did not collect information as to whether or not protective services was involved in a child's placement outside the home.

Therefore, it is likely that child placements reported in the CVAW study involved placements outside of the home that were not initiated by a protective service agency. A number of the child placements reported in the CVAW study may have been voluntarily initiated by primary caretakers versus a protective service agency. It is plausible, then, that protective services was not involved in a number of the cases studied by the CVAW study. This implies that the association between placement and cases being closed without prosecution may be more directly related to case and family characteristics than protective service decision-making.

In the CVAW study, the strong correlation between the placement and prosecution decisions for intrafamilial cases was driven by the highly significant association between non-prosecution and placement with a relative. Although placement of any type was found to be significantly associated to cases being closed without prosecution; separate examinations of placement in foster care, a shelter or in a hospital were not found to be statistically significant (Cross et al., 1999).

Most protective service removals involve the placement of a child in a foster home. The highly significant relationship between non-prosecution and placement with a relative versus a foster home in the CVAW study supports the idea that, in the prior study, the association may not have been directly linked to protective service intervention.

The results of the CVAW study may indicate that the case prosecution decision may be more directly related to family and case characteristics versus characteristics associated with protective service involvement and decision-making. Further research on the placement/prosecution relationship should be designed to examine this supposition.

Criminal Justice Impact on Child Removal

An indirect relationship was found which supports the idea that, at least for some cases, the involvement of the criminal justice system can assist protective services in their efforts to keep children in the homes. The Suffolk County study found that in many cases in which children were not removed and judicial involvement occurred, protective services reported that criminal justice actions were helpful in keeping the child in the home. The judicial actions found to be helpful in keeping the child in the home were the prosecution of the case, the arrest and jailing of the alleged perpetrator immediately following the report, and the issuance of restraining orders. These findings support the idea that the criminal justice system can act as an ally to protective services in their efforts to provide safeguards for the abused child with the least amount of disruption in their living arrangements.

The helpfulness of criminal justice activity in negating removal involves two questions. First, can criminal justice activity be initiated that will result in interfering with perpetrator access to the child? If so, judicial actions may remove the threat of continued abuse by the perpetrator. In this study, the helpfulness of criminal justice activity was found to be related to the relationship between the child and the perpetrator. Judicial interventions were more helpful in keeping children in the home when the perpetrator was a parent. This confirms that the way in which the judicial system can be most helpful in the removal decision is by eliminating the ability of the perpetrator to have access to the child. Criminal justice interventions can be of little help in negating the need for placement in cases of child abuse that involve offenders who do not have an automatic right to access, for example, a relative, family friend or neighbor.

The second question relates to the protective service evaluation of the home environment. Is the home environment of the child both safe and adequate? The answer to this question will depend upon the DSS assessment of the ability of the primary caretaker to provide ongoing protection for the child, and meet the basic psychological and physical needs of the child. A child may be removed from the home even if the threat of immediate abuse has been removed. For example, judicial interventions cannot negate the need for removal of a child who is being severely neglected or living with an actively substance abusing primary caretaker. The association between no neglect in the home and judicial involvement being helpful supports this assertion. Therefore, the results suggest that criminal justice interventions can be of greatest assistance in negating the need for removal when three conditions exist:

- an abused child is receiving adequate care from a primary caretaker
- the primary caretaker is not the perpetrator of the abuse
- criminal interventions can significantly interfere with perpetrator access to the child

The correlation between domestic violence and cases in which judicial actions were found to be helpful is an interesting finding. Over the past ten years, the criminal justice response to domestic violence has improved significantly. The swift response by law enforcement and the use of restraining orders have become standard practices in the nation. In addition, some protective service agencies, including the Massachusetts Department of Social Services, now have special units that specifically deal with case management and service provision in cases involving domestic violence (Whitney & Davis, 1999).

In Massachusetts, DSS investigators include in all of their initial screenings questions designed to uncover indicators of domestic violence in the family (Spath, 2001). If domestic violence is revealed in the initial investigation, a special protocol is utilized. Investigators are encouraged to ensure child protection by acting as an ally to the nonoffending parent, assisting them with the development of a safety plan and providing them with information regarding shelters for battered women and possible judicial interventions. If requested, assistance is provided by protective services in filing a criminal report and/or obtaining a restraining order (Spath, 2001).

The utilization of restraining orders in cases of domestic violence can help to keep abused children in the home by interfering with the perpetrator's access to the child. The active utilization of this criminal justice intervention by protective services in child abuse cases that involve family violence provides an opportunity for information sharing and collaboration between the two systems. In cases in which the abused spouse is willing to prosecute, the concurrent occurrence of domestic violence and child abuse in one family may allow the criminal justice system to target an alleged abuser on two fronts, adding weight to the prosecutor's case.

Cases in which domestic violence and child abuse overlap provide an ideal opportunity for testing models of interagency cooperation (Spath, 2001). The results of the Suffolk County study suggest that case outcomes in joint child abuse-domestic violence cases can improve through coordinated efforts between criminal justice and protective services.

The finding that the cases in which the judicial system was helpful were more likely to involve an allegation of assault and battery is, in part, related to the higher likelihood of initial arrests in cases of physical abuse versus sexual abuse. In this study, 60% of the physical abuse cases and 9% of the sexual abuse cases involved an arrest prior to the referral to the DA. This is very likely due to the different ways in which physical abuse and sexual abuse come to the attention of authorities. Physical abuse cases often involve eyewitness reports of assaults by outside individuals and observable physical injuries which can provide substantial evidence for the prosecutor's case (J. Fine, personal communication, May 22, 2001). The immediate report, arrest, and physical evidence empower law enforcement, protective services and prosecutors to intervene quickly and more effectively in many cases of physical abuse.

Sexual abuse cases, on the other hand, are often reported after the fact by a mandated reporter following disclosure by the child. An immediate arrest is rare and physical and medical evidence is often not available (Pence & Wilson, 1994). These factors can interfere with the ability of the criminal justice interventions to be useful in protective service decision-making about many sexual abuse cases.

The staff members of the Chelsea/Revere DSS area office found criminal justice involvement more helpful in keeping children in the home than all of the other DSS offices. This may due to demographic differences between this office and the other area offices as well as Chelsea area office's distinct approach to interagency collaboration. Chelsea/Revere is an urban area, however, it has fewer families living in poverty and less serious crime than all of the other Boston regions

(S. Goldfarb, personal communication, December 10, 1999). Therefore, families that come under the auspices of DSS in Chelsea are less likely to be impacted by multiple stressors and case management is likely to be of a less complex nature (S. Goldfarb, personal communication, December 10, 1999). Criminal justice involvement can be most influential in DSS cases that focus solely on the abuse incident versus other family or environmental factors.

Another explanation may relate to the strong emphasis that the Chelsea office reports to place on community involvement and proactive engagement. The Chelsea area office was found to be more prompt in their referral of cases to the District Attorney and more willing to participate in case reviews than other Boston region area offices (personal communication, J. Fine, Suffolk County District Attorney's Office, May 22, 2001). This focus on the importance of interagency collaboration may also explain why judicial interventions were found to be much more helpful by this area office.

Factors Influencing Child Removal

The final predictors of child removal both confirm and add to the findings of prior studies. Many of the variables found to be associated with child removal by previous researchers were verified by the present study. Cases involving primary caretakers as perpetrators, primary caretakers who do not support the complaint and a concurrent report of neglect are consistent with idea of removal as a function of primary caretaker functioning and the current risk to the child.

The relationship of child placement to the older victim replicates the findings of previous studies but contradicts protocols developed by protective services. Child protection recognizes age to be an important criteria in the assessment of risk. Limited self-protection abilities are believed to put the younger child at great risk for continued abuse (Meddin, 1985). This contrasts with research findings that older children are at a higher risk for removal.

It is possible that the present finding of an association between the older child and removal reflects in part the advanced verbal and cognitive abilities of older children. Older children who are maltreated may be more aware of the outside assistance that is available to them and better able to access resources and are better able to provide information about the abuse to investigators. This association may also partly reflect the fact that older children often experience more severe forms of sexual abuse. In the Suffolk County study, a much higher percentage of the older children were the victims of rape (50%), whereas only 29% of the children age 0-6 and 25% of the children age 7 to 12 this type of abuse.

Two new findings emerged from the Suffolk County study regarding predictors of placement. Both prior removal and primary caretaker ethnicity were found to be significantly related to child placement. It is logical that primary caretaker ethnicity could impact removal as it is the primary caretaker and his or her functioning which is judged by protective services when the child placement decision is made. It is possible that the finding of different removal rates for different primary caretaker ethnic groups relates to cultural-based child rearing practices that may be in conflict with the way in which child maltreatment is defined in the United States and/or bias on the part of the protective service caseworker. However, the small sub-samples involved in this finding suggest that the subject should be investigated further before conclusions are drawn.

Prior removal of the child is also identified as an important factor in protective service decision-making in the Suffolk County study. Previous contact between child protection and an abusive family is considered an important risk factor in the protective service investigation (Meddin, 1985). Prior removal of a child signifies to protective services the ongoing and serious nature of a particular case of abuse. Prior removal indicates that there is a history of maltreatment in the family. It reflects a history of the home environment being assessed as inadequate for the needs of the child and indicates that chronic abuse may be a characteristic of the family (Meddin, 1985). Protective services is likely to be less tolerant of the risk involved in keeping a child who has experienced prior removal in their home.

Factors Influencing Case Prosecution

The Suffolk County study is unique in that it includes in an examination of the factors that influence the criminal prosecution of child abuse, case characteristics and outcomes related to protective service involvement. However, the findings are limited by the exclusion of variables found to be related to prosecution in previous studies. The type of evidence available, perpetrators with prior criminal records, substance abusing perpetrators, and the presence of eyewitness or physical testimony, were not available for inclusion in this study. The study was unable to assess the importance of these variables in conjunction with protective service variables. However, the findings do provide a framework for identifying key family, case and system factors that influence prosecution.

The correlation between the age of the child victim and the likelihood of prosecution supports the results of previous studies. Children seven and older were found to be most likely to have their cases selected for prosecution in the Suffolk County study. However, this association was driven by and only significant for the sexual abuse cases. In the sexual abuse sub-sample, children seven to twelve were found to be more likely to have their cases selected for prosecution than the younger or older sub-samples of children in the study.

This reaffirms the difficulties expressed by prosecutors bringing cases of very young children and adolescents to trial. Typical jury perceptions of victims must be considered in the prosecutorial decision-making process (Bucci et al., 1998). Members of juries often find the details of sexual abuse cases difficult to believe and are reluctant to find a defendant guilty without corroborating evidence. Jurors express doubt regarding the ability of children under the age of six to distinguish between fact and fiction. Young children are sometimes viewed as being overly vulnerable to suggestion (Myers, 1994; Pence & Wilson, 1994). In response, prosecutors may find it difficult to prosecute with only the testimony of the child victim.

Reports of sexual abuse by adolescents may also be questioned in regards to their veracity (Pence & Wilson, 1994). Since many teenagers are sexually active, jurors often question whether the sexual act was one of abuse or mutual consent. This disbelief is in part fueled by a long history of public skepticism in regards to the issue of consent (Myers et al., 1999). Therefore, prosecutors may look for significant corroborating evidence before choosing to prosecute cases of adolescent sexual abuse victims.

The significance of referral source to case prosecution also confirms prior research results. Cases referred by protective services are less likely to be prosecuted. This may reflect differences in the way the systemic responses to cases of child abuse occur. The significance of referral source to case prosecution is very likely the result of a combination of including the types of cases that are referred to the police versus DSS, the ability of the police to collect evidence and make an arrest, the higher percentage of less serious cases for which DSS is the referral source and the ten day investigation period utilized by protective services.

Law enforcement is often the first agency to be called when physical injury of a critical nature occurs. The evidence and eyewitness accounts associated with these incidents can help to facilitate case prosecution. In contrast, DSS is usually the first agency to receive the report when there is only a suspicion of abuse or a less serious forms of physical injury. Suspicion of abuse rarely results in concrete evidence that can support the criminal case (D. Deakin, personal communication, D.Deakin, August 9, 1998). This variation in the types of cases reported first to law enforcement versus DSS may explain some of the difference in prosecution rates.

The type of intervention that occurs for each case plays a part in the likelihood of case prosecution. Although both the police and DSS are empowered to respond quickly to reports of abuse, the ability of law enforcement to gather evidence at the scene and immediately arrest ensures that a higher percentage of cases referred by the police will be more likely to be chosen for prosecution.

In addition, immediate arrests are most likely to occur in cases in which serious abuse has occurred, clear evidence is available and a perpetrator can be identified. Initial arrest is significantly associated with type of abuse. In the present study, initial arrests occurred in 77% of the physical abuse cases. In comparison, only 23% of the sexual abuse cases involved an initial arrest.

Cases in which arrests occur are referred quickly to District or Superior Court. Law enforcement is not obligated to inform the District Attorney of reports of cases in which arrests do not occur. However, the police must still file a 51A with DSS of all reports of abuse. Therefore, cases that do not involve an arrest, in essence, become DSS cases and DSS is required to forward all of their substantiated abuse cases to the DA. This results in a significant difference in the average level of severity of cases reported to the DA from the police versus DSS.

The delay inherent in the DSS referral policy may also account for the lesser rate of prosecution of protective service cases. DSS can take up to ten days to complete an investigation on non-urgent cases before referring it to the District Attorney's office. Although referral to the

District Attorney is allowed during the ten day period for cases of serious impairment or sexual assault of any type, most cases are forwarded following the investigation. Twenty-five percent of the cases in this study had more than 30 days between the DSS intake and referral to the District Attorney. A greater length of time between the initial referral to DSS and the DSS referral to the District Attorney, may lessen the ability of the District Attorney to successfully prosecute a case. All of these factors, taken together, provide some explanation for why cases referred by DSS are less likely to be prosecuted in comparison to cases referred by the police.

The Suffolk County study also found that the type of abuse inflicted on the child victim can influence the likelihood of case prosecution. Physical abuse cases were more likely to be prosecuted than sexual abuse cases. This differential rate of prosecution occurred even when controlling for referral source and initial arrest. Previous research has rarely examined the differences in systemic responses to physical versus sexual abuse, however, in contrast to the current finding, (Tjaden & Thoennes, 1992) found sexual abuse cases more likely to be chosen for prosecution. Variations in the type of abuse most likely to be prosecuted may relate to statuatory differences between states. At the time that data collection for the present study was being conducted, Massachusetts law allowed for the prosecution of only those assault and battery cases that involved substantial bodily injury (National Center for Prosecution of Child Abuse, 1999). In contrast, the prosecution of child sexual assault in Massachusetts encompassed all types of sexual abuse including penetration, oral or genital contact, sexual molestation and sexual exploitation (National Center for Prosecution of Child Abuse, 1999). Therefore, differing prosecution rates relating to type of abuse in the Suffolk County sample may reflect the broad variation present in severity of abuse in sexual abuse cases that are reported to the District Attorneys in Massachusetts.

The absence of concurrent neglect was also found to be an independent correlate to case prosecution in the Suffolk County study. Cases involving neglect were significantly less likely to be chosen for prosecution. This provides evidence that affirms the importance of familial support in the prosecution of child abuse cases. The presence of neglect may indicate that the child and the family may be impacted by multiple internal and external stressors such as poverty, low educational attainment, physical or mental illness, and/or substance abuse (Gaudin, Polansky, Kilpatrick & Shilton, 1993), and may lack necessary resources and supports. In this study, a concurrent finding of neglect was found to be statistically associated with the DSS assessment that the family had inadequate income to satisfactorily provide for the child.

It might be assumed that this association between neglect and cases being declined for prosecution represents the level of support of the primary caretaker for the child's complaint. Prior research has found maternal support for the child's complaint of abuse to be significantly associated with cases being chosen for prosecution (Cross et al., 1994). However, in the Suffolk County study, no association was found between familial neglect and the cooperation of the primary caretaker with DSS or the support of the primary caretaker for the prosecution of the complaint.

Primary caretakers in families in which neglect is occurring are not likely to have the skills or resources necessary to effectively negotiate the judicial system or provide support to their children through the processes of criminal court. Children who are neglected often have primary caretakers who suffer from numerous life stressors, depression, and loneliness. It is probable that the prosecutor's office might find neglectful families difficult to communicate with and less reliable than other families. It is also possible that, when dealing with neglectful families, the prosecution of the case becomes secondary to addressing the more pressing problems that are impacting the family.

In the Suffolk County study, the significance of this association between neglect and cases being declined for prosecution was driven by a strong correlation within the sexual abuse sub-sample. A relationship between prosecution and neglect was not found in the physical abuse sub-sample. In other words, when analyzed separately, a significant relationship was found between no neglect and case prosecution in the sexual abuse sub-sample but not in the physical abuse sub-sample. The relationship between this variable and case prosecution was considerable. None of the sexual abuse cases that involved neglect were chosen for prosecution. Therefore, it is possible that the relationship between neglect and cases not being chosen for prosecution is indicative of the unique problems District Attorneys face in the successful prosecution of sexual abuse cases. Sexual abuse cases that have no corroborating evidence rely heavily on the ability of the child to serve as a witness. Child abuse victims who are neglected may suffer from multiple stressors, including cognitive, psychological and social impairments, making it more difficult for them to function well as a witness.

Prosecutors have reported that child victims need to be able to rely on the support of family members in order to be effective witnesses. It is likely that many families that are substantiated for neglect do not have the knowledge, experience or strength, or social skills to meet the needs of the potential child witness. The successful prosecution of these cases will be hampered by these factors (J. Fine, personal communication, May 22, 2001).

It is also possible that prosecutors are declining to prosecute cases involving sexual abuse and neglect because of the ways in which the limitations of the victim or family could be used as a barrier to successful prosecution. For example, family members, as witnesses, may be portrayed as lacking credibility by the Defense Attorney. In addition, the neglectful behavior of the family could be blamed for creating the unsafe setting in which the sexual abuse occurred. For example, a mother may be blamed for making a poor decision in regards to the individual in whom she entrusted the care of the child.

The Relationship of Neglect to Removal and Prosecution

The significant association of the neglect variable to both child removal and case prosecution in cases of child sexual abuse is an important finding. The overlapping significance of neglect to both child placement and cases being declined for prosecution suggests that factors relating to the functioning of the family and overall home environment is connected to decision making by the two systems.

The presence of neglect in a sexual abuse case informs the protective service investigator that there are concerns relating to the ability of the family to provide adequate care for the child. In cases in which child protection also cannot be assured, removal of the child is likely to be necessary to ensure the child receives adequate care in a safe environment.

At the same time, the presence of neglect may impact the ability of the criminal justice system to prosecute the case of abuse. Child abuse victims who also are neglected may lack the internal strength and external support needed to negotiate the criminal justice processes or serve as witnesses.

The dual effect of neglect on the case prosecution and child placement decisions is a problem that has not been recognized or addressed by either system. This group of children, whose families are in crisis, are clearly at risk for further maltreatment. Removal may be necessary to ensure adequate care. The limitations of the child and family may create a barrier to successful case prosecution. Therefore, the child, who has already been victimized by the abuse, is likely to experience two difficult outcomes on two additional fronts, separation from family, friends and community and a lack of validation by the judicial system. In these cases, protective services may function as the bottom-line response system, acting to protect those children for whom criminal justice is unable to provide safety or justice.

Child abuse and neglect often occur simultaneously within families. The significant correlation between the concurrent presence of neglect and abuse and negative outcomes in both the criminal justice and child protection systems makes clear the importance of incorporating all possible case, family and environmental characteristics, and systemic interventions, into the design of child abuse research. Research studies that attempt to study child abuse and neglect in isolation are likely to result in model mispecification, providing a limited picture of the factors that influence outcomes for child abuse victims. Increasing support services within the criminal justice system to offset the limitations of families in which neglect occurs may be one possible avenue to obtain better judicial outcomes for children.

CHAPTER 7

Policy Recommendations

Child welfare and criminal justice agencies can greatly influence the well-being of maltreated children. The findings of the Suffolk County study and previous research suggest that policy and practice improvements could enable child protection, law enforcement and prosecutors to meet their systemic objectives more efficiently and effectively. Improved policies and practices within these systems could result in better outcomes for child victims and their families.

Three areas for future policy reform are apparent. First, when criminal justice interventions can potentially support improved outcomes for child victims, they should be actively utilized. Second, both the child protection and criminal justice systems should study and develop practices that aim to dismantle barriers to systemic effectiveness in cases involving families in crisis. Finally, collaborative responses to child maltreatment must be improved. All collaboration models should specify measurable, concrete goals and objectives and utilize practices that are evidence-based. In addition, in order for collaborative agreements to be effective, they must be fully integrated into organizational practice and formally incorporated within state statutes.

Utilizing Criminal Justice Interventions

Criminal justice interventions such as arrest, prosecution and the issuance of a restraining order can help to negate the need for child removal by protective services under specific conditions. These interventions are helpful when they interfere with perpetrator access to the child in cases in which the child has an adequate home environment and the perpetrator is not the primary caretaker for the child. In other words, when there are no concerns regarding the primary caretaker or the home, criminal justice interventions can help child protection investigators to keep children in their homes. Child outcomes could be improved through the dissemination and utilization of this information by both protective service and criminal justice agencies. Protocols that examine these case factors at the initial phase of case investigation could enable both law enforcement and child protection investigators to evaluate whether early referral to the prosecutor could be beneficial in a particular case.

Prosecutors and law enforcement officers should also be informed regarding the indirect ways in which criminal justice interventions can benefit children. Protective service workers report that arrest and prosecution can be helpful in preventing child removal in some cases. Criminal justice interventions can remove risk to the child by putting pressure on offenders. The filing of formal charges and/or a restraining order, even in cases with no corroborating evidence, sends the message that the offender's behavior is not acceptable, which can influence the behavior of both the accused and non-offending caretaker.

Judicial interventions can also be helpful to child victims. Child victims often believe they are responsible for the abuse that occurred and/or the family disruption that resulted from the report of abuse (Faller, 1993). This belief can impair psychological functioning and the healthy recovery of child victims (Faller, 1993). Accepting cases for prosecution sends child victims the message that a serious crime has been committed, affirming that the abuse was wrong. For these reasons, prosecutors should be encouraged to consider going forward with cases that are not clearly 'prosecutable' but may result in secondary benefits to the child. Recent pressure on the criminal justice system to address the needs of crime victims for 'justice' reflects a societal belief that all victims should be able to expect affirmation and support from the criminal justice system (Sebba, 1999; Shapland, 1986).

Improved child outcomes could also be attained through the use of specialized protocols in cases in which child abuse and domestic violence co-occur. Criminal justice interventions, such as immediate arrests and the use of restraining orders, can be helpful in negating the need for child placement when both child abuse and domestic violence are present. Child protection agencies can improve outcomes for children by addressing issues of domestic violence and child abuse together. Specific response guidelines can produce a more holistic and family-centered response on the part of child welfare. In creating specialized protocols for abuse cases involving domestic violence, protective services can reach their goal of quality care and protection for the child by providing information and tangible supports to the family and utilizing judicial interventions in place of child removal. The protocols encourage and facilitate case coordination with the criminal justice system, allowing for a more effective response to these cases. These policies may also serve as a model for other types of effective, systemic collaboration with public and nonprofit agencies that respond to and/or provide services to families impacted by both domestic violence and child abuse.

Child advocates continue to raise concerns regarding the impact of prosecution and a trial on the well-being of a child, especially in intrafamilial child sexual abuse cases. Although innovative methods for improving the judicial experience for child victims have lessened these barriers, concerns still remain regarding the benefit of criminal prosecution for the child victim (Office for Victims of Crime, 1999). However, the evidence that criminal justice interventions can help some children to remain in their home and can support them in their recovery (Henry, 1997) suggests that judicial involvement can often be in the best interest of many abused children. Future research should continue to examine the positive and negative ramifications of criminal court engagement with child victims.

Supporting Families in Crisis

The high rate of placement and absence of prosecution in sexual abuse cases involving child neglect in the Suffolk County study informs us that there is a specific group of victims who may require special attention from both the criminal justice and child protection systems. The presence of multiple forms of maltreatment suggests that these children may be living in families that are in crisis; experiencing difficulty in everyday functioning and lacking the skills and support systems to cope with environmental stressors. The child victims from these families are likely to experience both placement outside the home and a judicial system that is limited in its ability to address the crimes that have been committed against them. In many cases involving both chronic neglect and sexual maltreatment, it is likely that placement outside the home may initially be the best outcome for the child. Likewise, criminal justice involvement, which may exacerbate the multiple stressors already experienced by the child who is both abused and neglected, may not be an appropriate intervention for this group of children.

It is also possible that the finding of neglect may be the result of a protective service determination that the non-offending parent failed to protect the child from sexual abuse. If this is the case, child outcomes may be improved through the implementation of less punitive, family–centered approaches that attempt to bolster the ability of the non-offending parent to provide adequate protection. Further research should be undertaken to determine who these neglected and sexually abused children are, the internal and external stressors that are impacting their families, and the reasons underlying the outcomes they experience with both protective services and criminal justice.

In the Suffolk County study, the association of neglect with both removal and cases being declined for prosecution was found only for the sexual abuse cases. Therefore, it is probable that the combination of neglect with sexual abuse presents limitations that prosecutors find difficult to overcome. The challenge of prosecuting sexual abuse cases without corroborating evidence may be exacerbated by the presence of family functioning difficulties. The findings point to the need for discussion among criminal justice professionals about the impact of family functioning and the home environment on the successful prosecution of sexual abuse. The inclusion of protective services in this discussion would be beneficial given the experience that child protection has had with families in which both abuse and neglect occurs. Policy efforts in this area should focus on the creation, implementation and evaluation of criminal justice practice models that attempt to identify and provide specialized advocacy and support to neglected children and their families throughout the investigation and case prosecution process.

Improving Collaboration

Many states have created cooperative practices that engage multiple agencies in joint investigations and multidisciplinary teams on an informal basis. These practices have also been found to be effective when they follow the establishment of strong interagency relationships and are legitimated through written policies (Office for Victims of Crime, 1999). Collaborative policies that have been found to be beneficial to abused children include the joint training of child protection and criminal justice personnel, the use of child interview specialists, the establishment of child death review teams, the development of response protocols between investigatory systems and health and mental health service providers, joint child protection and law enforcement investigations, and the development of multidisciplinary teams and centers (Office for Victims of Crime, 1999).

In most states, however, formal policies that mandate cooperation between child welfare and criminal justice are lacking. By statutory authorization, child abuse reports are referred between agencies and interagency cooperation is allowed (U.S.D.H.H.S., 2003d). However, discretionary reporting and inconsistent collaboration between the two systems is currently the standard mode of practice in most jurisdictions. The discretion afforded protective services in regards to case referral and involvement in joint investigation teams limits the ability of law enforcement and prosecutors to conduct thorough forensic investigations and, therefore, provide effective criminal justice responses to many cases.

The Office for Victims of Crime (1999) strongly recommends that criminal justice agencies communicate with and work in collaboration with protective service agencies, juvenile courts, health and mental health providers and human service agencies to ensure that systemic decision-making is fully informed and in the best interest of the child. A number of states have found that legislative mandates that require collaboration in the form of joint investigations and multidisciplinary teams can be very effective in improving case assessments, fostering joint decision-making, identifying and accessing resources and helping multiple systems to work together to reach their goals (Office for Victims of Crime, 1999; Kolbo & Strong, 1997; Rogan, 1990).

However, most child abuse cases involving caretakers enter first through protective services. Child protection and criminal justice cannot collaborate in terms of systemic decision-making unless information on cases of abuse are promptly shared between the two systems. The swift referral of cases from child protection to the prosecutor is often allowed, but in practice, difficult. Rapid case referral requires extra effort on the part of the investigative caseworker, who may already be overburdened by a high caseload and impending deadlines.

Given their role and status in the child protection hierarchy, it is likely that most protective service front-line workers focus on those aspects of their role that are emphasized by their direct supervisor and agency director. Cooperative engagement is most likely to occur when it is emphasized by administrators, incorporated into the agency mission, and supported in everyday practice (Nevin & Roberts, 1990). Legislative and organizational initiatives that encourage and support the criminal prosecution of cases investigated by protective services would provide a basis for more child protection engagement with the criminal justice system (Snell, 2003).

The establishment of a coordinated approach will only be effective if individuals involved in the process are supportive of it (Kolbo & Strong, 1997). Obtaining the cooperation of individuals from diverse systems can be difficult to achieve. Barriers to cooperation include a lack of trust between individuals from different agencies, a lack of understanding of contrasting goals and objectives, variation in status roles, the allocation of insufficient resources to enable collaboration to occur and differences in public attitudes toward each agency (Nevin & Roberts, 1990). For this reason, it is essential that individuals at every level of each agency involved in the multidisciplinary effort, from direct service provider to program director, be involved in the planning process. Advisory councils consisting of representatives from all systems and joint, in-service training have been found to be very useful in overcoming the role confusion and misconceptions that can be associated with inter-agency collaboration (Kolbo & Strong, 1997).

Despite difficulties associated with multidisciplinary cooperation, reports from the field indicate that informal and formal collaboration has been improving (J. Fine, personal communication, May 22, 2001). Throughout the nation, collaborative efforts have been undertaken by individuals within both the child protection and criminal justice systems who see the necessity for information sharing and joint investigations. Children's advocacy centers represent one of the most promising initiatives.

Children's advocacy centers bring together multidisciplinary teams of child protection, law enforcement, criminal justice, and medical and mental health professionals to provide effective, coordinated responses to reports of child abuse in a child-affirming and family-centered manner (Snell, 2003; Walsh et al., 2003). Although much variation exists in the settings and program models utilized, children's advocacy centers share a philosophy that emphasizes the reduction of stress and secondary trauma to child victims through shared forensic interviews, coordinated interventions, and case management to secure services for the child and family (Snell, 2003; Walsh et al., 2003).

Throughout the nation, professionals in child protection and criminal justice are working to improve their responses to child abuse victims through the development of multidisciplinary advocacy centers. Currently, there are 460 registered children's advocacy centers operating throughout the United States (Walsh et al., 2003). Shortly after the completion of the Suffolk County study, a children's advocacy center was established in the Boston region through the leadership of the Suffolk County District Attorney's office and the support of individuals in law enforcement, health care and child protection (S. Goldfarb, personal communication, S. Goldfarb, March 4, 2004). It is reported that the establishment of this center resulted in more joint interviews and joint interviews occurring earlier (S. Goldfarb, personal communication, March 4, 2004). Interagency case reviews are now held on a monthly basis involving staff members from all agencies. New police protocols have been established that allow for prosecutors, law enforcement and child protection to collaborate in case investigation. The establishment of the center has also resulted in an improvement in the timing of case referrals from child protection to the district attorney (S. Goldfarb, personal communication, March 4, 2004). However, there is still much that is unknown about the effectiveness of children's advocacy centers in improving child and family well-being and investigative agency outcomes. Little formal research is available that can guide practitioners regarding those protocols and practices that have been found to be most successful and helpful to both victims and agencies (Snell, 2003). Fortunately, more information on the effectiveness of these collaborative initiatives should be available in the near future. Many children's advocacy centers are in the process of collecting and analyzing data on child and agency outcomes. In addition, the Crimes Against Children Research Center at the University of New Hampshire is currently in the process of analyzing data from a multi-site, national evaluation of children's advocacy centers (T. Cross, personal communication, October 4, 2004).

The preliminary results of the Crimes Against Children Research Center evaluation are encouraging. In this study, child maltreatment case information from four children's advocacy centers is being compared to case data from comparison communities within the same state. Initial findings indicate that sexually abused children who are served through children's advocacy centers receive more medical examinations and more likely to be referred to mental health providers (T. Cross, personal communication, October 4, 2004). Although the data do not indicate that the involvement of a children's advocacy center results in fewer interviews, there was little evidence suggesting duplicative interviewing (T. Cross, personal communication, October 4, 2004). The study has also found that children's advocacy positively influence case coordination and information sharing. Joint investigations and case reviews were much more likely to occur for cases that were served by children's advocacy centers (T. Cross, personal communication, October 4, 2004).

One outstanding question that must still be addressed by professionals involved in children's advocacy centers and other types of multidisciplinary teams is who is and is not being served. Referral protocols and practices vary tremendously by agency and region. In many areas referrals to children's advocacy centers or multidisciplinary teams are discretionary (Walsh et al., 2003) and the process by which cases are recommended for services is informal and subjective. This suggests that even in regions where specialized child advocacy services exist, some child maltreatment victims will not be afforded the benefits of multidisciplinary support and interventions.

Case referrals to multidisciplinary teams or children's advocacy centers must be standardized. The circumstances under which cases should be referred to a team or center should be stated clearly and unambiguously. These criteria should be easy to operationalize, specifically stating the conditions under which cases should be referred (T. Cross, personal communication, October 3, 2004). It is also important that referral criteria be clearly communicated to all agencies that respond to child abuse complaints. In addition, agency guidelines on referral practices should be developed and integrated into everyday practice.

As part of this process, multidisciplinary teams and children's advocacy centers will be called upon to clearly identify their goals and objectives. If case referral becomes a standard practice, children's advocacy centers could become overwhelmed by increasing caseloads (Simone, Cross, Jones, & Walsh, in press).

Given current and potential resources, these organizations must identify how many cases and which types of cases they are prepared to serve. Although all children's advocacy centers share a child-centered philosophy, they often differ in how they prioritize outcomes. For example, responding to the physical and mental health needs of children harmed by severe and chronic abuse may be the primary objective of a children's advocacy center housed in a medical institution. In contrast, an independent center established by criminal justice professionals may focus primarily on those cases in which case coordination and information sharing could result in better judicial outcomes. It appears that formal and informal screening processes are currently being utilized in those jurisdictions in which all child protection abuse cases are referred to the prosecutor's office. The criteria upon which this screening is based should also be articulated (Simone, Cross, Jones & Walsh, in press). Discussion and specification of goals and objectives will assist children's advocacy centers in developing appropriate referral criteria.

Better outcomes are possible for abused children through the collaborative efforts of the child welfare and criminal justice systems. Research that further clarifies the ways in which the case prosecution and child placement decisions are associated can assist professionals in both systems to better understand and utilize the benefits associated with systemic communication and cooperation. Future research should also examine which protective service cases are most likely to benefit from criminal justice interventions, the specific interventions that are most helpful, and how coordination between these two agencies can best be facilitated. In addition, research should focus on the design and effectiveness of multidisciplinary teams and children's advocacy centers in improving child outcomes. Future research in these areas and the development of policies that enhance multi-systemic goal achievement through inter-agency collaboration is essential to the development of a more effective societal response to the problem of child abuse.

Appendices

Appendix A

SUFFOLK COUNTY DISTRICT ATTORNEY'S OFFICE
___ REFERRAL

CAU LOG #_____   PROMIS #_____
INTAKE DATE_____ASSIGNMENT DATE_____
ADA_____   VWA_____   INTERVIEWER_____

VICTIM #____ OF ____ PARENTS_____
CONSUMER #_____
1. NAME_____   SEX____AGE____DOB_____
ADDRESS_____
TEL_____LANGUAGE_____   ETHNICITY_____

PERPETRATOR #____ OF ____ ADULT/JUVENILE
1. NAME_____   SEX____AGE____
    ADDRESS_____
    DOB_____SS#_____   RELATIONSHIP_____
    ETHNICITY_____

ABUSE ALLEGED

SEXUAL	PHYSICAL
RAPE IND. A&B	DEATH ABDW A&B
ASSLT. W/I RAPE	SERIOUS INJURY
EXPLOITATION	

OTHER:_____
ABUSE DATES:_____PLACE:_____CHILD'S AGE____
FACTS:_____
_____
_____

SPECIAL FACTORS:_____
_____

PROCEEDINGS: S.A.I.N. TEAM YES/NO DATE:_____

DSS OFFICE_____   OPEN: YES/NO   SW_____

POLICE DEPT_____INVOLVED: YES/NO OFFICER_____

ARRESTED: YES/NO   DATE:_____ CUSTODY: YES/NO

209A   NEW   PRIOR EXP.   PRIOR ACTIVE

DISTRICT CRT:_____ NEXT EVENT_____DATE_____

REFERRAL FORM CONTINUATION #___

CAU LOG#_____   PROMIS#_____

VICTIM #___ OF ___   PARENTS_____

2. NAME_____   SEX____AGE____DOB_____

ADDRESS_____

       TEL_____LANGUAGE_____ETHNICITY_____

ADDITIONAL FACTS:_____

_____

CAU LOG#_____   PROMIS#_____

VICTIM #___ OF ___   PARENTS

3. NAME_____   SEX____AGE____DOB_____

ADDRESS_____

       TEL_____LANGUAGE_____ETHNICITY_____

PERPETRATOR: #___ OF ___   ADULT/JUVENILE

2. NAME_____   SEX____   AGE____

       ADDRESS_____

       DOB_____SS#_____   RELATIONSHIP_____

PERPETRATOR: #___ OF ___   ADULT/JUVENILE

3. NAME_____   SEX____   AGE____

       ADDRESS_____

DOB_____SS#_____RELATIONSHIP_____

Appendix B

For Researcher Use Only: Case #_____ Date
Rec'd_____

A STUDY OF THE IMPACT OF CRIMINAL JUSTICE & CHILD WELFARE SYSTEM INVOLVEMENT ON CHILD SURVIVORS OF ABUSE AND THEIR FAMILIES

PART I: THE FIRST SET OF QUESTIONS PERTAIN TO ANY PAST CHILD ABUSE ISSUES IN THIS FAMILY

1. WAS THIS CHILD EVER REMOVED FROM HIS/HER HOME BY DSS FOR ANY REASON IN THE FIVE YEARS PRIOR TO THE CURRENT ABUSE REPORT?
    (PLEASE CHECK ONE)

    _____ Yes   _____ No   _____ Unknown

2. PRIOR TO THE CURRENT ABUSE REPORT, DOES DSS HAVE ANY REPORT OF THIS CHILD EXPERIENCING SEXUAL ABUSE, PHYSICAL ABUSE OR NEGLECT? **(PLEASE CHECK ONE)**

    _____ Yes   _____ No   _____ Unknown

    IF YES, CIRCLE EACH CATEGORY FOR WHICH DSS HAS A PRIOR REPORT FOR THIS CHILD: **(CIRCLE ALL THAT APPLY)**

    Sexual abuse   Physical Abuse   Neglect

```
╔══════════════════════════════════════════════╗
║   THE FOLLOWING SET OF QUESTIONS PERTAIN TO    ║
║         THE CURRENT REPORT OF ABUSE            ║
╚══════════════════════════════════════════════╝
```

3.   ON WHAT DATE WAS THIS REPORT RECEIVED BY
       THE DEPARTMENT OF SOCIAL SERVICES?

                    _____ / _____ / _____
                     (Month/Day/Year)

4.   FROM WHAT **SOURCE** DID THE DEPARTMENT OF
       SOCIAL SERVICES FIRST RECEIVE THIS REPORT?
       (PLEASE CHECK ONE)

       _____   District Attorney's Office
       _____   Individual (not a mandated reporter or agency
               representative)
       _____   Police Department
       _____   Mandated Reporter from another agency (Please
               specify)_____
       _____   Other   (Please specify)   _____

5.   WHEN THIS CURRENT REPORT OF ABUSE WAS
       RECEIVED, WHO WAS THE *PRIMARY CARETAKER*
       FOR THIS CHILD? *IF THIS CHILD HAS MORE THAN
       ONE PRIMARY CARETAKER, CHECK THE PERSON
       MOST RESPONSIBLE FOR THE DAY TO DAY CARE OF
       THE CHILD PRIOR TO THIS REPORT OF ABUSE.*

CHECK <u>ONLY ONE</u> PRIMARY CARETAKER

_____ Biological mother	_____ Biological father
_____ Step mother	_____ Step father
_____ Female foster parent parent	_____ Male foster
_____ Female partner of biol. Father	_____ Male partner of biol. mother
_____ Older female sibling sibling	_____ Older male
_____ Grandmother	_____ Grandfather
_____ Other female relative	_____ Other male relative
_____ Female friend of family	_____ Male friend of family

IF NONE OF THE ABOVE APPLIES, please describe below the
primary caretaker of this child:

6.   **PLEASE INDICATE THE RACE/ETHNICITY OF THE
      PRIMARY CARETAKER: (PLEASE CHECK ONE)**

_____ White	_____ Dominican	_____ Haitian
_____ African-American	_____ Cambodian	_____ Portuguese
_____ Latino	_____ Vietnamese	_____ Asian
_____ Puerto Rican	_____ Chinese	_____ Other

7.　WHERE WAS THIS CHILD'S PRIMARY PLACE OF
　　RESIDENCE PRIOR TO THIS REPORT OF ABUSE?
　　(PLEASE CHECK ONE)

_____ With primary caretaker (PC)　　_____ Youth shelter
_____ With relative (other than PC)　　_____ Group home
_____ Health or mental health facility　　_____ Foster home
_____ Other (specify)_____

8.　WAS THIS REPORT OF ABUSE SUBSTANTIATED BY
　　THE DEPARTMENT OF SOCIAL SERVICES?

　　_____ Yes　　_____ No　　**IF YOU CHECKED
NO, SKIP TO QUESTION 16**

9.　PLEASE CHECK ALL OF THE FOLLOWING CASE OR
　　FAMILY CHARACTERISTICS THAT APPLY TO THIS
　　CASE. **(CHECK ALL THAT APPLY TO THIS CASE.
　　ADD ADDITIONAL REASONS NEXT TO 'OTHER'
　　CATEGORY.)**

YES　　**NO**
_____　_____ substantiated report of physical abuse of this child
_____　_____ substantiated report of sexual abuse of this child
_____　_____ child has serious physical health or mental health
　　　　　　　problems
_____　_____ indications of physical or sexual abuse of other
　　　　　　　children in household

_____ _____ indications that primary caretaker neglects child
(inadequate housing, food, health care, schooling)

_____ _____ indications that primary caretaker emotionally abuses
child

_____ _____ primary caretaker is the alleged perpetrator of current
abuse report

_____ _____ primary caretaker has inadequate income to care for
child

_____ _____ primary caretaker not cooperating with DSS

_____ _____ primary caretaker does not support child's complaint
of abuse

_____ _____ primary caretaker does not support the prosecution of
the alleged perpetrator

_____ _____ primary caretaker has abandoned child

_____ _____ primary caretaker is in a hospital, mental health or
substance abuse treatment facility or in jail/prison

_____ _____ primary caretaker lacks adequate parenting skills

_____ _____ adult substance abuser in the household

_____ _____ adult with psychological problems in the household

_____ _____ domestic violence in household

_____ _____ alleged perpetrator lives with or is allowed to enter
child's home

_____ _____ alleged perpetrator has access to child

Other important case or family characteristics (please
specify)_____

10.   FOLLOWING THE REPORT OF ABUSE, DID THE DSS
        INVESTIGATION FIND THE PRIMARY CARETAKER
        ABLE TO ADEQUATELY PROTECT THIS CHILD FROM
        FURTHER ABUSE? **(PLEASE CHECK ONE)**

        _____ Yes   _____ No   _____ Yes, but
                                             conditionally

11.   FOLLOWING THE REPORT OF ABUSE, DID THE DSS
        INVESTIGATION FIND THE PRIMARY CARETAKER
        ABLE TO PROVIDE ADEQUATE CARE FOR THIS
        CHILD?   **(PLEASE CHECK ONE)**

        _____ Yes   _____ No   _____ Yes, but
                                             conditionally

12a.   WAS THIS CHILD REMOVED FROM THE HOME
        FOLLOWING THE CURRENT REPORT OF ABUSE?
        (PLEASE CHECK ONE)

        _____ Yes   _____ No   **IF YOU CHECKED
        NO, SKIP TO QUESTION 13**

        IF YES, PLEASE CHECK BELOW WHAT TYPE OF
        REMOVAL OCCURRED? **(PLEASE CHECK ONE)**

        _____ DSS removal   _____Juvenile Court removal
        _____ Voluntary removal by parent/guardian
        _____Other (specify) _____

12b.   IF THIS CHILD **WAS REMOVED** FROM THE HOME,
        WHERE WAS HE OR SHE PLACED? **(PLEASE CHECK
        ONE.   IF THE CHILD HAS HAD MULTIPLE
        PLACEMENTS, CHECK THE <u>FIRST</u> PLACEMENT
        ONLY.)**

      _____   Foster home   _____   With relative

      _____   Group home   _____   Health or mental health

      _____   Youth shelter   facility

      _____   Other (specify)_____

12c.   WHAT WAS THE EXACT DATE OF REMOVAL?
        ____ / ____ / _____

        (Month/Day/Year)

12d.   HAS THIS CHILD BEEN RETURNED TO THE HOME?

_____   Yes   _____   No   **IF YOU CHECKED <u>NO</u>, SKIP
        TO QUESTION 15**

12 e.   IF THIS CHILD HAS BEEN RETURNED TO THE HOME,
        WHAT WAS THE EXACT DATE OF THEIR RETURN?

        ____ / ____ / _____
        (Month/Day/Year)

12f.   DID ANY ACTIONS BY THE CRIMINAL JUSTICE
        SYSTEM HELP DSS TO RETURN THE CHILD TO THEIR
        HOME? **(PLEASE CHECK ONE)**

_____   Yes   _____   No   _____   Unknown

**IF YOU CHECKED YES OR UNKNOWN, SKIP TO
QUESTON 14.**
IF YOU CHECKED NO, SKIP TO QUESTION 15.

13.   IF THIS CHILD **WAS <u>NOT</u> REMOVED** FROM THE
      HOME FOLLOWING THIS REPORT OF ABUSE, DID
      ANY ACTIONS BY THE CRIMINAL JUSTICE SYSTEM
      HELP DSS TO KEEP THE CHILD IN THE HOME?
      (PLEASE CHECK ONE)

      _____ Yes _____ No _____ Unknown
      IF YOU CHECKED NO, SKIP TO QUESTION 15

14.   WHAT ACTIONS BY THE CRIMINAL JUSTICE SYSTEM
      HELPED TO KEEP THE CHILD IN THE HOME <u>OR</u>
      RETURN THE CHILD TO THE HOME?   **(CHECK ALL
      REASONS LISTED BELOW THAT APPLY TO THIS
      CASE.** ADD ADDITIONAL REASONS NEXT TO
      'OTHER' CATEGORY.)

YES   NO

_____ _____ the decision to prosecute the case

_____ _____ the decision to not prosecute the case

_____ _____ the arrest of the alleged perpetrator immediately
             following the report

_____ _____ the jailing of the alleged perpetrator immediately
             following the report

_____ _____ the conviction and sentencing of the perpetrator

_____ _____ the issuance of a no contact order to the perpetrator
             regarding the child

_____   _____ the perpetrator's receiving probation

_____   _____ the perpetrator's going to prison following conviction

_____   _____ the alleged perpetrator fled prosecution; whereabouts
                 unknown

Other Reasons: (please specify)

_____

_____

_____

_____

_____

_____

15.   IS THERE ANYTHING ELSE YOU WOULD LIKE TO
         TELL US ABOUT HOW THE DECISION OF WHETHER
         OR NOT TO PLACE THIS CHILD OUTSIDE THE HOME
         WAS AFFECTED BY THE ACTIONS OF THE CRIMINAL
         JUSTICE SYSTEM?

_____

_____

_____

_____

_____

_____

_____

PART II: THE FOLLOWING questions pertain to THE
***PRIMARY CARETAKER* FOR THIS CHILD**
WHEN THE ALLEGED CHILD ABUSE OCCURRED.

---

5. WHO WAS THE ***PRIMARY CARETAKER*** FOR THIS
    CHILD **WHEN THE ALLEGED ABUSE OCCURED?** *IF*
    THIS CHILD HAD MORE THAN ONE PRIMARY
    CARETAKER, CHECK THE PERSON MOST
    RESPONSIBLE FOR THE DAY TO DAY CARE OF THE
    CHILD WHEN THE ALLEGED ABUSE OCCURRED.

    CHECK <u>ONLY ONE</u> PRIMARY CARETAKER

_____ Biological mother	
Biological father	_____
_____ Step mother	_____ Step father
_____ Female foster parent	_____ Male foster parent
_____ Female partner of biological father	_____ Male partner of biological mother
_____ Older female sibling	_____ Older male s sibling
_____ Grandmother	_____ Grandfather
_____ Other female relative	_____ Other male relative
_____ Female friend of family	_____ Male friend of family

IF NONE OF THE ABOVE APPLIES, please describe below the
primary caretaker of this child:

_____

> **The following questions pertain to THE *PRIMARY CARETAKER* FOR THIS CHILD *WHEN THE ALLEGED CHILD ABUSE OCCURRED.***

Please check any symptoms or behaviors that you have OBSERVED OR HAVE BEEN NOTIFIED OF that may indicate that this PRIMARY CARETAKER has experienced partner violence.

16.   THE *PRIMARY CARETAKER* OF THE ALLEGEDLY ABUSED CHILD DISPLAYS THE FOLLOWING SYMPTOMS AND/OR BEHAVIORS THAT MAY INDICATE THAT THE *PRIMARY CARETAKER* HAS BEEN *PHYSICALLY ABUSED*: (PLEASE CHECK ALL THAT APPLY)

_____   has a current restraining order on file

_____   involved in a pending prosecution for a battering incident

_____   has a history of partner violence in past relationships

_____   has a history of restraining orders

_____   has a history of using shelter services

_____   has a history of repeated accidents

_____   has been hit, slapped, pushed, kicked, choked, and/or burned by partner

_____   displays visible evidence of physical injuries

_____   is unwilling to discuss injuries

_____   has a history of repeated emergency room visits

_____   displays a significant delay in seeking medical treatment

_____   has a history of police visits to the home

_____   is hyper-vigilant regarding child(ren)'s safety

_____   other (please specify)_____

_____   none of the above

17. THE *PRIMARY CARETAKER* OF THE ALLEGEDLY ABUSED CHILD DISPLAYS THE FOLLOWING SYMPTOMS AND/OR BEHAVIORS THAT MAY INDICATE THAT THE *PRIMARY CARETAKER* **HAS BEEN *CONTROLLED AND/OR MANIPULATED*: (PLEASE CHECK ALL THAT APPLY)**

_____ continually monitored by partner

_____ discouraged by partner from starting new friendships

_____ required to account to partner how money is spent

_____ discouraged and/or prevented by partner from working or going to school

_____ discouraged and/or prevented by partner from seeing friends or family

_____ phone calls monitored and/or controlled by partner

_____ wardrobe monitored and/or controlled by partner

_____ mail monitored and/or controlled by partner

_____ accused by partner of being unfaithful

_____ money stolen by partner

_____ hesitant to meet or talk alone

_____ defers decision making to partner

_____ indicates the presence of a weapon in the home

_____ indicates that child is asked by partner to assist in monitoring (partner asks child what primary caretaker did)

_____ partner threatened to take away child(ren)

_____ partner threatened to call DSS

_____ partner threatened to call the Immigration and Naturalization Service (INS) and report illegal immigrant status

_____ partner threatened to hurt and/or kill himself/herself

_____ partner threatened to harm parents of primary caretaker

_____ other (please specify)_____

_____ none of the above

18.   THE ***PRIMARY CARETAKER*** OF THE ALLEGEDLY ABUSED CHILD DISPLAYS THE FOLLOWING SYMPTOMS OR BEHAVIORS THAT MAY INDICATE THAT THE ***PRIMARY CARETAKER* HAS BEEN *VERBALLY, EMOTIONALLY, AND/OR SEXUALLY ABUSED*: (PLEASE CHECK ALL THAT APPLY)**

_____   called degrading names by partner

_____   humiliated at home and/or in public by partner

_____   possessions (clothing, photographs) destroyed by partner

_____   threatened with physical injury by partner

_____   children or other family members safety threatened by partner

_____   pets hurt by partner

_____   indicated existence of reckless behavior of partner (i.e. driving car too fast with passengers)

_____   forced to perform sexual acts and/or raped by partner

_____   prevented from using birth control

_____   hurt during a pregnancy

_____   forced to engage in prostitution or pornography

_____   forced to use drugs

_____   accused of being an unfit parent by partner

_____   expresses hostility toward partner

_____   expresses hostility towards others in family

_____   partner interfered with obtaining medical care

_____   deliberately awakened by partner during sleeping hours

_____   other (please specify)

_____

_____   none of the above

20. PLEASE CHECK THE **TYPE(S)** OF CONTACT THAT YOU HAVE HAD WITH THE **PRIMARY CARETAKER:** (**PLEASE CHECK ALL THAT APPLY**)

_____ letter contact   _____ phone contact

_____ face to face contact

_____ no contact with **primary caretaker**

21. PLEASE INDICATE IF ANY INDIVIDUALS **DIRECTLY PROVIDED YOU** WITH INFORMATION *ON INDICATORS OF PARTNER VIOLENCE* IN THIS CHILD ABUSE INVESTIGATION. (**PLEASE CHECK ONE**)

_____ **NO**:   No one provided information on partner violence issues (**SKIP TO QUESTION 23**)

_____ **YES**:   Information on indicators of partner violence was provided to me.

IF YOU ANSWERED NO - PLEASE SKIP TO QUESTION 23

22. PLEASE INDICATE WHAT INDIVIDUALS LISTED BELOW **DIRECTLY PROVIDED YOU** WITH INFORMATION ON INDICATORS OF PARTNER VIOLENCE IN THIS CHILD ABUSE INVESTIGATION: (**PLEASE CHECK ALL THAT APPLY**)

Family and/or Family Acquaintances:

_____ Biological mother   _____ Biological father

_____ Step mother   _____ Step father

_____	Female foster parent parent	_____	Male foster
_____	female partner of biological father	_____	male partner of biological mother
_____	Older female sibling	_____	Older male sibling
_____	Grandmother	_____	Grandfather
_____	Other female relative	_____	Other male relative
_____	Female friend of family	_____	Male friend of family
_____	Alleged child abuse victim	_____	Sibling of abused child
_____	Neighbor		
_____	Other (please specify)_____		

Social Service, Legal and Medical Professionals:

_____	Prosecutor school personnel	_____	Teacher/other
_____	Victim witness advocate medical professional	_____	Physician/other
_____	Therapist	_____	DSS
_____	Multidisciplinary team representative interviewer	_____	Police Dept. investigative
_____	Other (specify)		

23.   PLEASE INDICATE BELOW IF EITHER **YOU OR ANOTHER INDIVIDUAL** INVOLVED IN THE CHILD ABUSE INVESTIGATION PROVIDED INFORMATION AND/OR ASSISTANCE TO THE **PRIMARY CARETAKER TO ADDRESS POSSIBLE PARTNER VIOLENCE ISSUES. (PLEASE CHECK ONE)**

_____ **NO:**   Information and/or assistance **WERE NOT** provided to the primary caretaker for possible partner violence issues by either another investigator or myself **(SKIP TO QUESTION 25)**

_____ **YES:**   Information and/or assistance **WERE** provided to the primary caretaker for possible partner violence issues by either another investigator or myself

IF YOU ANSWERED NO - PLEASE SKIP TO QUESTION 25

24.   PLEASE INDICATE WHAT SERVICES AND/OR INFORMATION THAT YOU OR ANOTHER INDIVIDUAL INVOLVED IN THIS CHILD ABUSE INVESTIGATION PROVIDED TO THE PRIMARY CARETAKER FOR POSSIBLE PARTNER VIOLENCE ISSUES: **(PLEASE CHECK ALL THAT APPLY)**

_____   written information of rights

_____   education/general information about partner violence

_____   information on counseling/advocacy services

_____   information on local hot line services

_____   information on local shelter services

_____   information on partner violence offender treatment

_____   information on how to obtain a restraining order

_____ information on counseling and/or other services for
allegedly abused child

_____ information on how to obtain her own attorney

_____ referral to an attorney

_____ a completed safety plan

_____ developed family/neighbor contacts as part of the
safety plan

_____ referral for medical services

_____ referral to other social service agency

_____ other (please specify)

_____

25. PLEASE INDICATE HOW LIKELY YOU BELIEVE THAT
THE PRIMARY CARETAKER *HAS A PAST HISTORY* OF
PARTNER VIOLENCE: (CIRCLE ONE NUMBER)

1	2	3	4	5	6
Very Unlikely	Unlikely	Somewhat unlikely	Somewhat likely	Likely	Very likely

26. IF YOU DO THINK THAT *IT IS SOMEWHAT LIKELY,
LIKELY, OR VERY LIKELY THAT THE PRIMARY
CARETAKER HAS A PAST HISTORY OF PARTNER
VIOLENCE,* PLEASE EXPLAIN WHY:

_____
_____
_____

27. PLEASE INDICATE HOW LIKELY YOU BELIEVE THAT
THE PRIMARY CARETAKER *IS CURRENTLY
EXPERIENCING* PARTNER VIOLENCE: **(CIRCLE ONE)**

1	2	3	4	5	6
Very Unlikely	Unlikely	Somewhat unlikely	Somewhat likely	Likely	Very likely

28.   IF YOU DO THINK THAT *IT IS SOMEWHAT LIKELY,*
       LIKELY, OR VERY LIKELY THAT THE PRIMARY
       CARETAKER IS CURRENTLY EXPERIENCING
       PARTNER VIOLENCE, PLEASE EXPLAIN WHY:

       _____

       _____

29. PLEASE INDICATE THE DATE THIS SURVEY WAS
     COMPLETED:

                    _____/_____/_____
                    (Month / Day / Year)

30. IS THERE ANYTHING ELSE YOU WOULD LIKE TO TELL
     US ABOUT THIS CASE?

Appendix C

MEDIAN FAMILY INCOMES ASSOCIATED WITH THE REGIONAL OFFICES OF THE MASSACHUSETTS DEPARTMENT OF SOCIAL SERVICE

DSS Regional Office	Range of Median Incomes (by zip code of child abuse victim)
Jamaica Plain	$22,010 - $34644
Roxbury	$18,390 - $33,845
Boston	$18,390 - $27,742
Dorchester	$22,010 - $31,035
Chelsea/Revere	$22,925 - $36,019
Outside Boston Region	$22,925 - $53492

Source: 1990 Census of Population and Housing, U.S. Department of Commerce

Appendix D

EXPLANATORY VARIABLES TESTED
IN BIVARIATE ANALYSES

DOMAIN *Explanatory* *Variable*	*Question*	*Dependent* *Variable(s)*	*Level of* *Measurement*
CHILD VICTIM CHARACTERISTIC			
Victim's Age	What is child abuse victim's age?	Removal/ Prosecution	INTERVAL and NOMINAL
Victim's Sex	What is the sex of the child abuse victim?	Removal/ Prosecution	NOMINAL male/female
Victim's Ethnicity	What is the victim's ethnicity?	Removal/ Prosecution	NOMINAL White African-American Latino Puerto Rican Dominican Cambodian Vietnamese Chinese Haitian Portuguese Asian Other
Victim Language	What is the primary language of the child victim?	Removal/ Prosecution	NOMINAL English Spanish Unknown Other
Victim's residence	What was the child victim's primary place of residence prior to the abuse report?	Removal/ Prosecution	NOMINAL With primary caretaker With relative Health/mental health facility Youth shelter Group home Foster home Other

DOMAIN Explanatory Variable	Question	Dependent Variable(s)	Level of Measurement
Age at onset	What was the victim's age at onset of abuse?	Removal/ Prosecution	INTERVAL

FAMILY CHARACTERISTIC

DOMAIN Explanatory Variable	Question	Dependent Variable(s)	Level of Measurement
Residential zip code/ SES	What is the zip code/SES of the family's residence?	Removal/ Prosecution	NOMINAL
Primary caretaker	Who was the primary caretaker of victim, when this abuse report was received?	Removal/ Prosecution	NOMINAL (see survey)
Primary caretaker neglect	Any indications that primary caretaker neglects victim?	Removal/ Prosecution	NOMINAL yes/no
Primary caretaker emotional abuse	Any indications that primary caretaker emotionally abuses victim?	Removal/ Prosecution	NOMINAL yes/no
Primary caretaker not cooperative	Is the primary caretaker not cooperating w/ DSS?	Removal/ Prosecution	NOMINAL ye/no
Primary caretaker not support prosecution	Does the primary caretaker not support prosecution?	Removal/ Prosecution	NOMINAL yes/no
Primary caretaker is perpetrator	Is the primary caretaker the alleged perpetrator?	Removal/ Prosecution	NOMINAL yes/no

DOMAIN Explanatory Variable	Question	Dependent Variable(s)	Level of Measurement
Other abuse in family	Are there indications of of SA or PA of other children in the family?	Removal/ Prosecution	NOMINAL yes/no

FAMILY STRESSOR CHARACTERISTIC

Victim health problem	Does the victim have a serious phy/mental health problem?	Removal/ Prosecution	NOMINAL yes/no
Domestic violence	Is there domestic violence in household?	Removal/ Prosecution	NOMINAL yes/no
Adult psychological problem	Is there an adult with psychological problems in the household?	Removal/ Prosecution	NOMINAL yes/no
Adult substance abuse	Is there an adult substance abuser in the houshold?	Removal/ Prosecution	NOMINAL yes/no
Lack of parenting skills	Does the primary caretaker lack adequate parenting skills?	Removal/ Prosecution	NOMINAL yes/no
Inadequate Income	Does primary caretaker have an inadequate income to care for child victim?	Removal/ Prosecution	NOMINAL yes/no

DOMAIN Explanatory Variable	Question	Dependent Variable(s)	Level of Measurement
Abandoned child	Has the primary caretaker abandoned the child victim?	Removal/ Prosecution	NOMINAL yes/no
Hospital residence	Is the primary caretaker residing in hospital or mental health facility?	Removal/ Prosecution	NOMINAL yes/no
ABUSE CHARACTERISITC			
Abuse type	What is the abuse type?	Removal/ Prosecution	NOMINAL Sexual Physical Both Death
PERPETRATOR CHARACTERISTIC			
Perpetrator's sex	What is the sex of the perpetrator?	Removal/ Prosecution	NOMINAL male/female
Perpetrator's ethnicity	What is the ethnicity of the perpetrator?	Removal/ Prosecution	NOMINAL White African-American Latino Puerto Rican Dominican Cambodian Vietnamese Chinese Haitian Portuguese Other
Perpetrator's age	Age of the perpetrator?	Removal/ Prosecution	INTERVAL
Juvenile status	Is the perpetrator a juvenile?	Removal/ Prosecution	NOMINAL yes/no

DOMAIN Explanatory Variable	Question	Dependent Variable(s)	Level of Measurement
Relationship to child victim	What is the relationship of the perpetrator to the child victim?	Removal/ Prosecution	NOMINAL bio step sibling step sibling bio parent step parent foster parent grandparent mother's boyfriend caregiver teacher acquaintance stranger uncle aunt cousin victim's boyfriend other relative's boyfriend shared residence schoolmate other
Perpetrator lived with child	Has the perpetrator lived with the child?	Removal/ Prosecution	NOMINAL yes/no
Perpetrator access to child victim	Does the perpetrator have access to the child?	Removal/ Prosecution	NOMINAL yes/no
CASE CHARACTERISTIC			
DA Intake	Date District Attorney rece'd report.	Removal/ Prosecution	INTERVAL
DSS Intake	Date DSS received report.	Removal/ Prosecution	INTERVAL
DA referral source	What was the referral source of the report to the D.A.?	Removal/ Prosecution	NOMINAL DSS police DSS and police SAIN Self

DOMAIN Explanatory Variable	Question	Dependent Variable(s)	Level of Measurement
DSS referral source	What was the referral source of the report to DSS?	Removal/ Prosecution	NOMINAL DA individual police mandated reporter other
SAIN case	Was a SAIN investigation conducted?	Removal/ Prosecution	NOMINAL yes/no

CRIMINAL JUSTICE CHARACTERISTIC

Criminal Allegations	What are the abuse allegations?	Removal/ Prosecution	NOMINAL yes/no (See Appendix D
District Court	To which District Court was this case referred?	Removal/ Prosecution	NOMINAL Dorchester So. Boston Chelsea E. Boston Charlestown Brighton West Roxbury Roxbury BMC N/A
Assistant DA assigned	Which Assist. DA was assigned to the case?	Removal/ Prosecution	NOMINAL yes/no (See Appendix D
Arrest	Was the perpetrator arrested?	Removal/ Prosecution	NOMINAL yes/no
Prosecution	Was the case chosen for prosecution?	Removal	NOMINAL Yes No Pending

DOMAIN Explanatory Variable	Question	Dependent Variable(s)	Level of Measurement
PROTECTIVE SERVICE CHARACTERISTIC			
Prior maltreatment type	For what type of abuse does DSS have a prior report on this child victim?	Removal/ Prosecution	NOMINAL (yes/no) sexual abuse physical abuse neglect sexual abuse and neglect physical abuse and neglect sexual and physical abuse all three
Prior removal	Was the child victim temoved by DSS from their home in 5 years prior to this report?	Removal/ Prosecution	NOMINAL yes/no
Prior report	Was there a prior report of maltreatment for this child?	Removal/ Prosecution	NOMINAL yes/no
Abuse substantiation	Was the current report of abuse substantiated by DSS?	Removal/ Prosecution	NOMINAL yes/no
Adequate care	Can the primary caretaker provide adequate care for the child?	Removal/ Prosecution	NOMINAL yes/no
Protection	Can the primary caretaker protect the child from future abuse?	Removal/ Prosecution	NOMINAL yes/no

DOMAIN Explanatory Variable	Question	Dependent Variable(s)	Level of Measurement
Placement	Was this child placed outside the home following abuse report?	Prosecution	NOMINAL yes/no
Type of placement	Where was the child victim placed?	Prosecution	NOMINAL Foster home Group home With relative Health/mental hlth facility Youth shelter Other
Date of placement	Date of placement?	Prosecution	INTERVAL
Return to home	Was this child returned to the home?	Prosecution	NOMINAL yes/no
Date of return	Date that the child was returned to the home.	Prosecution	INTERVAL
CJS Assistance	Did any actions by the criminal justice system help to keep the child in the home or return the child to the home?	Used to identify Positive Effect Cases	NOMINAL yes/no
CJS Actions	What actions by the criminal justice system helped to keep the child in the home or return the child to the home?	Used to identify the factors that relate to the helpfulness of criminal justice system	NOMINAL Prosecution No prosecution Arrest Jailing Conviction/sentencing No contact order Probation Prison incarceration Flight of defendant during initial investigation Other (specify)

DOMAIN Explanatory Variable	Question	Dependent Variable(s)	Level of Measurement
MEDIA IMPACT CHARACTERISTIC			
High media coverage	Was there high media coverage of child abuse in the 30 days preceding the report?	Removal/ Prosecution	NOMINAL
CJS negative coverage	Was there negative coverage of CJS interventions in the 30 days preceding the report?	Prosecution	NOMINAL
DSS negative coverage	Was there negative coverage of DSS interventions in the 30 days preceding the report?	Removal	NOMINAL
Coverage of agency interventions	During the periods of negative DSS or CJS coverage, what agency interventions were negatively portrayed?	Removal/ Prosecution	NOMINAL (yes/no) -arrest or prosecution -no arrest/ no prosecution -placement -no placement

Bibliography

Agresti, A. (1992). A survey of exact inference for contingency tables. *Statistical Science, 7*(1), 131-177.

American Prosecutor's Research Institute. (2004). *Investigation and prosecution of child abuse* (3rd ed.). Thousand Oaks, CA: Sage.

Avery, L., Hutchinson, K. D. & Whitaker, K. (2002). Domestic violence and intergenerational rates of child sexual abuse: A case record analysis. *Child and Adolescent Social Work Journal, 19*(1), 77-90.

Axelrod, R. & Bennett, D. S. (1997). Choosing sides: A landscape theory of aggregation. In R. Axelrod (Ed.), *The complexity of cooperation: Agent-based models of competition and collaboration* (pp. 69-94). Princeton, NJ: Princeton University.

Bailey, K. D. (1994). *Sociology and the new systems theory: Toward a theoretical synthesis.* New York: State University of New York.

Baird, S. C. (1997, August). Child abuse and neglect: Improving consistency in decision-making. *Focus, 4,* 1-13.

Banyard, V. L., Williams, L. M. & Siegel, J. A. (2004). Childhood sexual abuse: A gender perspective on context and consequences. *Child Maltreatment, 9*(3), 223-238.

Barnett, O., Miller, C. L. & Perrin, R. D. (2004). *Family violence across the lifespan* (2nd ed.). Thousand Oaks, CA: Sage.

Bath, H. I. & Haapala, D. A. (1993). Intensive family preservation services with abused and neglected children: An examination of group differences. *Child Abuse and Neglect, 17*(2), 213-225.

Berliner, L. & Conte, J. R. (1995). The effects of disclosure and intervention on sexually abused children. *Child Abuse and Neglect, 19*(3), 371-384.

Besharov, D. (1990). *Combatting child abuse: Guidelines for cooperation between law enforcement and child protective agencies.* Washington, D.C.: The American Enterprise Institute.

Bevan, E. & Higgins, D. J. (2002). Is domestic violence learned? The contribution of five forms of child maltreatment to men's violence and adjustment. *Journal of Family Violence, 17*(3), 223-245.

Bishop, S. J., Murphy, J. M., Jellinek, M. S., Quinn, S. D., & Poitrast, J. F. G. (1992). Protecting seriously mistreated children: Time delays in a court sample. *Child Abuse & Neglect, 16,* 465-474.

Blush, G. J. & Ross, K. L. (1990). Investigation and case management issues and strategies. *Issues in Child Abuse Accusations, 2*(3), 152-160.

Bradshaw, T. L. & Marks, A. E. (1990). Beyond a reasonable doubt: Factors that influence the legal disposition of child sexual abuses cases. *Crime & Delinquency, 36*(2), 276-285.

Brannon, C. L. (1994). The trauma of testifying in court for child victims of sexual abuse versus the accused's rights to confrontation. *Law and Psychology Review, 18*, 439-460.

Brewer, K. D., Rowe, D. M., & Brewer, D. D. (1997). Factors related to prosecution of child sexual abuse cases. *Journal of Child Sexual Abuse, 6*(1), 91-111.

Briere, J. N. & Elliott, D. M. (1994). Immediate and long-term impacts of child sexual abuse. *The Future of Children, 4*(2), 54-69.

Bronstein, L. R. (2003). A model for interdisciplinary collaboration. *Social Work, 48*(3), 297-306.

Bross, D. C., Ballo, N., & Korfmacher, J. (2000). Client evaluation of a consultation team on crimes against children. *Child Abuse and Neglect, 24*(1), 71-84.

Bucci, L., Wall, J., Suarez, L., Coakley, M., & Soldati, L. (1998, November). *Meeting challenges of prosecuting child maltreatment.* Panel discussion at the Northeast Regional Child Maltreatment Conference, Providence, RI.

Bulkley, J. (1988). Legal proceedings, reforms and emerging issues in child sexual abuse cases. *Behavioral Sciences and the Law, 6*(2), 153-180.

Bulkley, J. A., Feller, J. N., Stern, P. & Roe, R. (1996). Child abuse and neglect laws and legal proceedings. In J. Briere, L. Berliner, J. A. Bulkley, C. Jenny & T. Reid (Eds.), *The APSAC handbook on child maltreatment* (pp. 271-296). Thousand Oaks, CA: Sage.

Bulkley, W. (1967). *Sociology and modern systems theory.* Englewood Cliffs, NJ: Prentice-Hall.

Butler, S., Atkinson, L., Magnatta, M. & Hood, E. (1995). Child maltreatment: The collaboration of child welfare, mental health, and judicial system. *Child Abuse and Neglect, 19*, 355-362.

Cantwell, H. B. (1997). The neglect of child neglect. In M. E. Helfer, R. S. Kempe & R. D. Krugman's (Eds.), *The battered child* (5th ed.) (pp. 347-373). Chicago: University of Chicago.

Ceci, S. J. & Bruck, M. (1995). *Jeopardy in the courtroom: A scientific analysis of children's testimony.* Washington, DC: American Psychological Association.

Chapman, J. R. & Smith, B. E. (1987). *Child sexual abuse: An analysis of case processing.* Washington, D.C: American Bar Association.

Cheit, R. E. & Goldschmidt, E. B. (1997). Child molesters in the criminal justice system: A comprehensive case-flow analysis of the Rhode Island docket (1985-1993). *New England Journal on Criminal and Civil Confinement, 23*(2), 267-301.

Child Abuse Prevention and Treatment Act of 1974, 42 U.S.C. § 5101 et seq; 42 U.S.C. § 5116 et seq.

Child Abuse Prevention and Treatment Act , as amended, 1996, 42 U.S.C. § 5101 et seq.

Cohen, J. & Cohen, P. (1983*). Applied multiple regression/correlation analysis for the behavioral sciences* (2nd ed.). Hillsdale, NJ: Lawrence Erlbaum.

Connell-Carrick, K. (2003). A critical review of the empirical literature: Identifying correlates of child neglect. *Child and Adolescent Social Work Journal, 20*(5), 389-425.

Conte, J. (1984). The justice system and sexual abuse of children. *Social Service Review, 58,* 557-568.

Continuing Medical Education. (2001, April 6). Third national incidence study of child abuse and neglect. *Healthier You* Retrieved August 10, 2004, from http://www.healthieryou.com/cabuse.html

Costin, L. (1972). *Child welfare: Policies and practices.* New York: McGraw-Hill.

Costin, L. B., Karger, H. J. & Stoesz, D. (1996). *The politics of child abuse in America.* New York: Oxford University.

Courtney, M. E. (1998). The costs of child protection in the context of welfare reform. *The Future of Children, 8*(1), 93-94.

Cramer, R. E. (1985). The district attorney as a mobilizer in a community approach to child sexual abuse. *University of Miami Law Review, 40*, 209-216.

Crittendon, P. M. (1999). Child neglect: Causes and contributors. In H. Dubowitz (Ed.), *Neglected children: Research, practice and policy* (pp. 89-108). Thousand Oaks, CA: Sage.

Cross, T., De Vos, E., & Whitcomb, D. (1994). Prosecution of child sexual abuse cases: Which cases are accepted? *Child Abuse and Neglect, 18*(8), 663-677.

Cross, T., Martell, D. & McDonald, E. (1995, July). *Child sexual abuse child placement and the criminal justice system.* Paper presented at the International Family Violence Research Conference, University of New Hampshire, Durham, N.H.

Cross, T., Martell, D. McDonald, E. & Ahl, M. (1999). The criminal justice system and child placement in child sexual abuse cases. *Child Maltreatment, 4,* 32-44.

Cross, T. & Spath, R. (1998). *Executive summary: Evaluation of Massachusetts' Sexual Abuse Intervention Network.* Unpublished report, Brandeis University, Waltham, MA.

Cross, T., Walsh, W. A., Simone, M. & Jones, L. M. (2003). Prosecution of child abuse: A meta-analysis of rates of criminal justice decisions. *Trauma, Violence and Abuse, 4*(4), 323-340.

Cross, T., Whitcomb, D. & De Vos, E. (1995). Criminal justice outcomes of prosecution of child sexual abuse: A case flow analysis. *Child Abuse and Neglect*, 19, 1431-1442.

Cullen, B. J., Smith, P. H., Funk, J. B. & Haaf, R. A. (2000). A matched cohort comparison of a criminal justice's response to child sexual abuse: A profile of perpetrators. *Child Abuse and Neglect, 24*(4), 569-577.

Daro, D. (1988). *Confronting child abuse: Research for effective program design.* New York: The Free Press.

Daro, D., Edleson, J. L. & Pinderhughes, H. (2004). Finding common ground in the study of child maltreatment, youth violence, and adult domestic violence. *Journal of Interpersonal Violence, 19*(3), 282-298.

Davidson, H. A. (1997). The courts and child maltreatment. In M. E. Helfer, R. S. Kempe & R. D. Krugman (Eds.), *The battered child* (5th ed.) (pp. 428-499) Chicago: The University of Chicago.

Davis, N. S. & Wells, S. J. (Eds.). (1996). *Justice system processing of child abuse and neglect cases. Final report.* Washington, DC: American Bar Association and National Institute of Justice.

Dawson, K. & Berry, M. (2002). Engaging families in child welfare services: An evidence-based approach to best practice. *Child Welfare, 81*(2), 293-318.

De Francis, V. (1970). *Child abuse legislation in the 1970's.* Denver: The American Humane Association.

DeJong, A. R., & Rose, M. (1991). Legal proof of child sexual abuse in the absence of physical evidence. *Pediatrics, 88*(3), 506-511.

DeVoe, E. R. & Faller, K. C. (2002). Questioning strategies in interviews with children who my have been sexually abused. *Child Welfare, 81*(1), 5-32.

DiLauro, M. D. (2004). Psychosocial factors associated with types of child maltreatment. *Child Welfare, 83*(1), 69-99.

Downs, S. W., Moore, E., McFadden, E. J. & Costin, L. B. (2000). *Child welfare and family services: Policies and practices.* Needham Heights, MA: Allyn and Bacon.

Drake, B. & Pandey, S. (1996). Understanding the relationship between neighborhood poverty and specific types of child maltreatment. *Child Abuse and Neglect, 20*, 1003-1018.

Dubowitz, H., Black, M., Starr, R. H. & Zuravin, S. (1993). A conceptual definition of neglect. *Criminal Justice and Behavior, 20*(1), 8-26.

Dubowitz, H., Klockner, A., Starr, R. H., & Black, M. M. (1998). Community and professional definitions of child neglect. *Child Maltreatment, 3*(3), 235-243.

Dziech, B. W. & Schudson, C. B. (1989). *On trial: America's courts and their treatment of sexually abused children.* Boston: Beacon Press.

Eamon, M. K. (1994). Poverty and placement outcomes of intensive family preservation services. *Child and Adolescent Social Work Journal, 11,* 349-361.

Ells, M. (2000, March). *Forming a multidisciplinary team to investigate child abuse.* Office of Juvenile Justice and Delinquency Prevention. Retrieved July 10, 2004 from w.ncjrs.org/html/ojjdp/portable_guides/forming/forward.html

English, D. (1995). Risk Assessment: What do we know? Findings from three research studies on children reported to child protective services. In E. Wattenberg (Ed.), *Children in the shadows: The fact of children in neglecting families* (pp. 85-112). Minneapolis: University of Minnesota.

Erikson, M. F., Egeland, B. & Pianta, R. (1996). The effects of maltreatment on the development of young children. In D. Cicchettia & V. Carlson (Eds.), *Child maltreatment: Theory and research on the causes and consequences of child abuse and neglect* (pp 647-684). New York: Cambridge University.

Ernst, J. S. (2000). Mapping child maltreatment: Looking at neighborhoods in a suburban city. *Child Welfare, 79*(5), 555-573.

Ethier, L. S., Courture, G. & Lacharite, C. (2004). Risk factors associated with the chronicity of high potential for child abuse and neglect. *Journal of Family Violence, 19*(1), 13-25

Everson, M., Hunter, W., Runyon, D., Edelsohn, G. & Coulter, M. (1989). Maternal support following disclosure of incest. *American Journal of Orthopsychiatry, 2,* 197-207.

Faller, K. (1988). Decision-making in cases of intrafamilial child sexual abuse. *American Journal of Orthopsychiatry, 1,* 121-128.

Faller, K. C. (1990). *Understanding child sexual maltreatment.* Newbury Park: Sage.

Faller, K. (1993). *Child sexual abuse: Intervention and treatment issues. The user manual series.* Washington, DC: U.S. Department of Health and Human Services.

Faller, K. (1991). What happens to sexually abused children identified by child protective services? *Children and Youth Services Review, 13,* 101-111.

Faller, K. C., & Henry, J. (2000). Child sexual abuse: A case study in community collaboration. *Child Abuse and Neglect, 24,* 1215-1225.

Fanshel, D. & Shinn, S. E. (1978). *Children in foster care: A longitudinal investigation.* New York: Columbia University.

Feeney, F., Dill, F. & Weir, A. (1983*). Arrests without conviction: How often they occur and why.* Washington, DC: Office for Victims of Crime, National Institute of Justice.

Finkelhor, D. (1979). *Sexually victimized children.* New York: The Free Press.

Finkelhor, D. (1983). Removing the child--prosecuting the offender in cases of sexual abuse. *Child Abuse and Neglect, 7,* 195-205.

Finkelhor, D. (1984). *Child sexual abuse: New theory and research.* New York: The Free Press

Finkelhor, D. & Hashima P. Y. (2001). The victimization of children and youth. In S. O. White (Ed.), *Handbook of youth and justice* (pp. 49-78). New York: Plenum.

Finkelhor, D., Hotaling, G., Lewis, I. A., & Smith, C. (1990). Sexual abuse in a national survey of adult men and women: Prevalence, characteristics, and risk factors. *Child Abuse & Neglect, 14,* 19-28.

Finkelhor, D. & Jones, L. M. (January, 2004). Explanations for the decline in child sexual abuse cases. *Juvenile Justice Bulletin* (1-11). U.S. Department of Justice. Office of Justice Programs. Office of Juvenile and Delinquency Prevention.

Finkelhor, D., Moore, D. Hamby, S. & Strauss, M. (1997). Sexually abused children in a national survey of parents: Methodological issues. *Child Abuse and Neglect, 21,* 1-9

Finkelhor, D. & Ormrod, R. (May, 2001). Child abuse reported to the police. *Juvenile Justice Bulletin* (1-7). U.S. Dept of Justice. Office of Justice Programs. Office of Juvenile Justice and Delinquency Prevention.

Finkelor, D., Wolak, J. & Berliner, L. (2001). Police reporting and professional help seeking for child crime victims: A review. *Child Maltreatment, 6*(1), 17-30.

Ford, J. D., Racusin, R., Ellis, C. G., Davis, W. B., Reiser, J. Fleischer, A. & Thomas, J. (2000). Child maltreatment, other trauma exposure, and posttraumatic symptomatology among children with oppositional defiant and attention deficit hyperactivity disorder. *Child Maltreatment, 5*(3), 205-218.

Froum, A. & Kendall-Tackett, K. (1998). Law enforcement officers' approaches to evaluations of child sexual abuse. *Child Abuse and Neglect, 2*(9), 939-942.

Gaines, R., Sandgrund, A., Green, A. & Power, E. (1978). Etiological factors in child maltreatment: A multivariate study of abusing, neglecting and normal mothers. *Journal of Abnormal Psychology, 5,* 531-540.

Gambrill, E. & Stein, T.J. (Eds.) (1994). *Controversial issues in child welfare.* Boston: Allyn and Bacon.

Garbarino, J. (1980). Preventing child maltreatment. In R.H. Price, R.F. Ketterer, B.C. Bader and J. Monahan (Eds) *Prevention in mental health: Research, policy and practice* (pp. 63-80) Beverly Hills: Sage.

Garbarino, J. (1992). The meaning of poverty in the world of children. *American Behavioral Scientist, 35*(3), 220-237.

Garbarino, J. & Collins, C. (1999). Child neglect: The family with a hole in the middle. In H. Dubowitz (Ed.), *Neglected children: Research, practice and policy.* Thousand Oaks, CA: Sage.

Garmezy, N. (1981). Children under stress: Perspectives on antecedents and correlates of vulnerability and resistance to psychopathology. In A. I. Rabin, J. Arnoff, A. M. Barclay & R. A. Zucker Eds.), *Further explorations in personality* (pp. 196-269). NY: Wiley.

Gaudin, J. M. (1993). Effective intervention with neglectful families. *Criminal justice and behavior, 20*(1), 66-88.

Gaudin, J. M. (1999). Child neglect: Short-term and long-term outcomes. In H. Dubowitz (Ed.), *Neglected children: Research, practice and policy* (pp. 89-108). Thousand Oaks, CA: Sage.

Gaudin, J. M., Polansky, N. A., Kilpatrick, A. C., & Shilton, P. (1993). Loneliness, depression, stress, and social supports in neglectful families. *American journal of orthopsychiatry, 63*(4), 597-605.

Geeraert, L., Van Den Noortgate, W., Grietens, H., Onghena, P. (2004). The effects of early prevention programs for families with young children at risk for physical child abuse and neglect: A meta-analysis. *Child Maltreatment, 9*(3), 277-292.

Gelles, R. J. (1996). *The book of David: How preserving families can cost children's lives.* New York: Basic Books.

Gelles, R. J. (1998). The youngest victims: Violence toward children. In R. Bergen (Ed.), *Issues in intimate violence* (pp. 5-24). Thousand Oaks, CA: Sage.

Gelles, R. J. (1999). Policy issues in child neglect. In H. Dubowitz (Ed.), *Neglected children: Research, practice and policy* (pp. 278-298). Thousand Oaks, CA: Sage.

Goldman, J. & Salus, M. (2003). *A coordinated response to child abuse and neglect: The foundation for practice (The Users Manual Series).* Washington, DC: U.S. Department of Health and Human Services.

Goodman, G. S., Taub, E. P., Jones D. P., England, P., Port, L. K., Rudy, L., & Prado, L. (1989). *Emotional effects of criminal court testimony on child sexual abuse victims.* (Final report, Grant No. 85-IJ-CX-0020) Washington, DC: National Institute of Justice.

Goodman, G. S., Taub, E. P., Jones, D. P., England, P., Port, L. K., Rudy, L. & Prado, L. (1992). Testifying in criminal court: Emotional effects on child sexual assault victims. *Monographs of the Society for Research in Child Development.* 57, (5, Serial No. 229).

Goodman, N. (1992). *Introduction to Sociology.* New York: Harper Collins.

Gothard, S. (1987). The admissibility of evidence in child sexual abusecases. *Child Welfare, 66,* 13-24.

Grauerholz, L. (2000). An ecological approach to understanding sexual revictimization: Linking personal, interpersonal, and sociocultural factors and processes. *Child Maltreatment, 5*(1), 5-17.

Graves, P. A., & Sgroi, S. M. (1982). Law enforcement and child sexual abuse. In S. M. Sgroi (Ed.). *Handbook of clinical intervention in child sexual abuse* (pp. 309-333). Lexington, Mass.: Lexington Books.

Gray, E. (1993). *Unequal justice: The prosecution of child sexual abuse.* New York: The Free Press.

Grosman, B. (1969). *The prosecutor: An inquiry into the exercise of discretion.* Toronto: University of Toronto.

Hagberg, R. B. & Greer, J. (2004, August). *Development, trauma and the brain: The neurobiological and psychological impact of childhood abuse and neglect.* Paper presented at the 6th Annual Parenting the Challenging Child Summer Symposium. Providence, Rhode Island.

Hamarman, S., Pope, K. H. & Czaja, S. J. (2002). Emotional abuse of children: Variations in legal definitions and rates across the United States. *Child Maltreatment, 7*(4), 303-311.

Harshbarger, S. (1987). Prosecution is an appropriate response in child sexual abuse cases. *Journal of Interpersonal Violence, 2,* 108-112.

Harvey, W. & Dauns, P. E. (1993). *Sexual offenses against children and the criminal process.* Toronto, Canada: Butterworths.

Hashima, P. Y. & Finkelhor, D. (1999). Violent victimization of youth versus adults in the National Crime Victimization Survey. *Journal of Interpersonal Violence, 14*(8), 799-820.

Hauggard, J. (1988). *The sexual abuse of children: A comprehensive guide to current knowledge and intervention strategies.* San Francisco: Jossey-Bass.

Haugaard, J. J. (2004). Recognizing and treating uncommon behavioral and emotional disorders in children and adolescents who have been severely maltreated: Reactive attachment disorder. *Child Maltreatment, 9*(2), 154-161.

Helfer, M. E., Kempe, R. S. & Krugman, R. D. (Eds.). (1997). *The Battered Child.* (5th ed.). Chicago: University of Chicago Press.

Henry, J. (1997). System intervention trauma to child sexual abuse victims following disclosure. *Journal of Interpersonal Violence, 12*(4), 499-512.

Herrenkohl, R. C. & Russo, M. J. (2001). Abusive early child rearing and early childhood aggression. *Child Maltreatment, 6,* 3-17.

Higgins, D. J. & McCabe, M. (2003). Maltreatment and family dysfunction in childhood and subsequent adjustment of children and adults. *Journal of Family Violence, 18*(2), 107-121.

Hooper, C. A. (1992). *Mothers surviving child sexual abuse.* London: Tavistock/Routledge.

Howell, J. C., Kelly, M. R., Palmer, J. & Mangum, R. L. (2004). Intergrating child welfare, juvenile justice and other agencies in a continuum of services. *Child Welfare, 83*(2), 143-157.

Hudson, C. G. (2000). At the edge of chaos: A new paradigm for social work? *Journal of Social Work Education, 36*(2), 215-230.

Hunter, W., Coulter, M., Runyan, D. & Everson, M. (1990). Determinants of placement for sexually abused children. *Child Abuse and Neglect, 14*, 407-417.

Jaudes, P. K. & Morris, M. (1990). Child sexual abuse: Who goes home? *Child Abuse and Neglect, 14*, 61-68.

Jellineck, M. S., Murphy, J. M., Poitrast, F., Quinn, D., Bishop, S. J. & Goshko, M. (1992). Serious child mistreatment in Massachusetts: The course of 206 children through the courts. *Child Abuse and Neglect, 16*, 179-185.

Jensen, J. M., Jacobson, M., Unrau, Y., & Robinson, R. L. (1996). Intervention for victims of child sexual abuse: An evaluation of the children's advocacy model. *Child and Adolescent Social Work Journal, 13*(2), 139-156.

Joa, D. & Edelson, M. G. (2004). Legal outcomes for children who have been sexually abused: The impact of child abuse assessment center evaluations. *Child Maltreatment, 9*(3), 263-276.

Johnson, K. (1998). *Trauma in the lives of children.* (2nd Ed.). Alamedo, CA: Hunter House.

Johnson, R. M., Kotch, J. B., Catellier, D. J., Winsor, J. R., Dufort, V. & Hunter, W. (2002). Adverse behavioral and emotional outcomes from child abuse and witnessed violence. *Child Maltreatment, 7*(3), 179-188.

Kaminer, B. B., Crowe, A. H., & Budde-Giltner, L. (1990). The prevalence and characteristics of multidisciplinary teams for child abuse and neglect: A national survey. In M. B. W. Sandra M. Stith, & Karen Rosen (Ed.), *Violence Hits Home: Comprehensive Treatment Approaches to Domestic Violence* (pp. 549-567). New York: Springer.

Kempe, C., Silverman, F., Steele, B., Proegmueller, W. & Silver, H. (1962). The battered child syndrome. *Journal of the American Medical Association, 181*, 17-24.

Kendall-Tackett, K. & Marshall, R. (1998). Sexual victimization of children: Incest and child sexual abuse. In R. Bergen (Ed.), *Issues in Intimate Violence* (pp. 47-64). Thousand Oaks, CA: Sage.

Kinard, E. M. (2001). Recruiting participants for child abuse research: What does it take? *Journal of Family Violence, 16*(3), 219-236.

King, N. M. P., Hunter, W. M. & Runyan, D. K. (1988). Going to court: The experience of child victims of intrafamilial sexual abuse. *Journal of Health Politics, Policy and Law, 13*(4), 705-721.

Knepper, P. E., & Barton, S. M. (1997). The effect of courtroom dynamics on child maltreatment proceedings. *Social Service Review, 71*(2), 288-308.

Knudsen, D.D. & Miller, J.L. (Eds.) (1991). *Abused and battered: Social and legal responses to family violence.* New York: Aldine de Gruyter.

Kohl, J. (1993). School-based child sexual abuse prevention programs. *Journal of family violence, 8,* 137-150.

Kolbo, J. R. & Strong, E. (1997). Multidisciplinary team approaches to the investigation and resolution of child abuse and neglect: A national survey. *Child Maltreatment, 2*(1), 61-72.

Kopels, S., Chariton, T. & Wells, S. (2003). Investigation laws and practices in child protective services. *Child Welfare, 82*(6), 661-685.

Krugman, R. D. (1990). Future challenges for child protection teams: Research, education, advocacy. In S. M. Stith, M. B. Williams, & K. Rosen (Eds.), *Violence Hits Home: Comprehensive Treatment Approaches to Domestic Violence* (pp. 616-624). New York: Springer.

La Fountaine, J. (1990). *Child sexual abuse.* Cambridge, UK: Polity Press.

Lentsch, K. A. & Johnson, C. F. (2000). Do physicians have adequate knowledge of child sexual abuse? The results of two surveys of practicing physicians, 1986 and 1996. *Child Maltreatment, 5*(1), 72-78.

Levesque, R. J. R. (1995). Prosecuting sex crimes against children: Time for "outrageous" proposals? *Law & Psychology Review, 19,* 59-91.

Lipovsky, J. A. (1994). The impact of court on children: Research findings and practical recommendations. *Journal of Interpersonal Violence, 9*(2), 238-257.

Lipovsky, J. & Stern, P. (1997). Preparing children for court: An interdisciplinary view. *Child Abuse and Neglect, 2*(2), 150-163.

Lipsky, M. (1980). *Street-level bureaucracy: Dilemmas of the individual in public services.* New York: Russell Sage.

Long, G. F. (1988). Legal issues in child sexual abuse: Criminal cases and neglect and dependency cases. In L. E. Auerbach (Ed.), *Handbook on sexual abuse of children: assessment and treatment issues* (pp. 137-151). New York: Springer.

Loomis, C. P. (1960). *Social systems: Essays on their persistence and change.* Princeton, New Jersey: D. Van Nostrand.

Loomis, C. P. & Dyer, E. D. (1976). *Social systems: The study of sociology.* Cambridge, MA: Schenkman.

Louthan, W. (1985). The politics of discretionary justice. In C.F. Pinkele & W.C. Louthan (Eds.), *Discretion, justice and democracy: A public policy perspective.* Ames, Iowa: Iowa State University.

Luhmann, N. (1995). *Social systems.* Stanford, California: Stanford University.

MacMurray, B. K. (1989). Criminal determination for child sexual abuse. *Journal of Interpersonal Violence, 4*(2), 233-244.

Mahady-Smith, C. M. (1985). The young victim as witness for the prosecution: Another form of abuse? *Dickinson Law Review, 89*(3), 721-749.

Malmgren, K. W. & Meisel, S. M. (2004). Examining the link between child maltreatment and delinquency for youth with emotional and behavioral disorders. *Child Welfare, 83*(2), 175-189.

Maney, A. & Wells, S. (Eds.) (1988). *Professional responsibilities in protecting children: A public health approach to child sexual abuse.* New York: Praeger.

Markowitz, F. E. (2001). Attitudes and family violence: Linking intergenerational and cultural attitudes. *Journal of Family Violence, 16*(2), 205-218.

Martin, S. E. & Besharov, D. (1991). *Police and child abuse: New policies for expanded responsibilities.* Washington, DC: Office for Victims of Crime, Office of Justice Programs.

Martone, M., Jaudes, P. K., & Cavins, M. (1996). Criminal prosecution of child sexual abuse cases. *Child Abuse & Neglect, 20*(5), 457-464

Massachusetts Citizens for Children – Kid's Count. (2001, April). *A state call for action: Working to end child abuse and neglect in Massachusetts.* Boston, MA: Author.

Massachusetts Department of Social Services, Domestic Violence Unit. *Domestic violence protocol for CPS.* Unpublished manuscript.

Massachusetts Department of Social Services, (2000, June). *Services for children and families..* Boston, MA: Author. Retrieved July 10, 2000 from http://www.magnet.state.ma.us/dss/info-pac/2.htm.

McCauley, M. & Parker, J. F. (2001). When will a child be believed? The impact of the victim's age and juror's gender on children's credibility and verdict in a sexual-abuse case. *Child Abuse and Neglect, 25*(2), 523-539.

McCauley, M., Schwartz-Kenney, B. M., Epstein, M. A., & Tucker, E. (2001). United States. In B. M. Schwartz-Kenney, M. McCauley, & M. A. Epstein's (Eds.), *Child abuse: A global view* (pp. 241-256). Greeenwood Press: Westport, CT.

McDonald, T.P. & Johnson, W. (1993). Tracking reported sexual abuse cases. *Journal of Child Sexual Abuse, 2*(2), 1-11.

McNamara, E. (1998, November). *Child abuse and the media: The case for working together.* Paper presented at the Northeast Regional Child Maltreatment Conference, Providence, RI.

Meddin, B. (1985). The assessment of risk in child abuse and neglect investigations. *Child Abuse and Neglect, 9*, 57-62.

Menard, S. (1995). *Applied logistic regression analysis.* Thousand Oaks, CA: Sage.

Mennerich, A., Cross, T. Martell, D. & White, A. (2001.) *Case and system predictors of prosecution of child abuse.* Unpublished manuscript.

Merrick, D. (1996). *Social work and child abuse*. London: Routledge.

Michaels, M.D. (1989). The chaos paradigm. *Organization Development Journal, 7*,(2), 31-35.

Miller-Perrin, C. L. & Perrin, R. D. (1999). *Child Maltreatment*. Thousand Oaks, CA: Sage.

Moore, D. W., Gallup, G. H. & Schussel, R. (1995). *Disciplining children in America: A Gallup Poll report*. Princeton, NJ: The Gallup Organization.

Mori, K. (1994). The adoption assistance and child welfare act of 1980. *Child Welfare Perspectives, 4*(2), 33-36.

Myers, J. E. B. (1994). Adjudication of child sexual abuse cases. *The Future of Children, 4*(2), 8-101.

Myers, J. E. B. (1996). A decade of international reform to accommodate child witnesses. *Criminal Justice and Behavior, 23*(2), 402-422.

Myers, J. E. B. (1998). Legal issues in child abuse and neglect practice. (2nd ed.). Thousand Oaks, CA: Sage.

Myers, J. E. B. (1999). Professional writing on child sexual abuse from 1900 to 1975: Dominant themes and impact on prosecution. *Child Maltreatment, 4*(3), 201-216.

Myers, J. E. B., Diedrich, S., Lee, D., Fincher, K. M. & Stern, R. (1999). Professional writing on child sexual abuse from 1900 to 1975: Dominant themes and impact on prosecution. *Child Maltreatment, 4*(3), 201-216.

Naar-King, S., Silvern, L., Ryan, V. & Sebring, D. (2002). Type and severity of abuse as predictors of psychiatric symptoms in adolescence. *Journal of Family Violence, 17*(2), 133-149.

National Center on Child Abuse and Neglect (1978). *National analysis of official child abuse and neglect reporting*. Washington, D.C.: Author.

National Center on Child Abuse and Neglect. (1981). *Child sexual abuse: Legal issues and approaches: A monograph*. Washington, D.C.: American Bar Association.

National Center on Child Abuse and Neglect. (1999, November). *What is child abuse?* Washington, D.C.: Author. Retrieved March 3, 2004, from http://www.canb.com/nccanch/pubs/factsheets/whatis.htm.

National Center for the Prosecution of Child Abuse. (1999). *Child abuse and neglect state statutes elements, crimes*. US Department of Health and Human Services. Retrieved March 3, 2003 from http://www.ndaaapri.org/apri/NCPCA/State_Statutes/State_Statutes_List.html

National Clearinghouse on Child Abuse and Neglect Information. (2000). *Child Abuse and Neglect State Statute Series*. Washington, DC.: Author.

National Clearinghouse on Child Abuse and Neglect Information. (2003). *Child Abuse and Neglect State Statute Series*. Washington, DC.: Author.

National Institute of Justice Update. (1995, May). *Prosecuting child physical abuse cases: Lessons learned form the San Diego experience.* Washington, DC: Office for Victims of Crime, Office of Justice Programs.

National Research Council, Panel on Research on Child Abuse and Neglect. (1993). *Understanding child abuse and neglect.* Washington, DC: National Academy Press.

Nelson, B. J. (1984). *Making an issue of child abuse: Political agenda setting for social problems.* Chicago: The University of Chicago.

Netting, F. E., Kettner, P. M., & McMurtry, S. L. (1998). *Social work macro practice.* New York: Longman.

Nevin, R.S. & Roberts, A.R. (1990). Models of community coordination in the treatment of abused and neglected children. In S.M. Stith, M.B. Williams and K. Rosen (Eds.)., *Violence hits home: Comprehensive treatment approaches to domestic violence* (pp. 151-178). New York: Springer.

Newberger, E. H. (1987). Prosecution: A problematic approach to child abuse. *Journal of Interpersonal Violence,2,* 112-117.

Norlin, J.M. & Chess, W.A. (1997). *Human behavior and the social environment: Social systems theory* (3rd ed.). Boston: Allyn and Bacon.

Office for Victims of Crime. (1999). *Breaking the cycle of violence: Recommendations to improve the criminal justice response to child victims and witnesses* (U.S.Department of Justice, Office of Justice Programs Publication NCJ # 176983). Retrieved February 14, 2003, from http://www.ojp.usdoj.gov/ovc/publications/factshts/monograph.htm

Office of Human Research Protections. (2001, May). *IRB Guidebook.* US Dept. of Health and Human Services, Washington, DC: Author. Retrieved March 23, 2003 from http://ohrp.osophs.dhhs.gov/irb_guidebook.htm.

Office of Juvenile Justice and Delinquency Prevention. (1994). *The child victim as a witness research report.* Washington, DC: Office for Victims of Crime.

Orr, S. (1999, October). *Child protection at the crossroads: Child abuse, child protection and recommendations for reform.* (Policy Study No. 262). Los Angeles, CA: Reason Public Policy Institute.

Pecora, P. J., Whittaker, J. K., Maluccio, A. N. & Barth, R. P. (with Plotnick, R.) (2000.) *The child welfare challenge: Policy, practice and research.* New York: Walter de Gruyter.

Pellegrin, A. & Wagner, W. (1990). Child sexual abuse: Factors affecting victims' removal from home. *Child Abuse and Neglect, 14,* 53-60.

Pelton, L. H. (Ed.). (1985). *The social context of child abuse and neglect.* New York: Human Sciences Press.

Pence, D. M. & Wilson, C. A. (1994). Reporting and investigating child sexual abuse. *The Future of Children, 4*(2), 70-83.

Polansky, N. A., Chalmers, M. A., Buttenweiser, E., & Williams, D. P. (1982). *Damaged parents: An anatomy of child neglect.* Chicago: University of Chicago.

Polansky, N. A., Gaudin, J. M., Ammons, P. W. & Davis, K. B. (1985). The psychological ecology of the neglectful mother. *Child Abuser and Neglect, 9,* 265-267.

Portwood, S. G. (1999). Coming to terms with a consensual definition of child maltreatment. *Child Maltreatment, 4,* 1, 56-68.

Portwood, S. G., Grady, M. T. & Dutton, S. E. (2000). Enhancing law enforcement identification and investigation of child maltreatment. *Child Abuse and Neglect, 24*(2), 195-207.

Portwood, S. G. (1999). Coming to terms with a consensual definition of child maltreatment. *Child Maltreatment, 4*(1), 56-68.

Protection and Care of Children and Proceedings Against Them, 119 M.G.L. § 51A-51D (1993).

Ramanathan, R. (1995). *Introductory econometrics with applications.* San Diego: The Dryden Press.

Randolph, J. M. (1994). From community care to ward of the state. *Child Welfare Perspectives, 4*(2), 9-15.

Reichard, R. D. (1993). Dysfunctional families in dysfunctional systems? Why child advocacy centers may not be enough. *Journal of Child Sexual Abuse, 2*(4), 103-109.

Rittner, B. (1995). Children on the move: placement patterns in children's protective services. *Families in Society: The Journal of Contemporary Human Services. 76,*(3), 469-477.

Rogan, M. S. (1990). The multidisciplinary team approach to child abuse and neglect. In S.M. Stith, M.B. Williams & K. Rosen (Eds.). *Violence hits home: Comprehensive treatment approaches to domestic violence.* (pp. 105-114). New York: Springer.

Rossi, P., Schuerman, J. & Budde, S. (1999). Understanding decisions about child maltreatment. *Evaluation Review, 23*(6), 579-598.

Runyan, D. K., Everson, M. D., Edelsohn, G. A., Hunter, W. M. & Coulter, M. L (1988). Impact of legal intervention on sexually abused children. *Journal of Pediatrics, 113,* 647-653.

Runyan, D. K., Gould, C., Trost, D. & Loda, F. (1981). Determinants of foster care placement for the maltreated child. *American Journal of Public Health, 7,* 706-710.

Runyan, D. K., Hunter, W. M., Everson, M. D., Whitcomb, D., & DeVos, E. (1994). The intervention stressors inventory: A measure of the stress of intervention for sexually abused children. *Child Abuse and Neglect, 18*(4), 319-329.

Runyon, M. K. & Kenny, M. C. (2002). Relationship of attributional style, depression and posttrauma distress among children who suffered physical or sexual abuse. *Child Maltreatment, 7*(3), 254-265.

Runyan, D.K. & Toth, P.A. (1991). Child sexual abuse and the courts. In R.D. Krugman & J.M. Leventhal (Eds.). *Child sexual abuse.* (Report of the Twenty-Second Roundtable on Critical Approaches to Common Pediatric Problems). Columbus, Ohio: Ross Laboratories.

Ryan, G. (1997). The sexual abuser. In M. E. Helfer, R. S. Kempe & R. D. Krugman (Eds.), *The battered child.* (5th ed.). (pp. 329-346) Chicago: The University of Chicago.

Sagatun, I. J. & Edwards, L. P. (1995). *Child abuse and the legal system.* Chicago: Nelson-Hall.

Salzinger, S., Felman, R. S., Ng-Mak, D. S., Mojica, E., Stockhammer, T. & Rosario, M. (2002). Effects of partner violence and physical child abuse on child behavior: A study of abused and comparison children. *Journal of Family Violence, 17*(1), 23-52.

Saunder, B. E., Villeponteaux L. A., Lipovsky, J. A., Kilpatrick, D. G., and Veronen, L. J. (1992). Child sexual assault as a risk factor for mental disorders among women: A community survey. *Journal of Interpersonal Violence, 7,* 189-204.

Saywitz, K. J. & Snyder, L. (1993). Improving children's testimony with preparation. In G. S. Goodman & B. L. Bottoms (Eds.), *Child victims, child witness: Understanding and improving testimony* (pp. 117-146). NY: Guilford.

Sebba, L. (1999). Victim's rights-whose duties? In J.J.M. van Dijk, R.G.H. van Kaam, and J.M. Wemmer (Eds.). *Caring for crime victims: Selected proceedings of the ninth international symposium on victimology* (pp. 141-158). Monsey, NY: Criminal Justice Press.

Sedlack A. J. & Broadhurst, D. (1996). *Third national incidence study of child abuse and neglect. Final report.* Washington, DC: U.S. Department of Health and Human Services. National Center on Child Abuse and Neglect.

Shapland, J. (1986). Victims and the criminal justice system. In Fattah, E.A. (Ed.). *From crime policy to victim policy: Reorienting the justice system.* New York: St. Martin's Press.

Shephard, J. R. (1997). The role of law enforcement in the investigation of child abuse and neglect. In M. E. Helfer, R. S. Kempe & R. D. Krugman (Eds.), *The battered child* (pp. 451-459). Chicago: The University of Chicago.

Sheppard, D. I. & Zangrillo, P. A. (1996). Coordinating investigations of child abuse. *Public Welfare, 54*(1), 21-32.

Simone, M., Cross, T. P., Jones, L. M. & Walsh, W. (in press). Children's advocacy centers: Understanding the impact. In K. Kendall-Tackett & S. Giacomoni (Eds.). *Victimization of children and youth: Patterns of abuse, response strategies.* Kingston, NJ: Civic Research Institute.

Smelser, N.J. (1994). *Sociology.* Cambridge, Massachusetts: Blackwell.

Smith, P. (1994). Family preservation: A policy analysis. *Child Welfare Perspectives, 4(*2), 25-29.

Smith, B. E. (1995). *Prosecuting child physical abuse cases: A case study in San Diego* (Research in Brief NCJ 152978). San Diego: National Institute Justice.

Smith, B. E., & Elstein, S. G. (1993). *The prosecution of child sexual and physical abuse cases* (Final Report). Washington, D.C.: The National Center on Child Abuse and Neglect.

Smith, B. E. & Goretsky, S. R. (1994). The prosecution of child sexual abuse cases. Part I and Part II. *ABA juvenile and child welfare law reporter, 11*, 78-80 and 94-96.

Snell, L. (2003). *Child advocacy centers: One stop on the road to performance-based child protection. Policy study 306.* Los Angeles: Reason Foundation.

Spath, R. (2001). *The detection of intimate partner violence indicators by child maltreatment professionals.* Unpublished doctoral dissertation. Brandeis University, Waltham, MA

Stark, D. R. (1999). Collaboration basics: Strategies from six communities engaged in collaborative efforts among families, child welfare and children's mental health. Washington, DC: National Technical Assistance Center for Children's Mental Health, Georgetown University Child Development Center.

Starling, S. P. & Boos, S. (2003). Core content for residency training in child abuse and neglect. *Child Maltreatment, 8*(4), 242-247.

Steele, B. F. (1975). *Working with abusive parents from a psychiatric point of view.* US Department of Health, Education and Welfare Publication Number (OHD) 75-70. Washington, DC: US Government Printing Office.

Straus, M. A. & Gelles, R. J. (1990). How violent are American families? Estimates from the National Family Violence Resurvey and other studies. In M.A. Straus & R. J. Gelles (Eds.), *Physical violence in American families: Risk factors and adaptations to violence in 8,145 families* (pp. 95-112). New Brunswick, NJ: Transaction Books.

Stroud, D. D., Martens, S. L. & Barber, J. (2000). Criminal investigation of child sexual abuse: A comparison of cases referred to the prosecutor to those not referred. *Child Abuse and Neglect, 24*(5), 689-700.

Suffolk County District Attorney's Office, Child Abuse Unit. (1996a). *1995 Statistics.* Unpublished manuscript.

Suffolk County District Attorney's Office, Child Abuse Unit. (1996b). *Policies, protocols and procedures.* Unpublished manuscript.

Swerson, C. C., Brown, E. J., Sheidow, A. J. (2003). Medical, legal and mental health service utilization by physically abused children and their caregivers. *Child Maltreatment, 8*(2), 138-144.

Tedesco, J. F. & Schnell, S. V. (1987). Children's reactions to sex abuse investigation and litigation. *Child Abuse and Neglect, 11,* 267-272.

The Children's Law and Policy Initiative, Massachusetts Citizen's for Children. (2002). *The children's bench book. Improving court responses to child victims of intra-familial violence and sexual abuse.* Boston, MA: Author.

Tjaden, P. & Thoennes, N. (1992). Predictors of legal intervention in child maltreatment cases. *Child Abuse and Neglect, 16,* 807-821.

Tjaden, P. G., & Anhalt, J. (1994). *The impact of joint law enforcement-child protective services investigations in child maltreatment cases.* Denver, CO: Center of Policy Research.

U.S. Department of Health and Human Services. (2000). *Rethinking child welfare practice under the adoption and safe families act of 1997: A resource guide.* Washington, DC: U.S. Government Printing Office.

U.S. Department of Health and Human Services. (2003a). *Child Abuse and Neglect State Statute Series: Statutes at a glance.* Washington, DC: U.S. Government Printing Office.

U.S. Department of Health and Human Services. (2003b). *Child Maltreatment 2001: Reports from the states to the National Center on Child Abuse and Neglect.* Washington, DC: U.S. Government Printing Office.

U.S. Department of Health and Human Services. (2003c). *Emerging practices in the prevention of child abuse and neglect.* Washington, DC: U.S. Government Printing Office. Retrieved March 29, 2004 from http://nccanch.acf.hhs.gov/topics/prevention/emerging/effective.cfm

U.S. Department of Health and Human Services. (2003d). *National study of child protective services systems and reform efforts.* Washington, DC: U.S. Government Printing Office. Retrieved February 16, 2004 from http://aspe.hhs.gov/hsp/CPS-status03/

U.S. Department of Health and Human Services. (2004). *Definitions, Scope, and Effects of Child Sexual Abuse.* Retrieved July 24, 2004, from http://nccanch.acf.hhs.gov/pubs/usermanuals/sexabuse/effects/cfm

U.S. Department of Health and Human Services. (2004*). Child Maltreatment 2002: Reports from the states to the National Center on Child Abuse and Neglect.* Washington, DC: U.S. Government Printing Office.

U.S. Finds Fault in All 50 States' Child Welfare Programs, and Penalties May Follow. (2004, April 26). *The New York Times,* p. A17.

Vander Mey, B. J. & Neff, R. L. (1986). *Incest as child abuse: Research and applications.* New York: Praeger.

Walker, L. E. A. (1988). *Handbook on sexual abuse of children.* New York: Springer.

Walsh, W., Jones, L. & Cross, T. (2003). Children's advocacy centers: One philosophy, many models. *The APSAC Advisor, 15*(3), 3-6.

Ward, T. (2003). The explanation, assessment and treatment of child sexual abuse. *International Journal of Forensic Psychiatry, 1*(1), 10-25.

Watkins, S. A. (1990a). The double victim: The sexually abused child and the judicial system. *Child and Adolescent Social Work, 7*(1), 29-43.

Watkins, S. A. (1990b). The Mary Ellen myth: Correcting child welfare history. *Social Work, 35*(6), 500-503.

Weber, M. (1997). The assessment of child abuse: A primary function of child protective services. In M. E. Helfer, R. S. Kempe & R. D. Krugman's (Eds.).*The battered child.* (5th ed.). (pp. 120-149). Chicago: University of Chicago.

Weiss, E. H., & Berg, R. F. (1982). Child victims of sexual assault: Impact of court procedures. Journal of the American Academy of Child Psychiatry, 21(5), 513-518.

Westcott, H. L. & Page, M. (2002). Cross-examination, sexual abuse and child witness identity. *Child Abuse Review, 11*, 137-152.

Whitcomb, D., Runyan, D., DeVos, E., Hunter, W., Cross, T., Everson, M., Peeler, N., & Porter, C. (1992). *When the victim is a child.* (2 ed.). Washington, D.C.: U.S. Dept. of Justice, Office of Justice Programs, National Institute of Justice.

Whitcomb, D., Goodman, G. S., Runyan, D. K., & Hoak, S. (1994). *The emotional effects of testifying on sexually abused children* (NIJ: Research in Brief NCJ 146414). Washington, D. C.: Department of Justice.

Whitcomb, D. & Hardin, M. (1996). *Coordinating criminal and juvenile court proceedings in child maltreatment cases* (NIJ Research Preview). Washington, DC: Department of Justice.

Whitcomb, D., Runyan, D., DeVos, E., Hunter, W., Cross, T., Everson, M., Peeler, N., & Porter, C. (1994). *The child victim as witness.* Washington, DC: Office of Juvenile Justice and Delinquency Prevention.

Whitney, P., & Davis, L. (1999). Child abuse and domestic violence in Massachusetts: Can practice be integrated in a public child welfare setting? *Child Maltreatment, 4*(2) 158-166.

Widom, C. S. (2000). Understanding the consequences of childhood victimization. In R. M. Reese (Ed.) *The treatment of child abuse* (pp. 339-370). Baltimore: John Hopkin University.

Widom, C. S. (2001). Child Abuse and Neglect. In S.O. White (Ed.), *Handbook of Youth and Justice* (pp. 31-47). New York: Plenum.

Wilber, N. R. (1987). Dilemmas of addressing child sexual abuse: The implementation of Chapter 288 in Middlesex County. Dissertation Abstracts International. (UMI No. 87722710).

Wilson, J. Q. (1989). *Bureaucracy: What government agencies do and why they do it.* New York: Basic Books.

Winton, M.A. & Mara, B. A. (2001). *Child abuse and neglect.* Needham Heights, MA: Allyn and Bacon.

Wong, D. S. (1998, February 16). DSS sees progress: Problems remain. *The Boston Globe.* pp.A-1.

Wood, J. M. & Garven, S. (2000). How sexual abuse interviews go astray: Implications for prosecutors, police and child protection services. *Child Maltreatment, 5*(2), 109-129.

Woodhouse, B. B. (2001). Children's Rights. In S.O. White (Ed.).,*Handbook of Youth and Justice* (pp. 377-410). New York: Plenum Publishers.

Zastrow, C. & Kirst-Ashman, K. K. (1997*). Understanding human behavior and the social environment* (4ᵗʰ ed.). Chicago: Nelson/Hall

Index